- THE ART OF -
PEAK PERFORMANCE

Hacking the Body and Mind for Peak Success

DR. K. JAYANTH MURALI

Best selling author of
"Enkindling the Endorphins of Endurance"

INDIA • SINGAPORE • MALAYSIA

ISBN

Hardcase 979-8-89133-780-0
Paperback 979-8-89133-778-7

To the pillars of my world,
my mom and dad,
who have held me up through every chapter of my life.

Contents

Dr. A. Amalraj, IPS.,
Commissioner of Police

Tambaram City Police,
Sholinganallur,
Chennai – 600 119.
044 - 2450 2525

Foreword

Life has bestowed us all with an incredible gift- 'the potential to excel against all odds'.

Life is also a wonderful canvas, waiting for us to paint it with the vibrant strokes of our ambitions, dreams, aspirations and performances. Often we find ourselves wondering how to unlock the immense potential that lies within us. When it comes to the art of unravelling human potential, Dr. Jayanth Murali stands out for his knowledge and wisdom.

In this book "The Art of Peak Performance" the author delves into the pillars of physical well-being - nutrition, sleep, and exercise - with focus on optimizing health for peak performance. He also provides guidance on harnessing the power of mindfulness and meditation to tame thoughts and preserving focus and calm. A fine balance between scientific rigor and accessibility is brought out, making complex concepts easy to understand and implement.

The book brings out the practical techniques required for developing mental toughness which is always a daunting professional and personal goal. Emotions are powerful forces that can either propel a person to greatness or hinder his progress. The author offers techniques to regulate emotions effectively, converting them into allies that fortify performance.

The book journeys through hormones and their role in peak performance. Understanding their influence can optimize potential. Breath, a normally unrecognized phenomenon, is examined for its remarkable impact on performance. The author also emphasises on harnessing technology to amplify abilities, using wearables and devices to elevate performance.

"The Art of Peak Performance" explains the ways in which environment can affect performance. Practical tips are given to optimize surroundings, enhancing performance and propelling a person towards difficult goals. It sheds light on the science behind social bonds and provides actionable advice on nurturing positive relationships that catalyze ones journey to excellence.

The author also infuses the wisdom of positive psychology. Positive emotions can infuse life with positivity and augment performance. Setting and achieving goals, a fundamental component of success, is detailed with the science behind effective goal-setting and practical insights into tracking progress. In a world where time management and productivity are critical, the book offers guidance on optimizing time, increasing productivity, and achieving a balance between work and rest. How unlocking creativity brings out peak performance is a must read for anyone.

Dr. Jayanth has addressed ethics and its role in performance enhancement. He gives insight into responsible use of morals that accompany the pursuit of peak performance. I invite all readers to embark on this voyage through the book with an open heart and an eager mind. In a world where the boundaries of human potential are continually being pushed, this book guides through to enhancing and optimizing of own potential.

Imagine a life where a person wakes up with boundless energy and ready to tackle any challenge. Picture him accomplishing his goals with remarkable ease, his mind a wellspring of clarity and creativity. Envision a world where stress is not a burden but a stepping stone to greater achievements. This is the world that the author invites the reader to enter.

Dr. Jayanth Murali has dedicated many years to understand the secrets of peak performance and presented them in this beautifully crafted book. Each page provides mind blogging information on peak performance. It will surely bound to gladden all those who lay their hands on and flips its pages.

With best wishes,

Dr.A. Amalraj, IPS 7/9/23.

Foreword

Welcome to the wondrous realm of knowledge, where we embark on a captivating exploration of "The Art of Peak Performance: Hacking the Body and Mind for Peak Success" authored by Dr. K. Jayanth Murali. This transformative journey transcends the boundaries of age, gender, and occupation.

Dr. Murali's words are akin to the elixir of wisdom brewed by a master alchemist, beckoning us into a world where the human potential knows no constraints. Within the pages of this treasure trove, you'll discover an array of bio-hacks and concepts meticulously crafted to unlock your full potential, promising a perpetual journey of growth and self-improvement.

In "The Art of Peak Performance," you'll explore the labyrinthine corridors of the human brain, unveiling the secrets of neuroplasticity and the immense power of your thoughts. You'll submerge yourselves in the realms of mental fortitude and practical strategies to conquer adversity. The art of visualization will become your ally, transforming your desires into tangible realities, and you'll uncover the mystical role of hormones as catalysts for transformation.

This expedition is not merely about personal excellence; it is a way of life. It signifies an unswerving commitment to relentless growth, awakening each day with purpose and passion, to navigate gracefully the intricate maze of life.

In a world captivated by fleeting desires, this book rekindles the flames of discipline and dedication. It serves as a poignant reminder that true greatness emerges from unwavering effort, the weaving together of strategic wisdom, and an unyielding pursuit of self-improvement.

"The Art of Peak Performance" is your magical grimoire, tailor-made for your ambitions, whether you are a scholar, an entrepreneur, an artist, or a guardian of the night. It is a celebration of the boundless capacity of the human spirit for growth and transcendence.

The author, a sage of peak performance, stands as your trusted guide, infusing each word with the enchantment needed for your journey to greatness.

In a world where mediocrity reigns, you have chosen a different path – the path of peak performance. As you embark on this enchanting odyssey, embrace this book as the key to unlocking your inherent potential. Apply these principles with diligence and enthusiasm, and witness your life transform into a tapestry of dreams woven seamlessly into reality.

Your journey towards peak performance commences now, and this fabulous effort by Dr. K. Jayanth Murali is your enchanted passport to a life of boundless accomplishment and profound fulfillment. Welcome to a world where dreams breathe and reality dances harmoniously. Your potential is immeasurable, and the pursuit of excellence is both an aspiration and a way of life. Welcome to "The Art of Peak Performance." Your extraordinary adventure awaits.

Sreedhar Bevara
Author, Leadership Expert & Motivational Speaker

Renowned for his compelling journey from a humble street vendor to the boardrooms of corporate giants, Sreedhar Bevara, an alumnus of the prestigious IIM Ahmedabad, stands as an acclaimed author of leadership bestsellers. His works, including *"Moment of Signal"* and *"The Roaring Lambs,"* which earned the coveted title of Amazon's Popular Book of 2021, that was published by HarperCollins.

TEDx speaker Sreedhar's exceptional thought leadership and dedication to empowering the youth have earned him recognition from esteemed leaders worldwide, including the Hon'ble Prime Minister, Mr. Narendra Modi. Presently, he serves as the head of the international consulting firm, BMR Innovations, and offers valuable counsel to the Goa State Innovation Council under the Government of Goa.

Acknowledgements

In the enchanting realm of literary creation, where words pirouette and thoughts intertwine, I humbly extend boundless gratitude to the luminous souls who have woven their essence into the very fabric of this opus, "The Art of Peak Performance: Hacking the Body and Mind for Peak Success". Their contributions shine like radiant stars adorning the velvety canvas of night, infusing this endeavour with an iridescent brilliance that defies description.

At the forefront of this symphony of acknowledgement stands my cherished partner, my beloved wife Jayanthi. Her presence has been an exquisite symphony of unwavering support and boundless patience, fortifying my spirit with a grace that transcends words. To you, my dearest, I extend a cascade of gratitude that surges like an ocean wave.

To my revered parents, whose footsteps laid the foundation of my being, my gratitude knows no bounds. Their wisdom, tender love, and unwavering guidance have sculpted my soul's very contours. Within their nurturing embrace, I discovered the seeds of integrity, diligence, and resilience that have blossomed into the literary tapestry before you. To my dear father and mother, words fall short of expressing the depth of my appreciation.

Enveloped in the embrace of paternal love, I extend heartfelt thanks to my treasured daughters, Tanya and Sonya. Their radiant presence has infused vibrant hues onto the canvas of my existence. Their unwavering affection, support, and encouragement have nourished my creative spirit, igniting a fervent passion within. Each heartbeat resonates with gratitude for the gift of their boundless love.

To my dear siblings, Ashok and Priya, you are celestial companions who have embarked on this extraordinary odyssey by my side. Your unwavering belief, camaraderie, and inspiration have been the gentle winds propelling this book to majestic heights. With heartfelt reverence, I extend my deepest thanks for the unique threads of brilliance you've woven into this exquisite tapestry.

A radiant beam of appreciation lights the path of Vidhya, whose unwavering enthusiasm, unparalleled dedication, and meticulous attention to detail have enriched this literary opus immeasurably. Her pursuit of perfection has ignited an eternal flame of gratitude within my heart. To her, I offer an effusion of heartfelt thanks that dances upon the wind.

Amidst this symphony of support, I am embraced by the unwavering friendship of my dear Rafiq Bhaiya, an unyielding pillar of strength through tumultuous tides. In uncertain waters, his presence has shone as a beacon of hope and solace. And to Bhaskar, a wellspring of inspiration, whose resolute belief in my abilities has alchemised doubt into steadfast determination. To both of you, I extend my deepest appreciation and unwavering gratitude.

With reverential awe, I bestow my sincere gratitude upon the entire constellation of souls at Notion Press, including luminaries like Mr. Kushagara and Ms. Surekha Thamannan guided under the visionary leadership of Mr. Naveen. Their orchestration of efficiency, unwavering commitment to excellence, and relentless dedication have propelled this project to breathtaking heights, where dreams transcend the intangible and manifest into palpable reality. I am eternally indebted to their stellar contributions.

To my cherished team, Murali, Govindan, Suresh, and my steadfast drivers, Thiyagarajan and Arun Prasad, you've stood as unyielding pillars fortifying the very scaffold of this literary venture. Amidst the whirlwind of countless moving parts, your unwavering support and tireless dedication have been sculpted into the essence of this creation.

With profound reverence, I extend heartfelt gratitude to all who have contributed, knowingly or unknowingly, to the kaleidoscope of inspiration gracing these pages. Your presence is interwoven with the essence of every word, forever a part of this narrative's magnificent tapestry.

Lastly, to you, dear reader, I extend my heartfelt thanks. As you embark upon this literary voyage, you breathe life into these words, and your hearts resonate with their melodies. Your presence, dear reader, completes the alchemical equation, transforming ink and paper into an immersive experience—a transformative journey of the soul that dances upon the canvas of the written word.

Endorsements

'The Art of Peak Performance' book transformed my approach to training and mindset. It's a game-changer for athletes seeking to break through performance plateaus and reach their highest potential.

– International athlete S.Arokiarajv, JCO,
Arjun awardee, Asian games gold medalist
& two time Olympian.

In *'The Art of Peak Performance,'* I found a treasure trove of insights into the human brain and its incredible potential. This book is a masterpiece that will empower you to unlock your true abilities.

– Dr. Karthik Mathivanan Senior Consultant
& Co Director MGM Institute Of Liver and
Multi-organ Transplant , MGM Health care , Chennai

Happiness is the elixir of life, and this book is The Alchemist's guide to brew it. It reveals the secrets of positive psychology and the art of crafting a life overflowing with joy and fulfilment.

– Gowrishankar Natesan, Vice President,
NewGen Publishing Company Limited, India.

The environment and performance are deeply entwined, and this book is the alchemical recipe for harnessing nature's forces. It unveils the secrets of harmonizing with the world around us to amplify our achievements.

– Dr. Jayanthi Murali, IFS, Chairperson,
Tamilnadu Pollution Control Board, Chennai.

For those who dare to dream, this book is a compass pointing toward the stars. 'The Art of Peak Performance' is a journey through uncharted territories of innovation, guiding visionaries to turn their boldest ideas into reality.

– R. Sudhakar, IPS, Additional Commissioner of Police,
Traffic, Greater Chennai City, Police .

The exploration of genetics and its role in peak performance is fascinating in this book. It offers a fresh perspective on tailoring your approach to achieve optimal results based on your genetic makeup.

– V. Balakrishnan, IPS,
Commissioner of Police, Coimbatore.

This book is a goldmine of information. It's the perfect resource for anyone who wants to improve their performance in any area of their life.

Mr Pavan Kumar Reddy, IPS,
Deputy Commissioner of Police, Tambaram

The Art of Peak Performance is a must-read for anyone who wants to take their performance to the next level. The book is packed with proven actionable advice that one can start using today.

Ashok Krish Founder and CEO Kaizen Secure Voiz| Yale alum
Serial Entrepreneur| Scale literal and figurative mountains | Philanthropist

As an entrepreneur, we face numerous challenges on a daily basis. This book provided me with practical strategies to overcome obstacles, enhance my creativity, and achieve peak performance in business and life.

Sam Paul, Paulsons Group,
Successful Entrepreneur

Mindfulness is the magic wand, and the book *'The Art of Peak Performance'* is the spellbook. It enchants readers with the ancient art of mindfulness, empowering them to create a reality filled with serenity and presence. I found the chapters on mindfulness and meditation to be a gem in this book. They provide practical techniques to readers to harness the power of the mind and improve focus and clarity.

Dhivya Kannan, Mindfulness Life Coach,
NI-Nurturing Institute, Chennai, India.

"Technology plays a pivotal role in achieving peak performance, and this book offers actionable strategies to foster well-being and success using technology. This book is a must-read for anyone who wants to live a healthier, happier, and more successful life."

Premnath Subramani, Chairman
& Managing Director, Invent softlabs.

Sleep is often overlooked, but its importance cannot be overstated. 'The Art of Peak Performance' offers invaluable insights into optimizing sleep for enhanced cognitive function and physical vitality." Further, Emotions are the colours of our lives, and I found this book to be a canvas inviting readers to explore the depths of their emotions, transforming them into a palette for painting their life's masterpiece.

Shri Hariram, Advocate, Madras High Court, Chennai.

The Art of Peak Performance is a literary masterpiece that has revolutionized my outlook on training and mindset, serving as a powerful agent of change for athletes aiming to transcend performance plateaus and ascend to their utmost potential.

Ragunathan, Inspector of Police,
Security Branch, Chennai - South Asian Silver Medallist
and Senior Open National Medallist in 10,000Mts
and 5,000Mts. Coach Junior Indian Athletic Team.

Introduction

Hello and welcome to "The Art of Peak Performance: Hacking the Body and Mind for Peak Success." I am excited to share with you a comprehensive guide that will help you achieve your highest potential in all areas of your life. The purpose of this book is to provide you with the knowledge and tools to biohack your way to peak performance.

As human beings, we all have the potential to achieve greatness in various aspects of our lives. Whether we are athletes striving to break records, business professionals seeking to climb the corporate ladder, or students aiming to excel academically, we all share a common goal: the goal of wanting to achieve our highest level of performance.

As someone who has always been interested in unlocking the full potential of my body and mind, I've spent years studying and experimenting with various techniques and practices to improve my performance in all aspects of my life. I have spent years researching and experimenting with various techniques and strategies to optimise physical and mental performance. I have worked with athletes, entrepreneurs and individuals from all walks of life to help them achieve their full potential. And through my journey, I've learnt that peak performance isn't just reserved for elite athletes or high-powered executives; it's something that anyone can achieve with the right mindset, tools and strategies.

That's why I wrote this book, "The Art of Peak Performance: Hacking the Body and Mind for Peak Success." I wanted to share everything I've learnt about optimising performance, from the biology of the brain to the impact of social connections and everything in between. The Art of Peak Performance is a comprehensive guide that takes a holistic approach to hacking your body and mind for success.

The book is divided into 29 chapters, each focusing on a specific area that is crucial for achieving peak performance. Each chapter in this book delves into a different aspect of peak performance, exploring the underlying science and providing practical tips and strategies for improving your performance in that area.

In the first chapter, I have provided an introduction to the science of peak performance, explaining the concept of biohacking and how it can be used to optimise performance. It lays the foundation for the rest of the book, providing a framework for understanding the various aspects of performance optimisation.

In the next chapter, I delve into the biology of the brain and how it influences our performance. I explain how the brain works, its potential for optimisation and the latest research on neuroplasticity. By understanding how the brain works, we can learn how to optimise its performance and achieve our goals.

In the third chapter, I focus on the role of genetics in peak performance. I explain how our genetic makeup influences our performance and how we can use genetic testing to optimise our performance. By understanding our genetic predispositions, we can tailor our approach to biohacking for optimal results.

In the next chapter on the role of epigenetics in peak performance. I explain how environmental factors can influence our gene expression and how we can use this knowledge to optimise our performance. By understanding how our environment affects our gene expression, we can create an optimal environment for peak performance.

The fifth chapter of the book is on the impact of nutrition on peak performance. I dwell on how our diet affects our brain and body and I provide practical strategies for optimising our nutrition for peak performance. By optimising our nutrition, we can fuel our brain and body for optimal performance.

Chapter 6 explores the role of sleep in peak performance. I explain here how sleep affects our brain and body and I provide practical strategies for optimising our sleep for peak performance. By optimising our sleep, we can improve our cognitive function and physical performance.

In the following seventh chapter, I delve into the science of exercise for optimal performance. I have explained how exercise affects our brain and body and I provide practical strategies for optimising our exercise routine for peak performance. By optimising our exercise routine, we can improve our physical and cognitive performance.

In Chapter 8 I delve into mindfulness and meditation, which can be powerful tools for achieving peak performance. By learning to quiet the mind and focus on the present moment, we can reduce distractions and improve our ability to concentrate, leading to better performance. We will explore various meditation techniques, including breath awareness, body scan and visualisation, and how they can be incorporated into a daily routine to improve mental clarity, focus, and overall well-being.

The next chapter is on nootropics, which are cognitive enhancers that can improve cognitive function, memory, creativity and motivation. While these substances can be highly effective, it's important to understand their potential risks and limitations. We will explore various types of nootropics, their mechanisms of action, and how they can be safely and responsibly used to support peak performance.

The following Chapter 10 addresses the impact of stress on performance and provides strategies for managing stress effectively. Chronic stress can negatively impact physical and mental health, reduce productivity and impair cognitive function. We will discuss the different types of stress, their effects on the body and mind, and how to develop healthy coping mechanisms to mitigate stress and promote peak performance.

In chapter 11, I dwell on the profound influence of mindset on achieving peak performance. Delving into the intricate interplay between mindset and performance, the chapter uncovers how one's mental outlook shapes ones capabilities and outcomes. Through compelling anecdotes and scientific insights, I demonstrate how mindset empowers individuals to navigate challenges with resilience, embrace continuous learning, and unlock their true potential. By exploring the transformational power of mindset, this chapter underscores the pivotal role it plays in propelling individuals towards unparalleled levels of achievement and success.

In chapter 12, I dwell on how to cultivate a growth mindset. By cultivating a growth mindset, individuals can perform at their peak by embracing challenges, persisting through setbacks, and pursuing learning and development opportunities. Individuals with a growth mindset view challenges as opportunities for learning, persist through setbacks, and seek out new experiences and opportunities for growth .

Chapter 13 provides insights into developing mental toughness, which is critical for peak performance. Mental toughness is the ability to persevere in the face of adversity, maintain focus and motivation and push through physical and mental barriers. We will discuss practical techniques for developing mental toughness, including visualisation, goal-setting and positive self-talk.

Chapter 14 explores the role of emotions in performance and how to regulate them. Emotions are a natural part of our human experience and can significantly impact our performance, both positively and negatively. In this chapter, I dive deep into the science behind emotions and the techniques to regulate them to maximise our performance potential. I provide practical examples and strategies for dealing with difficult emotions and turning them into productive energy.

Chapter 15 focuses on the role of visualisation and mental rehearsal in performance. Visualisation and mental rehearsal have been proven to be powerful tools for achieving peak performance. In this chapter, I explain how visualisation and mental rehearsal work and provide tips for using them effectively. I also share real-life examples of athletes and performers who have used visualisation and mental rehearsal to reach their peak potential.

In Chapter 16, I discuss the Role of hormones and their impact on peak performance. Understanding the role of key hormones and optimising hormone levels are critical aspects of achieving peak performance.

In Chpter 17 I explore the power of breath in achieving peak performance is analysed. Various kinds of breathwork techniques for physical and cognitive performance and their impact on emotional intelligence and well-being are discussed.

In chapter 18, I discuss the impact of the environment on performance. Our surroundings can have a significant impact on our performance and ability to achieve our goals. In this chapter, I delve into the science behind environmental factors and their effects on performance, including lighting, sound, temperature and more. I also provide tips for optimising our environment to enhance our performance and reach our goals.

Chapter 19 explores the impact of social connections on performance. Human beings are social creatures and our relationships with others can significantly impact our ability to achieve peak performance. In this chapter, I discuss the science behind social connections and how they can enhance or hinder our performance. I also provide tips for building positive social connections that can help us reach our peak potential.

Chapter 20 explains the benefits of cold exposure. Cold exposure offers a multitude of benefits for physical and mental well-being. The practice of cold exposure can optimise overall health and performance.

Chapter 21 focuses on biohacking your brainwaves. Various techniques of brainwave entrainment are analysed. By biohacking your brainwaves through the practice of brainwave entrainment, you can unlock your true potential.

In Chapter 22 I explore the impact of technology on performance. Technology has revolutionised the way we live and work, and it can also enhance our ability to achieve peak performance. In this chapter, I discuss the science behind technology and its effects on performance, including the use of wearables and other devices. I also provide practical tips for using technology effectively to optimise our performance and reach our goals.

Chapter 23 focuses on the role of positive psychology in peak performance. Positive psychology is the scientific study of human flourishing and well-being, and it has many practical applications for achieving peak performance. In this chapter, I delve into the science behind positive psychology and its effects on performance, including the benefits of positive emotions, gratitude and mindfulness. I also provide tips for applying positive psychology techniques to enhance our performance and achieve our goals.

Chapter 24 is all about setting and achieving goals for peak performance. Goal-setting is a critical component of achieving peak performance, and in this chapter, I explain the science behind effective goal-setting and provide tips for setting goals that are challenging, yet achievable. I also discuss the importance of tracking progress and making adjustments to our goals as needed.

Chapter 25 explores time management and productivity for peak performance. Effective time management and productivity are critical for achieving peak performance, and in this chapter, I provide tips for optimising our time and increasing our productivity. I also discuss the importance of taking breaks and the role of rest and relaxation in achieving peak performance.

In Chapter 26, I discuss the role of creativity in peak performance. Creativity is a vital component of achieving peak performance, and in this chapter, I delve into the science behind creativity and how it can be enhanced. I also provide tips for unlocking our creativity and using it to achieve our goals.

Chapter 27 is all about developing a personalised peak performance plan. In this chapter, I discuss the importance of developing a plan that is tailored to our individual needs and goals. I provide practical tips for developing a personalised plan that incorporates the strategies and techniques discussed throughout the book.

Finally, in Chapter 28, I explore the importance of measuring and tracking performance progress. Measuring and tracking your progress is essential to achieving peak performance. Without tracking your progress, you will not be able to identify areas of improvement, and you will not be able to celebrate your successes. In this chapter, we will discuss different ways to measure and track your progress, such as setting SMART goals, keeping a journal, using apps and tools to track your progress and creating a performance dashboard. By the end of this chapter, you will have a clear understanding of how to measure and track your progress and how to adjust your strategies to achieve your goals more effectively.

Ethics of performance enhancement and the importance of responsible use is dealt with in Chapter 29. As with any new technology or advancement, there are ethical considerations to be taken into account when it comes to performance enhancement. In this chapter, we will discuss the importance of responsible use of performance-enhancing techniques and tools, and how to balance the pursuit of peak performance with the ethical and moral considerations that come with it. We will also explore the role of regulations, governing bodies and laws when it comes to performance enhancement, and how to navigate this complex landscape. By the end of this chapter, you will have a clear understanding of the ethical considerations that come with performance enhancement, and how to be a responsible user of performance-enhancing techniques and tools.

In writing this book, my goal was to provide a comprehensive guide to achieving peak performance by hacking your body and mind for success. Each chapter is important because it provides valuable insights and practical strategies for optimising different aspects of your physical and mental performance. By understanding the biology of the brain, the role of genetics and epigenetics, the impact of nutrition and sleep and the science of exercise, you can develop a solid foundation for peak performance. Additionally, by exploring the role of mindset, mental toughness, emotion regulation, visualisation, social connections and positive psychology, you can cultivate the mental skills necessary for achieving peak performance. Finally, by developing a personalised peak performance plan, measuring and tracking your progress and using performance enhancement tools responsibly, you can achieve your goals and maximise your potential.

Each chapter explains the importance of the topic and provides practical tips, strategies, and techniques that can be applied to enhance performance. The book aims to provide readers with a comprehensive understanding of the various factors that influence performance and equip them with the tools necessary to optimise their performance.

I am confident that this book will be a valuable resource for anyone looking to improve their performance, whether in their personal or professional lives. I encourage you to read each chapter thoroughly, take notes, and apply the knowledge and strategies to your life. By doing so, you will be well on your way to unlocking your full potential and achieving your goals.

The mission of the book is to help individuals unlock their full potential and achieve success in their personal and professional lives. The vision is to create a world where individuals have the knowledge and resources to optimise their performance and achieve their goals.

But this book is more than just a guide to achieving peak performance. It is a call to action, a challenge to take control of your destiny and unleash your ultimate potential. It is about embracing the power of biohacking and using it to create the life you want. It is about pushing past your limits and becoming the best version of yourself.

The importance of the book lies in the fact that peak performance is not just about achieving success but also about living a fulfilling life. By optimising performance, individuals can achieve their goals, increase their productivity and improve their overall well-being.

Overall, "The Art of Peak Performance: Hacking the Body and Mind for Peak Success" is a must-read for anyone who is looking to enhance their performance and achieve success in various aspects of life. So, join me on this journey of self-discovery and transformation. Let's explore the science of peak performance and unlock the secrets to achieving greatness. Let's biohack our way to superhuman performance and become the best we can be.

CHAPTER 1

The Science of Peak Performance

INTRODUCTION

Humans are naturally curious and driven to seek improvement and growth in various areas of their lives, including their performance. Peak performance refers to a state of optimal functioning in which individuals can perform at their best, whether it be in sports, academics, work, or other areas of life.

Whenever I think of Peak Performance one real-life story that crosses my mind is that of the retired US Navy SEAL David Goggins. David Goggins overcame mediocrity to become a peak performer. As a child, Goggins was overweight and struggled academically. He faced racism and abuse at home and school, and his father was physically abusive towards him and his mother. Despite these challenges, Goggins knew he was capable of more and decided to join the military.

After completing his service in the military, Goggins struggled to find his purpose in life. He gained weight and became complacent until one day he saw a TV programme about the Navy SEALs and was inspired to become one of them. However, at that time, he was overweight, had never swum before, and had very little experience with physical exercise. He started swimming and training for the Navy SEALs. But the road was far from easy. He suffered numerous injuries, including stress fractures and shin splints. He failed the SEAL training three times, and it seemed like he would never be able to achieve his dream. But Goggins refused to give up. He developed an unbreakable mindset and turned his weaknesses into strengths. He started visualising success and set specific, measurable goals to achieve his dreams. He also developed an intense work ethic and pushed himself beyond his limits.

Eventually, Goggins achieved his dream of becoming a Navy SEAL and went on to serve in the United States Air Force Tactical Air Control Party. But his achievements didn't stop there. He continued to push himself to the limit, completing multiple ultramarathons, including the Badwater 135, which is considered one of the toughest races in the world.

Goggins' story is a testament to the power of perseverance, hard work and an unbreakable mindset. He overcame his weaknesses and transformed himself from a mediocre person to a peak performer, achieving success in multiple dimensions of performance. He continues to inspire others to push themselves beyond their limits and achieve their dreams, no matter how impossible they may seem. David Goggins continues to inspire people like me to scorn lives of mediocrity and become peak performers.

There are several reasons why people are fascinated by peak performance. First, achieving peak performance can be incredibly rewarding and satisfying, as it allows individuals to experience a sense of accomplishment and mastery. This can be especially true if the individual has worked hard and overcome challenges to reach their peak performance level.

Additionally, peak performance can lead to various benefits, such as increased confidence, greater success in personal and professional endeavours and improved physical and mental health. When people experience the benefits of peak performance, they often become motivated to continue striving for excellence in other areas of their lives as well.

Finally, embracing the pursuit of peak performance can lead to a more fulfilling and meaningful life. When people are actively engaged in pursuing their goals and working towards their full potential, they often feel more purposeful and satisfied with their lives overall.

Therefore, everyone needs to embrace the pursuit of peak performance, as it can lead to a richer, fuller life. Whether it be through setting challenging goals, engaging in deliberate practice, or seeking out resources and support, there are many ways to work towards achieving peak performance and reaping the benefits that come with it.

My journey from mediocrity to where I am today has some elements of David Goggins's journey though it lacks the toughness and intensity of what Goggins has so far endured and achieved in his life. When I reflect on my life, I am reminded of a journey that was marked by its twists and turns, highs and lows, and above all, an unwavering determination to achieve peak performance. Born into a family of modest means, I was brought up with the values of hard work and perseverance. These values served me well as I navigated my way through life, facing challenges and overcoming obstacles, and ultimately transforming myself into a peak performer.

My journey began in college, where I struggled to keep pace with my peers. Despite my mediocrity, I persevered and completed my PhD in Microbiology from the prestigious and premier Indian Agricultural Research Institute, New Delhi. To become a Scientist, I wrote the ARS (Agricultural Research Service examination) in 1991 conducted by the Indian Council for Agricultural Research (ICAR) and topped the examination. I then took the Indian Forest Service examination in 1991 and secured an all-India rank of number 6. Following this, I appeared in the Indian Civil Services examination conducted by the Union Public Service Commission in 1991 and passed it successfully with the 146th all-India rank and joined the Indian Police Service (IPS) in 1991.

At first, my professional journey was marked by success and achievement. I was proud of what I had accomplished and the position of authority that came with it. However, as the years passed, I found myself slipping into a life of comfort and mediocrity. The allure of the perks and the power that came with the job had seduced me into a complacent existence, and I was content to simply exist without challenging myself.

It wasn't until my 50th year that I realised the error of my ways. I realised I was happy, but I was not fulfilled. There was a void in my life that could only be filled by a new challenge, a new goal to pursue. I decided to change my life and began my journey into peak performance.

I started by waking up early, meditating, working out, running and reading and writing all simultaneously. These personal investments in the form of the above activities and discipline started transforming my life. Within a year, I had run my first full marathon at Auroville in February 2013 at 3 hrs 48 minutes, and I soon started writing a column in the Deccan Chronicle. Professionally, I started getting entrusted with more challenging and sensitive assignments. I got posted as ADGP Administration and a little later with the prestigious post of ADGP CBCID. There was no looking back after that. I found myself getting posted to the most prestigious and plum assignments like Director Vigilance and Anti-Corruption not once but twice and also as ADGP Law and Order not once but twice.

In CBCID as Secretary of the All-India Police Duty Meet, I led Tamil Nādu Police to first place among the different police forces in the country. And in 2019, I published my first book, 42 Mondays. I was able to achieve so much because of adopting habits of peak performance. I am today an author of four books and have given back so much to society by raising funds for Covid 19 pandemic, Kidney Foundation and organ donation in Chennai.

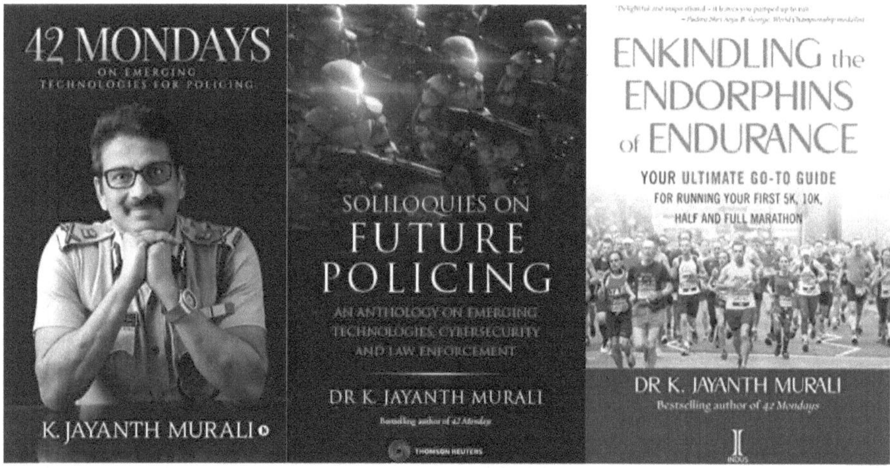

Through my journey, I have come to understand that peak performance is not just about achieving success or setting goals. It is about adopting a mindset of constant self-improvement, of always striving to be better than you were yesterday. It is about taking control of your life and your destiny and not being content to simply exist.

As I look back on my life, I am grateful for the challenges I faced, the struggles I overcame and the opportunities that lay ahead. My journey has taught me that with hard work, determination and a willingness to push yourself to your limits, anything is possible.

PEAK PERFORMANCE—DEFINITION AND SCIENCE OF PEAK PERFORMANCE

Peak performance can be defined as the state of being at one's best, achieving optimal performance in a particular task or activity. The science of peak performance seeks to understand the underlying mechanisms that enable individuals to perform at their highest potential and how these mechanisms can be optimised to improve performance. This book provides an overview of the scientific basis of peak performance, exploring key concepts, theories and evidence-based approaches for optimising human performance across various dimensions.

Dimensions of Peak Performance

Peak performance involves multiple dimensions of performance, including cognitive, emotional, social and physical dimensions. Each of these dimensions plays a critical role in enabling individuals to perform at their best.

Cognitive Performance

Albert Einstein is perhaps the most famous example of someone who has achieved peak cognitive performance. His groundbreaking work in physics and mathematics revolutionised our understanding of the universe. His ability to think critically, creatively and deeply about complex problems has inspired generations of scientists and thinkers. Cognitive performance refers to the ability to process and use the information to perform mental tasks effectively. This dimension of performance includes attention, memory, perception and decision-making. Research has shown that cognitive performance can be improved through various interventions, such as cognitive training, brain stimulation and mindfulness practices.

Emotional Performance

Emotional performance refers to the ability to regulate emotions effectively and maintain a positive emotional state, even in the face of stress or adversity. Emotional performance is essential for individuals in high-stress environments, such as athletes, military personnel and emergency responders. Techniques such as relaxation, cognitive restructuring and emotion regulation have been shown to improve emotional performance. One of the most inspiring examples of emotional performance is Kobe Bryant. The basketball legend was known for his intense focus and ability to perform at his best under immense pressure. Despite facing setbacks and obstacles, Kobe remained dedicated and focused, and his emotional intelligence helped him navigate through difficult times.

Social Performance

Oprah Winfrey is a prime example of someone who has mastered social performance. As a media mogul and philanthropist, she has built a successful brand by connecting with her audience and using her platform to bring about positive change. Her ability to build strong relationships and communicate effectively has been the foundation of her success. Social performance refers to the ability to communicate effectively, work collaboratively, and build positive relationships with others. Social performance is essential in various domains, including business, education and sports. Strategies such as communication skills training, team-building exercises and coaching have been shown to improve social performance.

Physical Performance

Physical performance refers to the ability to perform physical tasks effectively, such as running, jumping and lifting weights. Physical performance is critical in sports, military and first responder contexts. Strategies such as strength training, aerobic exercise and nutrition have been shown to improve physical performance. Usain Bolt is one of the greatest athletes of all time and a prime example of someone who has achieved peak physical performance. His speed and agility on the track have been unmatched, and he has broken numerous records throughout his career. His rigorous training and dedication to his craft have made him a true champion.

Interactions Between Dimensions

The various dimensions of performance are interconnected, and optimal performance requires a balance between them. For example, cognitive performance can be influenced by emotional and physical factors. Stress can impair cognitive performance, while exercise and good nutrition can enhance it. Similarly, emotional performance can be influenced by cognitive and social factors. Cognitive reappraisal, a cognitive strategy for changing emotional responses, can improve emotional regulation. Building positive relationships and social support can also improve emotional performance.

KEY CONCEPTS IN PEAK PERFORMANCE

Several key concepts underpin the science of peak performance, including the following:

Expertise

Expertise refers to the level of knowledge and skill an individual has in a particular domain. Research has shown that expertise is a critical predictor of performance in various domains, including sports, music and chess. Expertise is developed through deliberate practice, which involves engaging in focused, repetitive practice with specific goals and feedback. Steve Jobs was a visionary entrepreneur and a master of expertise. He built one of the most successful companies in history, Apple, by innovating and pushing the boundaries of technology. His deep knowledge of design, engineering and marketing was the foundation of his success.

Flow

Flow is a state of intense focus and absorption in an activity, where individuals feel fully engaged and in control of their actions. Michael Jordan is an example of someone who achieved peak performance through flow. He was known for his ability to get into the zone on the basketball court, where he felt completely immersed in the game and time seemed to slow down. This state of flow allowed him to perform at his best and become one of the greatest athletes of all time. Flow is often described as being "in the zone" and is associated with optimal performance in various domains, including sports, music and work. Flow is characterised by a balance between challenge and skill, where the task is challenging enough to be engaging but not so difficult that it causes anxiety or frustration.

Grit

Grit is the ability to persevere and maintain an effort towards long-term goals despite setbacks and obstacles. Grit is a critical predictor of success in various domains, including education, sports and business. Grit involves a combination of passion, persistence and resilience. J.K. Rowling is an inspiring example of someone who achieved peak performance through grit. She faced rejection after rejection before finally getting her first book, Harry Potter and the Philosopher's Stone, published. Her perseverance and determination to succeed have made her one of the most successful authors of all time.

Mindset

Mindset refers to the beliefs and attitudes individuals hold about their abilities and potential. Serena Williams is an example of someone who has achieved peak performance through a winning mindset. She has a strong belief in her abilities and can maintain a positive attitude even in the face of adversity. Her mental toughness has helped her become one of the greatest tennis players of all time. Research has shown that mindset can influence performance in various domains, including sports, education and business. Individuals with a growth mindset believe that their abilities can be developed through effort and hard work, while those with a fixed mindset believe that their abilities are fixed and unchangeable. A growth mindset is associated with better performance, greater persistence and more positive emotional experiences.

Goal-Setting

Goal-setting is the process of identifying specific, measurable and challenging goals that motivate and guide behaviour. Research has shown that goal-setting is an effective strategy for improving performance in various domains, including sports, education and business. Effective goal-setting involves setting clear and challenging goals, monitoring progress and providing feedback. Elon Musk is a visionary entrepreneur who has achieved peak performance through goal-setting. His ambitious goals, such as colonising Mars and revolutionising transportation, have inspired his team and pushed them to achieve great things. His ability to set big, audacious goals and then work tirelessly to achieve them is a testament to his success.

Without clear and specific goals, it is difficult to know what steps to take to achieve success. To set effective goals, I follow the SMART criteria, which stands for Specific, Measurable, Achievable, Relevant and Time-bound. One of my personal goals was to write a book, and I used the SMART criteria to guide me. I set a specific goal to write a 50,000-word novel, with measurable progress tracked through word count and achievable milestones set for each week. The goal was relevant to my passion for writing and time-bound by setting a deadline to finish within six months. A famous example of goal-setting is Michael Jordan, who famously set a goal to win six NBA championships. He used this goal to guide his training, practice and game-day performance, ultimately leading him to achieve his goal and become one of the greatest basketball players of all time. Setting clear and measurable goals is also critical to achieving peak performance. Olympic swimmer Michael Phelps is an excellent example of someone who has mastered the art of goal-setting. Throughout his career, he set both short-term and long-term goals for himself, and he consistently achieved them through dedication and hard work.

EVIDENCE-BASED APPROACHES FOR PEAK PERFORMANCE

There are several evidence-based approaches for optimising performance across various dimensions:

Cognitive Training

Cognitive training involves engaging in specific exercises designed to improve cognitive abilities, such as attention, memory and decision-making. Brain games, such as crossword puzzles, Sudoku and memory games, are popular forms of cognitive training. These games challenge different aspects of cognitive function and can improve overall cognitive performance with practice. Research has shown that cognitive training can improve cognitive performance in healthy adults, older adults and individuals with cognitive impairments.

One famous personality who achieved peak performance through cognitive training is chess grandmaster Magnus Carlsen. Carlsen is known for his exceptional memory and ability to calculate complex moves quickly. He attributes his success in part to his regular practice of solving chess puzzles and studying game strategies. He also incorporates mindfulness meditation into his training routine to improve his focus and reduce stress during tournaments. Through his dedicated cognitive training, Carlsen has achieved numerous accolades, including becoming the youngest chess player to reach the number-one ranking at the age of 19.

Brain Stimulation

Brain stimulation involves using non-invasive techniques, such as transcranial magnetic stimulation (TMS) and transcranial direct current stimulation (tDCS), to modulate brain activity and improve cognitive performance. A famous example of brain stimulation is chess grandmaster Garry Kasparov. He used visualisation techniques to prepare for matches, mentally playing out various scenarios to improve his strategic thinking and decision-making skills. Research has shown that brain stimulation can improve various cognitive abilities, such as working memory, attention and decision-making. Leonardo da Vinci is an example of someone who achieved peak performance through brain stimulation. He was a polymath who excelled in multiple fields, including art, science and engineering. He believed in constantly challenging his mind and seeking out new experiences to stimulate his creativity and intellect.

Mindfulness Practices

Mindfulness practices involve engaging in activities that promote present-moment awareness and non-judgemental acceptance of thoughts and feelings. Mindfulness practices, such as meditation and yoga, have been shown to improve cognitive, emotional and physical performance in various domains. Arianna Huffington is an example of someone who achieved peak performance through mindfulness. She is a successful entrepreneur and media personality who has written extensively on the importance of mindfulness and meditation for improving productivity and well-being. Her commitment to mindfulness has been a key factor in her success.

Relaxation Techniques

Relaxation techniques, such as progressive muscle relaxation and deep breathing, have been shown to improve emotional and physical performance. These techniques can reduce stress and promote relaxation, which can improve emotional regulation and physical performance. One technique I use is deep breathing exercises, taking slow, deep breaths to calm my mind and body. Another technique is progressive muscle relaxation, which involves tensing and releasing muscles throughout the body to reduce tension and promote relaxation. LeBron James is an example of someone who achieved peak performance through relaxation techniques. He is known for his rigorous training regimen, but he also understands the importance of rest and recovery. He uses techniques such as meditation, yoga and massage to relax his body and mind and stay relaxed.

Strength Training

Strength training involves engaging in resistance exercises, such as weightlifting, to build muscle strength and endurance. Strength training has been shown to improve physical performance in various domains, including sports, military and first responder contexts. To optimise performance, it is important to vary your workouts and focus on compound exercises, which work for multiple muscle groups at once.

One of my favourite strength training exercises is the deadlift, which works the entire body, improving strength and power. I also incorporate bodyweight exercises, such as push-ups and squats, to improve endurance and overall fitness. A famous example of strength training is Arnold Schwarzenegger, who famously incorporated weightlifting into his bodybuilding routine to become one of the most successful bodybuilders of all time.

Aerobic Exercise

Aerobic exercise involves engaging in activities that increase heart rate and breathing, such as running, swimming, or cycling. One of my favourite aerobic exercises is running, which improves cardiovascular fitness and endurance. I also incorporate HIIT workouts, such as sprint intervals, to improve overall fitness and performance. A famous example of aerobic exercise is Usain Bolt, who incorporated sprinting into his training routine to become one of the fastest runners in history.

Aerobic exercise has been shown to improve physical and cognitive performance in various domains. Aerobic exercise is another important component of physical performance, improving cardiovascular fitness and endurance. To optimise performance, it is important to vary your workouts and include both high-intensity interval training (HIIT) and steady-state cardio.

Nutrition

Nutrition is a crucial component of peak performance, providing the body with the fuel it needs to perform at its best. To optimise performance, it is important to eat a well-balanced diet, focusing on whole foods and avoiding processed and sugary foods. I follow a diet rich in lean protein and complex carbohydrates.

Nutrition plays a critical role in physical performance, as it provides the necessary nutrients for muscle growth and repair. A balanced diet that includes adequate protein, carbohydrates and fats is essential for optimal physical performance.

CONCLUSION

The science of peak performance seeks to understand the underlying mechanisms that enable individuals to perform at their highest potential and how these mechanisms can be optimised to improve performance. Peak performance involves multiple dimensions of performance, including cognitive, emotional, social and physical dimensions. These dimensions are interconnected, and optimal performance requires a balance between them. Key concepts in peak performance include expertise, flow, grit, mindset and goal-setting. There are several evidence-based approaches for optimising performance, including cognitive training, brain stimulation, mindfulness practices, relaxation techniques, strength training, aerobic exercise and nutrition. I've also found that brain stimulation, such as through reading or learning a new skill, can help to enhance cognitive performance. By challenging my brain, I've been able to improve my memory, focus and creativity. Additionally, practising mindfulness and relaxation techniques, such as meditation and deep breathing, have helped me to reduce stress and improve my overall well-being.

Lastly, I believe that nutrition and exercise play a vital role in achieving peak performance. Eating a healthy diet and staying active can help to boost energy levels and improve physical and mental health. I make sure to incorporate both strength training and aerobic exercise into my routine, and I fuel my body with nutritious foods that provide the nutrients I need to perform at my best.

In conclusion, achieving peak performance is a multifaceted process that requires a combination of emotional, social, physical, cognitive and nutritional factors. By focusing on developing grit, embracing a growth mindset, setting clear goals, engaging in brain stimulation and mindfulness practices and maintaining a healthy lifestyle, anyone can achieve their peak potential. By understanding the science of peak performance and implementing evidence-based approaches, individuals can improve their performance across various domains and achieve their goals.

CHAPTER 2

Biology of the Brain: Understanding How the Brain Works and Its Potential for Optimisation

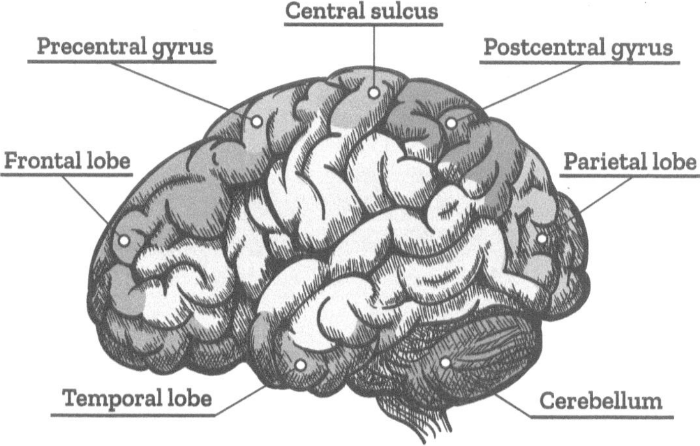

INTRODUCTION

The brain is the most complex organ in the human body. It is responsible for all our thoughts, emotions and actions. It is made up of different regions that work together to carry out specific functions. The brain can be divided into three main parts: the cerebrum, the cerebellum and the brainstem.

The cerebrum, which is the largest part of the brain, is responsible for higher cognitive functions such as perception, reasoning, memory and decision-making. It is divided into two hemispheres, the left and right, and these hemispheres are connected by a bundle of nerve fibres called the corpus callosum. The cerebrum is further divided into lobes, including the frontal, parietal, temporal and occipital lobes, each with its unique functions.

The cerebellum, located at the back of the brain, plays a crucial role in coordinating movement, balance and posture. It also contributes to motor learning and fine motor skills, such as hand-eye coordination and precise movements.

The brainstem, often referred to as the oldest and most primitive part of the brain, is responsible for basic functions that are essential for survival, such as breathing, heart rate and digestion. It also serves as a pathway for nerve signals to and from the rest of the brain, facilitating communication between different brain regions.

The thalamus, located in the centre of the brain, acts as a relay station for sensory information. It receives sensory inputs from various parts of the body and routes them to the appropriate areas of the brain for processing, allowing us to perceive and interpret the world around us.

The hypothalamus, a small but crucial region located below the thalamus, plays a pivotal role in regulating various body functions, including body temperature, hunger, thirst and sleep-wake cycles. It also controls the release of hormones from the pituitary gland, which in turn regulates various physiological processes in the body.

The hippocampus, an essential region for memory formation and consolidation plays a vital role in learning and spatial navigation. It helps us encode and store new memories, as well as retrieve them when needed.

The amygdala, often associated with emotions, particularly fear, is involved in processing emotional responses to stimuli. It plays a crucial role in our emotional experiences and responses to various situations.

The brain is made up of billions of neurons, which are specialised cells that transmit information through electrical and chemical signals. Neurons communicate with each other through synapses, which are small gaps between neurons. Neurotransmitters are chemicals that transmit signals between neurons. They play a crucial role in regulating mood, appetite and other bodily functions. Examples of neurotransmitters include dopamine, serotonin and acetylcholine.

Neurons, also known as nerve cells, are the fundamental building blocks of the nervous system, including the brain. They are specialised cells that are responsible for transmitting and receiving signals, allowing for communication and coordination within the brain and throughout the body.

STRUCTURE OF NEURONS

Neurons have a unique structure that is optimised for their function of transmitting signals. The main parts of a neuron include:

Cell body (soma): The cell body contains the nucleus, which houses the genetic material of the neuron and other organelles necessary for its survival and function.

Dendrites: Dendrites are branch-like structures that extend from the cell body and are covered with specialised structures called dendritic spines. Dendrites receive incoming signals from other neurons and transmit them towards the cell body.

Axon: The axon is a long, slender projection that extends from the cell body and carries outgoing signals away from the neuron. Axons can be several centimetres to metres in length in some cases.

Axon terminals: At the end of the axon, there are small branches called axon terminals, which contain specialised structures called synaptic terminals or boutons. These terminals form synapses, which are the points of communication between neurons.

Neurotransmitters

Neurons communicate with each other through specialised chemicals called neurotransmitters. Neurotransmitters are stored in vesicles in the synaptic terminals of the axon and are released into the synapse when an electrical signal, known as an action potential, reaches the axon terminals.

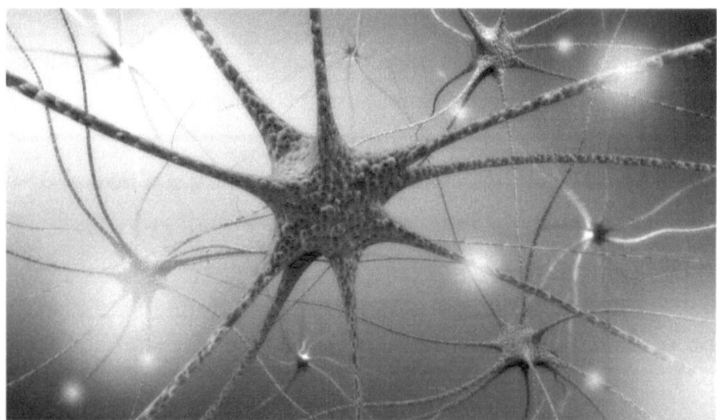

The released neurotransmitters then bind to receptors on the dendrites or cell body of the neighbouring neuron, transmitting the signal across the synapse. This binding of neurotransmitters to receptors can either excite or inhibit the receiving neuron, depending on the type of neurotransmitter and the specific receptors involved.

There are many different types of neurotransmitters, each with its unique properties and functions. Some common neurotransmitters include:

- **Acetylcholine:** Involved in muscle contraction, learning and memory.
- **Dopamine:** Associated with reward, motivation and movement.
- **Serotonin:** Regulates mood, appetite and sleep.
- **GABA (Gamma-aminobutyric acid):** Inhibitory neurotransmitter that helps regulate neuronal excitability and plays a role in anxiety and relaxation.
- **Glutamate:** Excitatory neurotransmitter that is involved in learning and memory.

Neurotransmitters play a crucial role in the communication and coordination of neuronal activity within the brain, allowing for complex information processing and integration of signals from various regions of the brain. Imbalances or dysfunctions in neurotransmitters have been implicated in various neurological and psychiatric disorders, highlighting their importance in brain function and health.

External factors such as drugs, alcohol and stress can affect neurotransmitter levels and alter brain function and behaviour. For example, drugs like cocaine and amphetamines can increase the levels of dopamine in the brain, leading to feelings of euphoria and increased energy. Alcohol can depress the central nervous system, leading to impaired judgement, slowed reflexes and poor coordination. Stress can cause the release of cortisol, a hormone that can damage neurons in the hippocampus and impair memory.

Overall, neurons and neurotransmitters are essential components of the brain's intricate communication system, enabling the complex functions of the nervous system, including perception, cognition, emotion and behaviour.

Neural networks are groups of interconnected neurons that work together to carry out specific functions. They are responsible for processes such as learning and memory.

These networks allow for the complex processing of sensory input, integration of information from different brain regions and generation of appropriate motor outputs and behaviours. Neural networks are responsible for many cognitive functions, including learning, memory, perception, decision-making and emotion.

Neural networks are formed through a process called synaptic plasticity, which involves the strengthening or weakening of connections between neurons based on their activity. When neurons are repeatedly activated together, the connections between them are strengthened, forming a functional network. This process allows for the formation of complex and specialised networks that are tailored to specific functions.

Different brain regions are interconnected in specific ways to form distinct neural networks. For example, the prefrontal cortex, which is involved in decision-making and cognitive control, is connected to the hippocampus, which plays a crucial role in memory formation. These interconnected networks allow for the integration of information from different brain regions and the coordination of complex cognitive processes.

Learning and memory are two important functions that rely on neural networks. Learning involves the acquisition of new information or skills, while memory is the ability to store and retrieve information from the past. Neural networks play a crucial role in the formation, consolidation and retrieval of memories. For example, the hippocampus, along with other brain regions, is involved in the formation of new memories, while the prefrontal cortex is important for working memory and long-term memory retrieval.

Brainwaves are patterns of electrical activity in the brain that can be measured using an electroencephalogram (EEG), which records the electrical signals produced by the brain. Different mental states and activities are associated with specific patterns of brainwave activity.

There are several types of brainwaves, categorised based on their frequency, which refers to the number of cycles of electrical activity that occur per second. The main types of brainwaves are:

- **Delta waves (0.5-4 Hz):** Delta waves are associated with deep sleep and are typically the slowest brainwaves. They are important for restorative processes in the body, such as tissue growth and immune system function.

- **Theta waves (4-8 Hz):** Theta waves are associated with deep relaxation, daydreaming and creativity. They are also observed during the early stages of sleep and during REM (rapid eye movement) sleep, which is associated with dreaming.
- **Alpha waves (8-13 Hz):** Alpha waves are associated with a relaxed and calm state of mind. They are often observed when a person is awake but in a relaxed state, such as during meditation or when the eyes are closed.
- **Beta waves (13-30 Hz):** Beta waves are associated with focused mental activity, concentration and alertness. They are typically observed during wakefulness and active mental tasks.
- **Gamma waves (30-100 Hz):** Gamma waves are the fastest brainwaves and are associated with high-level cognitive processes, such as perception, learning and memory.

Brainwaves can provide valuable information about the state of the brain and can be used in various clinical and research settings, such as studying sleep disorders, cognitive function and brain disorders. However, it's important to note that brainwave patterns are complex and can vary depending on many factors, including the individual, the specific task or activity and other environmental factors. Further research is ongoing to better understand the relationship between brainwave patterns and cognitive function.

The brain is a highly complex organ that processes vast amounts of information, controls behaviour, and constantly adapts to new challenges in the environment. Understanding how the brain processes information, controls behaviour, and adapts to new challenges is a fundamental goal of neuroscience, the scientific study of the nervous system, and involves interdisciplinary research spanning multiple fields, including biology, psychology, physics and computer science.

Information Processing in the Brain

The brain processes information from the external environment and internal states through its billions of neurons, which are specialised cells that transmit electrical and chemical signals. Neurons receive input from sensory organs, process the information, and generate appropriate outputs in the form of electrical signals that are transmitted to other neurons or muscles to produce behaviour.

Information processing in the brain involves complex and hierarchical processing, where information is processed in different brain regions in parallel and integrated to generate coherent perceptions, thoughts and actions. Sensory information, such as visual, auditory and tactile stimuli, is processed in specialised regions of the brain, such as the visual cortex, auditory cortex and somatosensory cortex. Higher-order brain regions, such as the prefrontal cortex, integrate information from different sensory modalities and are involved in higher cognitive processes, such as decision-making, problem-solving and planning.

The brain also engages in continuous feedback loops, where information is processed in a cyclical manner, with recurrent connections between brain regions facilitating ongoing processing and integration of information. This dynamic and interactive nature of information processing in the brain allows for flexible and adaptive behaviour in response to changing environmental conditions.

Behavioural Control by the Brain

The brain plays a central role in controlling behaviour, as it generates motor outputs that drive movements and actions. Motor control involves the coordination of various brain regions, including the motor cortex, basal ganglia, cerebellum and brainstem, which work together to plan, initiate and coordinate movements.

Motor control in the brain involves the generation of motor commands that are transmitted through descending pathways to the spinal cord, which then sends signals to muscles to produce movements. These motor commands are generated based on sensory information from the environment, internal states and cognitive processes, such as decision-making and intention.

Behavioural control by the brain also involves higher-level cognitive processes, such as motivation, emotion and reward, which influence the generation and execution of behaviour. For example, the brain's reward system, which involves regions such as the ventral tegmental area and nucleus accumbens, plays a crucial role in motivating behaviour and reinforcing certain actions or decisions.

Adaptation to New Challenges

The brain is highly adaptable and has the ability to change and reorganise its structure and function in response to new challenges and experiences. This phenomenon is known as neuroplasticity and is fundamental to learning, memory and recovery from brain injury.

Neuroplasticity can occur at different levels, including cellular, synaptic and network levels. At the cellular level, neurons can change their structural and functional properties in response to changes in their activity patterns or input. This can result in the strengthening or weakening of synaptic connections between neurons, which underlies learning and memory processes.

At the synaptic level, synapses, which are specialised connections between neurons, can undergo changes in their strength and structure in response to activity patterns. This can result in synaptic plasticity, which is a fundamental mechanism underlying learning and memory.

At the network level, the connections and interactions between different brain regions can change in response to new challenges or experiences. This can result in the reorganisation of neural networks and the development of new functional connections between brain regions.

Neuroplasticity is not limited to the developmental period but occurs throughout life in response to learning, environmental changes and brain injury. This adaptive capability of the brain allows for the acquisition of new skills. Neuroplasticity also plays a role in recovery from brain injury or stroke. The brain can reorganise itself to compensate for the damage caused by injury, allowing individuals to regain lost functions to some extent. The brain is a complex organ that controls behaviour through a network of neurons and neural networks, and different areas of the brain are responsible for different behaviours and emotions. Understanding the relationship between brain function and behaviour is a central focus of neuroscience research.

Memory

The brain uses different types of memory to store and retrieve information. Short-term memory is used to hold information temporarily, such as a phone number. This type of memory is limited in capacity and lasts only for a few seconds to a minute.

Long-term memory, on the other hand, is used to store information for a longer period, such as personal experiences and facts. Long-term memory is divided into two types: declarative and non-declarative memory. Declarative memory is used to store factual information such as names, dates and events. Non-declarative memory, on the other hand, is used to store skills and habits such as riding a bike or playing an instrument.

Prefrontal Cortex

The prefrontal cortex, located in the frontal lobe of the brain, is involved in higher cognitive functions that are critical for decision-making, planning and impulse control. It allows us to engage in complex reasoning, problem-solving and goal-directed behaviour. The prefrontal cortex receives input from various sensory and cognitive sources, integrates this information and generates appropriate responses and actions. It is responsible for executive functions, such as working memory, cognitive flexibility and inhibitory control, which are essential for adaptive behaviour in complex and changing environments.

Limbic System

The limbic system, located in the central part of the brain, is involved in emotions, motivation and memory. It includes several interconnected brain regions, such as the amygdala, hippocampus and hypothalamus. The amygdala plays a key role in processing emotions, particularly fear and anxiety, and is involved in the formation of emotional memories. The hippocampus is crucial for the formation and retrieval of explicit memories, such as episodic memories of events and facts. The hypothalamus is involved in regulating physiological functions, such as hunger, thirst, body temperature and stress responses. Together, the limbic system plays a critical role in shaping our emotions, motivation and memory processes, which in turn influence our behaviours and actions.

External Factors

External factors such as drugs, alcohol and stress can significantly impact brain function and behaviour. Drugs and alcohol can alter neurotransmitter levels in the brain, which are chemicals that transmit signals between neurons. For example, drugs that affect the dopamine system, such as stimulants or addictive substances, can lead to changes in reward processing and motivation, resulting in altered behaviour. Alcohol can affect various neurotransmitters, including gamma-aminobutyric acid (GABA), glutamate and dopamine, leading to changes in mood, cognition and behaviour.

Stress, both acute and chronic, can also have profound effects on brain function and behaviour. Stress activates the hypothalamic-pituitary-adrenal (HPA) axis, leading to the release of stress hormones, such as cortisol, which can impact brain function, including impairments in memory, cognitive flexibility and emotional regulation. Chronic stress can also result in structural changes in the brain, particularly in areas such as the hippocampus, leading to long-term alterations in brain function and behaviour.

In summary, the brain controls behaviour through a complex interplay of neural networks and different regions of the brain, including the prefrontal cortex and limbic system. External factors such as drugs, alcohol and stress can also significantly impact brain function and behaviour, highlighting the intricate relationship between brain function and behaviour.

Enhancing brain function is a topic of great interest in neuroscience, and several strategies have been explored to optimise brain health and cognitive performance. Here are some of the commonly studied strategies for enhancing brain function:

Neurofeedback

Neurofeedback is a technique that uses real-time feedback to train the brain to regulate its own activity. It typically involves measuring brain activity using electroencephalography (EEG) or other brain imaging techniques and providing feedback to individuals about their brain activity in real-time. Through this feedback, individuals can learn to modulate their brain activity and optimise brain function. Neurofeedback has been studied for a variety of conditions, including attention deficit hyperactivity disorder (ADHD), anxiety, depression and cognitive impairments. It has shown promise as a non-invasive and drug-free approach to enhancing brain function in some cases.

Brain Stimulation

Brain stimulation involves the use of electrical or magnetic fields to modulate the activity of specific brain areas. Transcranial magnetic stimulation (TMS) and transcranial direct current stimulation (tDCS) are two examples of brain stimulation techniques that have been studied for their potential to enhance brain function. TMS uses magnetic fields to stimulate specific regions of the brain, while tDCS applies a weak electrical current to the scalp to modulate brain activity. These techniques have been investigated for various conditions, including depression, chronic pain, stroke and cognitive enhancement. While the results are promising in some cases, further research is needed to determine their effectiveness and safety.

Brain-Boosting Supplements

Certain supplements have been studied for their potential to improve brain function. For example, omega-3 fatty acids, commonly found in fatty fish and flaxseed, have been associated with better cognitive function and brain health. Ginkgo biloba, a herbal supplement, has also been studied for its potential cognitive-enhancing effects. However, it's important to note that the evidence for the effectiveness of brain-boosting supplements is mixed, and more research is needed to establish their benefits and safety.

Lifestyle Factors

Engaging in healthy lifestyle habits can also contribute to enhanced brain function. Regular exercise has been associated with better cognitive performance and brain health. Exercise promotes neuroplasticity, which is the brain's ability to adapt and change throughout life. Getting enough sleep is also crucial for brain function, as sleep is essential for memory consolidation and cognitive processes. Additionally, maintaining a healthy diet that is rich in nutrients, antioxidants, and healthy fats can support brain health and cognitive function.

DIFFERENT WAYS IN WHICH BIOHACKERS ARE HACKING THEIR BRAIN

Biohacking is the process of using science, technology, and experimentation to optimise and enhance human performance, including brain function. Biohackers use various methods to hack the brain, including the following:

Nootropics: Nootropics, also known as "smart drugs," are supplements or drugs that enhance cognitive function. These supplements can improve memory, focus and mental clarity. However, some of these supplements may have side effects, and their long-term effects are not well-understood.

Transcranial Direct Current Stimulation (tDCS): tDCS involves applying a low electrical current to the brain using electrodes placed on the scalp. This technique is thought to enhance cognitive function and treat depression and other neurological disorders. However, its long-term effects and safety are still under investigation.

Meditation: Meditation is a technique that involves training the brain to focus and quiet the mind. It has been shown to reduce stress, improve emotional regulation and enhance cognitive function. However, it can be difficult to master and requires consistent practice.

Biofeedback: Biofeedback involves using technology to monitor physiological processes such as heart rate, breathing and brain activity. The feedback can be used to train the brain to regulate these processes, leading to improved mental and physical health.

Exercise: Exercise has been shown to improve brain function by increasing blood flow to the brain and promoting the growth of new neurons. It can also reduce stress and improve mood. However, the type and intensity of exercise required for optimal brain function are still being studied.

The benefits of brain-hacking techniques include enhanced cognitive function, improved mood and better overall health. However, some techniques may have side effects, and their long-term effects are not well-understood. It is important to approach brain-hacking with caution and to consult with a healthcare professional before trying any new techniques.

As technology continues to advance, there are many exciting and futuristic biohacking tools and methods being developed. Here are some examples:

Implanted devices: There are already devices that can be implanted in the brain to help with conditions such as epilepsy and Parkinson's disease. In the future, we may see more advanced devices that can enhance cognitive function, memory and even mood.

Gene editing: CRISPR-Cas9 technology allows for precise gene editing, which could be used to treat genetic diseases and enhance certain traits. However, there are ethical concerns about the potential misuse of this technology.

Virtual and augmented reality: These technologies can be used to simulate experiences and provide immersive training environments. They may also be used for therapeutic purposes, such as treating phobias and PTSD.

Wearable technology: Wearable devices such as smartwatches and fitness trackers can monitor vital signs and provide feedback on health and fitness goals. In the future, we may see more advanced devices that can monitor brain activity and provide real-time feedback.

Artificial intelligence: AI can be used to analyse large amounts of data and provide personalised recommendations for improving health and cognitive function. It may also be used to develop personalised treatment plans for neurological disorders.

While these technologies hold a lot of promise, there are also potential risks and ethical concerns associated with them. It is important to carefully consider the potential benefits and disadvantages of each tool or method before using them for biohacking purposes.

As our understanding of the brain continues to advance, new strategies and technologies are emerging that have the potential to revolutionise our ability to enhance brain function and treat neurological conditions. Here are some promising areas of research that may shape the future directions of brain research:

Optogenetics

Optogenetics is a cutting-edge technique that combines genetics and optics to enable the control of neural activity using light. This technique involves introducing light-sensitive proteins called opsins into specific neurons in the brain. These opsins can then be activated or inhibited by light, allowing researchers to precisely control the activity of neurons in real-time. Optogenetics has been used to study neural circuits and behaviours in animal models, and it holds promise for potential therapeutic applications in humans. For example, it could be used to develop new treatments for neurological conditions such as Parkinson's disease and epilepsy, by selectively modulating the activity of affected neurons in the brain.

Brain-Computer Interfaces (BCIs)

Brain-computer interfaces (BCIs) are devices that allow direct communication between the brain and a computer. BCIs can enable individuals to control external devices, such as prosthetic limbs or computer cursors, using their brain activity. BCIs can also be used to record and interpret neural activity for various applications, such as restoring movement to individuals with paralysis or improving cognitive function. BCIs can use different techniques to measure brain activity, including invasive methods such as implantable electrodes and non-invasive methods such as electroencephalography (EEG) and functional magnetic resonance imaging (fMRI). BCIs have the potential to greatly enhance the quality of life for individuals with neurological conditions and have exciting possibilities for future developments.

Artificial Intelligence and Machine Learning

Advancements in artificial intelligence (AI) and machine learning have the potential to greatly impact brain research. AI algorithms can analyse and interpret large datasets generated by brain imaging techniques, such as functional MRI and EEG, to uncover patterns and relationships in brain activity that may not be apparent to human researchers. Machine learning algorithms can also be used to develop predictive models for brain function and behaviour, leading to a deeper understanding of how the brain processes information and controls behaviour. Furthermore, AI can assist in optimising brain stimulation techniques, neurofeedback protocols and other interventions to enhance brain function and treat neurological conditions.

Neuropharmacology and Gene Therapy

Advancements in neuropharmacology and gene therapy hold potential for the development of novel treatments for neurological conditions. New drugs and gene therapies can be designed to specifically target and modulate the activity of neurons, neurotransmitters and other molecular targets in the brain. Gene editing technologies such as CRISPR-Cas9 have the potential to correct genetic mutations that cause neurological disorders, opening up possibilities for precision medicine approaches. Additionally, advances in drug delivery techniques, such as nanoparticles and gene editing tools, could enable targeted delivery of therapeutic agents to specific areas of the brain, minimising side effects and maximising therapeutic efficacy.

Brain Network Mapping

Mapping the connectivity and functional networks of the brain is a rapidly-evolving field of research. Advanced neuroimaging techniques, such as diffusion tensor imaging (DTI) and resting-state functional MRI (rs-fMRI), can provide detailed information about the connections between different brain regions and their functional interactions. These advances in brain network mapping can shed light on how the brain processes information, how different brain regions communicate with each other and how these networks are disrupted in neurological conditions. Such knowledge can lead to the development of targeted interventions to optimise brain function and treat neurological disorders.

CONCLUSION

In conclusion, the study of the brain's biology is a captivating and intricate field that continues to unveil the mysteries of its workings and optimisation potential. The brain is comprised of specialised regions with distinct functions and billions of neurons that communicate through neurotransmitters, enabling complex information processing and integration. Understanding the structure and function of neurons, as well as the role of neurotransmitters, provides valuable insights into how the brain processes information, regulates emotions, controls bodily functions and forms memories. Furthermore, rapid advancements in brain research, such as optogenetics, brain-computer interfaces, artificial intelligence and machine learning, hold promising prospects for enhancing brain function and treating neurological conditions in the future. These groundbreaking discoveries are propelling the field forward and opening new horizons for understanding and optimising the brain.

Furthermore, the brain is a dynamic organ that can be influenced by external factors such as drugs, alcohol, stress and other environmental factors. Imbalances or dysfunctions in neurotransmitters have been implicated in various neurological and psychiatric disorders, underscoring the critical role of neurotransmitters in brain function and health.

Advancements in our understanding of the biology of the brain have the potential for optimising brain function and improving brain health. Research in areas such as neuroplasticity, neuropharmacology, and neurotechnology is paving the way for new interventions and therapies that can enhance cognitive function, treat neurological disorders and improve overall brain health.

As our understanding of the brain continues to advance, there is great potential for harnessing this knowledge to optimise brain function and unlock the full capabilities of the human brain. By understanding the intricacies of how the brain works at the cellular and molecular level, we can develop interventions and strategies to enhance brain function, improve mental health and ultimately improve the quality of life for individuals. The study of the biology of the brain holds immense promise for the future of neuroscience and has the potential to revolutionise our understanding of the human brain and its optimisation.

CHAPTER 3

The Role of Genetics in Peak Performance

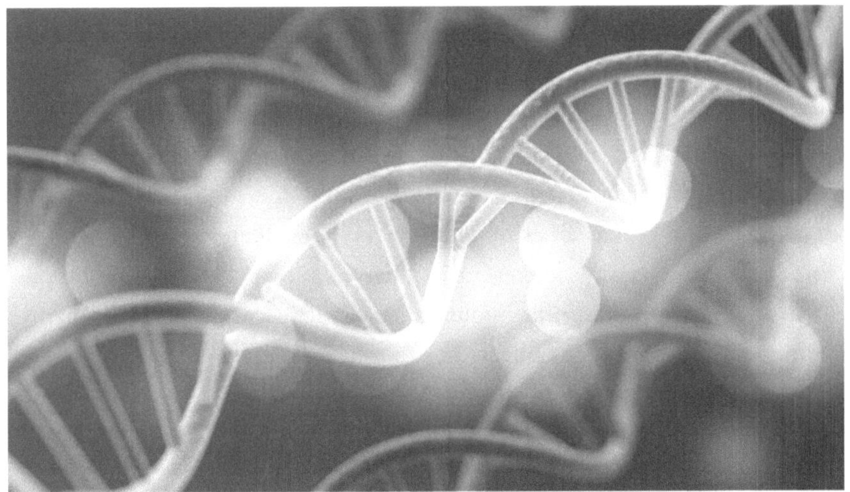

INTRODUCTION

Peak performance has always been a subject of interest among researchers, athletes and the general public. The question of what makes some individuals perform better than others has led to a lot of research in the field of genetics. This chapter will explore the genetic basis of human performance, discussing the influence of inherited traits on physical, cognitive and emotional abilities. It will also explore the latest research on gene expression, gene editing and gene therapy and how they can be used to enhance performance.

Physical Abilities

Physical abilities such as strength, endurance and speed are often considered to be the most important factors in peak performance. These traits are determined by the interplay of genetic and environmental factors. For example, genes that control the production of certain muscle fibres can influence an individual's strength and endurance. Similarly, genes that affect the metabolism of carbohydrates and fats can influence an individual's ability to sustain prolonged physical activity.

One of the most famous examples of genetic influence on physical performance is the Jamaican sprinters. Jamaica, a small island nation, has produced a disproportionate number of world-class sprinters. Researchers have found that this is due to a combination of genetic and environmental factors. The Jamaican population has a high frequency of a gene variant that enhances muscle power, which gives them a natural advantage in sprinting.

Cognitive Abilities

Cognitive abilities such as memory, attention and problem-solving are also important factors in peak performance. These abilities are influenced by a complex interplay of genetic and environmental factors. For example, genes that control the production of certain neurotransmitters can influence an individual's cognitive abilities.

The study of identical twins has been one of the most powerful tools for understanding the genetic basis of cognitive abilities. Identical twins have nearly identical genomes, so any differences in their cognitive abilities must be due to environmental factors. Studies have found that cognitive abilities are highly heritable, with up to 80% of the variation being due to genetic factors.

Emotional Abilities

Emotional abilities such as motivation, resilience and stress management are also important factors in peak performance. These abilities are influenced by a complex interplay of genetic and environmental factors. For example, genes that control the production of certain hormones can influence an individual's emotional responses to stress.

One of the most famous examples of genetic influence on emotional abilities is the warrior gene. This gene, also known as MAOA, has been linked to aggressive behaviour in some individuals. However, research has also shown that this gene can have positive effects, such as increasing resilience and reducing the risk of depression.

Gene Expression

Gene expression is the process by which genes are turned on or off. It is influenced by a complex interplay of genetic and environmental factors. For example, genes that control the production of certain enzymes can be turned on or off by environmental factors such as diet and exercise.

The study of epigenetics has been one of the most exciting developments in the field of genetics. Epigenetics refers to changes in gene expression that are not due to changes in the DNA sequence. These changes can be influenced by environmental factors such as diet, stress and exercise.

Gene Editing and Gene Therapy

Gene editing and gene therapy are emerging technologies that have the potential to enhance performance. Gene editing involves making precise changes to the DNA sequence, while gene therapy involves introducing new genes into the body to replace or supplement faulty genes.

One of the most promising applications of gene therapy is the treatment of genetic disorders such as muscular dystrophy. Researchers have also explored the use of gene therapy to enhance physical performance, such as increasing muscle mass or improving endurance.

For example, in recent years, researchers have been exploring the use of gene therapy to enhance muscle growth and strength in individuals with muscular dystrophy. By introducing a functional copy of the gene that is mutated in individuals with muscular dystrophy, researchers have been able to increase muscle strength and function in animal models.

While the potential benefits of genetic enhancement are significant, there are also ethical and social considerations that must be taken into account. One concern is the potential for genetic enhancement to exacerbate existing social inequalities. If only a select group of individuals have access to genetic enhancement technologies, it could lead to further disparities in society.

Additionally, there are concerns about the unintended consequences of genetic enhancement. For example, if a gene therapy designed to enhance athletic performance were to have unintended effects on other aspects of an individual's health, such as increasing the risk of heart disease, it could have serious negative consequences.

While genetics can play a significant role in an individual's abilities and potential for peak performance, it is important to approach the topic with caution and careful consideration of ethical and social implications. By continuing to study the role of genetics in performance and developing responsible guidelines for its use, we can unlock the full potential of human abilities while minimising potential harm.

BIOHACKING OF INHERITED TRAITS TO ENHANCE HUMAN PERFORMANCE

Biohacking is the practice of using technology and science to optimise and enhance the human body beyond its natural capabilities. With the advancement of technology and the increasing understanding of the human genome, there is now the possibility of biohacking inherited traits to enhance human performance.

One way inherited traits can be hacked is through the use of gene editing technologies such as CRISPR. CRISPR is a revolutionary gene editing tool that allows scientists to precisely edit specific genes in the genome. By editing genes related to physical, cognitive and emotional abilities, researchers can potentially enhance an individual's natural abilities.

For example, researchers have used CRISPR to edit genes associated with muscle growth in mice, resulting in increased muscle mass and strength. Additionally, researchers have used CRISPR to modify genes associated with memory and cognitive function in mice, resulting in improved learning and memory.

Another way inherited traits are being biohacked is through the use of gene expression analysis. Gene expression analysis involves measuring the activity of specific genes in an individual's genome. By analysing gene expression patterns, researchers can potentially identify inherited traits that may limit an individual's abilities and develop targeted interventions to enhance those abilities.

For example, researchers have used gene expression analysis to identify specific genes associated with elite athletic performance. By identifying these genes, researchers can potentially develop targeted interventions to enhance athletic performance in individuals who do not possess the same genetic advantages.

In the future, biohacking inherited traits may become more common and accessible as technology and understanding of the human genome continue to advance.

MODIFYING GENETICS FOR PEAK PERFORMANCE

Modifying genetics for peak performance is a complex process that involves advanced technologies and a thorough understanding of the human genome. Here are some of the steps involved in modifying genetics for peak performance:

Identify the genes associated with the desired trait: The first step in modifying genetics for peak performance is to identify the specific genes associated with the desired trait. This can be done through various methods such as genome-wide association studies, gene expression analysis, or CRISPR-mediated gene editing.

Modify the genes: Once the genes associated with the desired trait have been identified, they can be modified using various gene editing technologies such as CRISPR. Gene editing allows scientists to make precise changes to the DNA sequence, which can alter the function of the gene and potentially enhance the desired trait.

Test the modifications: After the genes have been modified, they need to be tested to ensure that the modifications have the desired effect. This can be done using animal models or in vitro experiments to assess the function of the modified genes.

Develop targeted interventions: Once the modifications have been validated, targeted interventions can be developed to enhance the desired trait in humans. This may involve the use of gene therapy, which involves delivering modified genes directly to a patient's cells to replace or supplement the non-functional or missing genes.

It is important to note that modifying genetics for peak performance is a complex and potentially risky process. There are many ethical and social considerations that need to be taken into account when developing and implementing these technologies. It is essential to ensure that any genetic modifications are safe, effective and do not exacerbate existing social inequalities.

ATHLETES WITH GENETIC ADVANTAGES

While genetics can play a significant role in athletic performance, it is important to note that the relationship between genetics and performance is complex and multifactorial. While some athletes may have genetic advantages that contribute to their success, other factors such as training, nutrition and environmental factors also play a critical role. Here are a few world-class athletes who succeeded because of having been blessed with genetic advantages.

Eliud Kipchoge: Eliud Kipchoge is a Kenyan long-distance runner and the current world record holder for the marathon. Kipchoge is known for his meticulous training and nutrition regimen, but he also has a genetic advantage. He has a rare genetic mutation that allows him to produce less lactic acid during exercise, which can contribute to better endurance performance.

Michael Phelps: Michael Phelps, as mentioned earlier, is known for his extraordinary success in swimming, winning 28 Olympic medals. Phelps has a unique physical profile, including a long torso, short legs and large hands and feet, that is well-suited for swimming. He also has a genetic advantage in producing less lactic acid during exercise, which can contribute to better endurance performance.

Hicham El Guerrouj: Hicham El Guerrouj is a Moroccan middle-distance runner and the current world record holder for the mile and the 1500 metres. El Guerrouj has a genetic advantage in his lung capacity, which is larger than average, allowing him to take in more oxygen during exercise.

Ashton Eaton: Ashton Eaton is an American decathlete and two-time Olympic gold medallist. Eaton has a genetic advantage in his fast-twitch muscle fibres, which are better suited for explosive movements required in events such as the 100-metre sprint and long jump.

These athletes demonstrate that genetics can play a role in athletic performance, but it is also important to note that other factors, such as training and nutrition, also play a critical role. Although some athletes have genetic advantages, it is important to remember that success in sports is not solely determined by genetics. Hard work, discipline and dedication are also critical components.

Genetic biohacking is still a relatively new and rapidly evolving field, and the long-term effects and ethical implications of these technologies are not yet fully understood. It is essential to approach these technologies with caution and ensure that they are used safely and ethically. Some genetic biohacks have been attempted so far such as:

Myostatin inhibition: Myostatin is a protein that regulates muscle growth, and inhibiting it can lead to increased muscle mass and strength. In animal studies, scientists have used gene editing techniques to inhibit myostatin expression, resulting in larger and stronger muscles. This technology has also been used in clinical trials for the treatment of muscle-wasting disorders.

Genetic testing for athletic performance: Some companies offer genetic testing services that claim to provide insights into an individual's athletic performance potential based on their genetic makeup. These tests look at genetic variations associated with factors such as muscle fibre type, endurance and recovery time.

Cognition enhancement: Various studies have identified genes that are associated with cognitive function, and some scientists have explored the use of gene editing to modify these genes to enhance cognitive performance. For example, some studies have looked at modifying the COMT gene, which is involved in dopamine regulation, to improve working memory.

Gene therapy for genetic disorders: Gene therapy involves delivering functional genes to replace or supplement non-functional or missing genes that cause genetic disorders. This technology has been used successfully to treat diseases such as spinal muscular atrophy and haemophilia.

CONCLUSION

In conclusion, the genetic basis of human performance is a complex and fascinating field of study. The interplay between genetics and environmental factors influences physical, cognitive and emotional abilities, ultimately shaping an individual's performance potential. The latest research on gene expression, gene editing and gene therapy has opened up new possibilities for enhancing performance through biohacking inherited traits.

From the Jamaican sprinters with their genetic advantage in muscle power to the studies on identical twins that highlight the heritability of cognitive abilities, evidence suggests that genetics play a significant role in determining an individual's performance potential. However, it is important to approach the topic of genetic enhancement with caution and ethical considerations.

Gene editing and gene therapy offer promising avenues for enhancing performance, but ethical and social concerns must be addressed. The potential for exacerbating existing social inequalities and unintended consequences of genetic enhancement raise important ethical questions. Responsible guidelines and regulations must be in place to ensure that genetic enhancement is used in an ethical and equitable manner.

By considering the latest research on genetics, gene expression, gene editing and gene therapy and addressing ethical and social concerns, we can unlock the full potential of human performance while minimising potential harm. Understanding the genetic basis of human performance and its implications for genetic enhancement can contribute to the development of responsible approaches to enhance performance and improve the lives of individuals while upholding ethical principles and social values.

CHAPTER 4

The Epigenetics Revolution: Hacking Your Genes for Peak Performance

INTRODUCTION

Epigenetics is the study of how environmental factors can influence the expression of genes without changing the underlying DNA sequence. Epigenetic modifications can be passed down from one generation to the next and can play a significant role in the development of various diseases and disorders.

Epigenetics has a significant impact on peak performance as well. For instance, exercise can lead to epigenetic modifications that enhance physical performance. In one study, researchers found that endurance exercise led to changes in DNA methylation patterns in genes related to muscle development and function, resulting in improved athletic performance.

Similarly, a healthy diet has been linked to positive epigenetic modifications as well. For example, a study showed that individuals who followed a Mediterranean diet had lower levels of DNA methylation in genes related to inflammation, leading to a reduced risk of chronic diseases such as heart disease and diabetes.

Stress can also have a significant impact on epigenetic modifications, which can ultimately impact peak performance. Chronic stress has been shown to lead to changes in DNA methylation patterns in genes related to the stress response and inflammation, leading to an increased risk of mental health issues such as anxiety and depression.

In my life too Epigenetics played a significant role and lifestyle interventions such as exercise, a healthy diet and stress management techniques have led to positive epigenetic modifications which ultimately enhanced all aspects of my life, especially during my police training days.

Before I joined the Police Academy in 1991, I was in a bit of a rut. I had just got married the previous year, but I had started to put on weight and develop a bit of a pot belly. My diet was not the healthiest and I wasn't getting much exercise. I was feeling pretty down and lacked confidence in myself.

However, all of that changed when I joined the Academy. Suddenly, I was surrounded by brilliant and hardworking trainees who were all dedicated to health and fitness. I was forced to undergo 4-5 hours of outdoor training every day, which was a big change from my previous sedentary lifestyle. But I was determined to keep up with my peers and as a result, I started eating much healthier in the police mess.

The competition with my fellow cadets pushed me to my limits both physically and mentally, but I discovered a newfound sense of discipline and resilience that I never knew I had. I was able to shed the excess weight and regain my physical fitness. It was amazing how much better I felt, both physically and mentally.

Being in such an environment of hardworking and driven individuals also helped me to adopt healthy sleeping habits, ensuring that I was well-rested and ready for the challenges of each day. I found myself retiring early at night and waking up early in the morning to run and practice a parade.

As a result of all these changes, my confidence and energy levels skyrocketed. I started to look smart and handsome with a short crew cut, and I was a hundred times fitter than I had been prior to my marriage. My productivity went through the roof, and I always felt like I could conquer the world. Despite the grind at the Academy, I was always in an upbeat mood.

In conclusion, changing my environment had a huge impact on my life. By surrounding myself with like-minded and driven individuals at the Police Academy, I was able to adopt healthy habits, build resilience and achieve my goals. I went from feeling down and lethargic to feeling energised and confident, and it was all thanks to the positive environment that surrounded me.

One of the most inspiring movies about transformation through diet and exercise is "Rocky" directed by John G. Avildsen. This iconic film tells the story of Rocky Balboa, a struggling boxer who gets a shot at the world heavyweight championship. Rocky is a small-time fighter who works as an enforcer for a loan shark. He lives in a rundown apartment and survives on a diet of cheap food and beer.

However, everything changes when Rocky is given the chance to fight Apollo Creed, the reigning world champion. To prepare for the fight, Rocky completely transforms his lifestyle. He starts eating healthy food, abstains from alcohol and starts training intensely. He runs up the steps of the Philadelphia Museum of Art, lifts weights and practices punching.

Through his intense training and healthy lifestyle, Rocky becomes a completely different person. He sheds the extra weight, gains incredible strength and develops impressive stamina. His transformation is not just physical, but also mental. He gains self-confidence, determination and a sense of purpose.

When the day of the big fight arrives, Rocky is in the best shape of his life. His hard work pays off as he goes the distance with Apollo Creed, taking the fight to the final bell. Although he loses the fight, Rocky has become a winner in life. He gains the respect of his community, earns the love of his girlfriend and becomes a role model for people all over the world.

The success of "Rocky" inspired a whole generation of people to get into shape and start exercising. The movie shows that with hard work, dedication and a healthy lifestyle, anyone can achieve their dreams. Rocky's transformation is a testament to the power of environment, discipline and positive change. Similarly, once a struggling student with a difficult childhood, Frank Shorter's life changed when he discovered his passion for running. His dedication to training led to epigenetic modifications that improved his athletic performance, and he eventually became a world-class marathon runner and gold medallist. Along the way, he also found that the discipline and focus required for running translated into other areas of his life, leading to a transformation that went beyond physical fitness. Despite the challenges he faced, Shorter's epigenetic modifications allowed him to rewrite his story and become the best version of himself.

But how do epigenetics impact an individual's performance? Epigenetic modifications, including DNA methylation, histone modifications and non-coding RNA molecules influence gene expression patterns and alter cellular function. For instance, research has suggested that DNA methylation patterns can be altered by exercise, leading to changes in gene expression that promote performance improvements. Similarly, the effect of diet on epigenetic modifications has also been studied, and it has been found that certain nutrients can affect DNA methylation patterns and gene expression related to performance.

Stress can also have a significant impact on epigenetic modifications and performance. Chronic stress can lead to epigenetic changes that negatively affect cognitive function and mental health, while short-term stress can trigger beneficial epigenetic modifications that enhance performance.

The potential for epigenetic interventions to enhance performance is an area of active research. For instance, some studies have investigated the use of dietary supplements that target specific epigenetic modifications to improve performance. Additionally, research has explored the potential use of gene therapy to alter epigenetic patterns and enhance performance.

Overall, understanding the role of epigenetics in performance and exploring interventions that target these mechanisms could provide new opportunities for enhancing human performance. Epigenetic modifications have been linked to a variety of health conditions, including cancer, heart disease, diabetes and neurological disorders. They can also impact cognitive function, mood and behaviour.

Therefore, it is important to adopt healthy lifestyle habits to promote positive epigenetic modifications. This can include regular exercise, a healthy diet, stress management techniques and adequate sleep. These interventions can lead to improved physical and mental health and ultimately, enhanced performance in all aspects of life.

IMPORTANT EPIGENETIC INTERVENTIONS THAT CAN MAXIMISE PERFORMANCE

Several epigenetic interventions can potentially lead to peak performance. Incorporating the following interventions could have a massive impact on one's life.

Exercise

Regular exercise has been shown to have positive effects on epigenetic modifications, particularly DNA methylation and histone modifications. Aim for at least 150 minutes of moderate-intensity exercise or 75 minutes of vigorous-intensity exercise per week. You can incorporate exercise into your daily routine by walking or cycling to work, taking the stairs instead of the elevator, or joining a fitness class.

Nutrition

A balanced and healthy diet can also influence epigenetic modifications. For example, a diet rich in fruits, vegetables and whole grains can increase DNA methylation and histone acetylation. On the other hand, a diet high in processed and sugary foods can lead to epigenetic changes associated with chronic diseases. Aim for a balanced diet that includes plenty of fruits, vegetables, whole grains, lean proteins and healthy fats.

Stress Reduction

Chronic stress has been shown to affect epigenetic modifications and lead to negative health outcomes. Incorporating stress-reducing practices such as meditation, yoga, or deep breathing exercises can potentially lead to positive epigenetic changes. Try to set aside some time every day for stress-reducing activities.

Sleep

Adequate sleep is important for overall health and has been shown to affect epigenetic modifications. Aim for 7-8 hours of sleep per night and establish a regular sleep routine. This can include going to bed and waking up at the same time every day, avoiding caffeine and electronics before bed and creating a relaxing sleep environment.

Mindfulness

Mindfulness practices such as meditation and deep breathing exercises have been shown to have positive effects on epigenetic modifications, particularly telomere length. Incorporate mindfulness practices into your daily routine by setting aside time for meditation or practising deep breathing exercises during breaks.

Incorporating these epigenetic interventions into your daily routine can potentially lead to positive epigenetic changes and enhance performance. It's important to remember that epigenetic modifications are influenced by a combination of environmental and genetic factors, so these interventions may have varying effects on different individuals. It's also important to consult with a healthcare professional before making any significant changes to your lifestyle or diet.

EPIGENETICS OF EXERCISE

The latest research suggests that exercise can induce changes in gene expression and DNA methylation patterns related to peak performance. For instance, studies have found that acute exercise can lead to increased expression of genes involved in energy metabolism and muscle contraction, while long-term exercise training can result in changes in gene expression related to mitochondrial biogenesis and muscle fibre type.

Furthermore, exercise has been shown to alter DNA methylation patterns in various tissues, including skeletal muscle, adipose tissue and blood cells. These changes can affect gene expression and cellular function, potentially contributing to improved performance.

Recent research has also investigated the effects of different types of exercise on epigenetic modifications and performance. For instance, one study found that high-intensity interval training (HIIT) led to greater changes in DNA methylation patterns and gene expression related to mitochondrial function and muscle growth compared to moderate-intensity continuous training (MICT).

Another study examined the effects of resistance exercise on DNA methylation patterns and gene expression in skeletal muscle, finding that this type of exercise induced changes in gene expression related to muscle hypertrophy and metabolism.

Overall, these findings suggest that exercise-induced changes in gene expression and DNA methylation patterns may contribute to improved performance and that different types of exercise may have unique effects on these epigenetic mechanisms.

EPIGENETICS OF DIET AND SLEEP

Recent research has demonstrated that diet and sleep can also influence gene expression and DNA methylation patterns related to peak performance.

Regarding diet, studies have shown that specific nutrients can impact DNA methylation patterns and gene expression related to performance. For instance, research has indicated that omega-3 fatty acids found in fish can affect DNA methylation patterns and gene expression in the brain, potentially improving cognitive function and mood.

Similarly, research has demonstrated that the consumption of dietary polyphenols, such as those found in fruits and vegetables, can affect DNA methylation patterns and gene expression related to inflammation and oxidative stress, potentially improving athletic performance and recovery.

Regarding sleep, research has found that sleep deprivation can lead to changes in DNA methylation patterns and gene expression that negatively impact cognitive function and mood. For example, one study found that sleep deprivation was associated with altered DNA methylation patterns in genes related to stress response and inflammation.

On the other hand, getting adequate sleep has been linked to positive changes in gene expression related to athletic performance and recovery. For instance, one study found that sleep extension improved basketball performance and was associated with changes in gene expression related to inflammation and immune function.

Overall, these findings suggest that diet and sleep can impact gene expression and DNA methylation patterns related to peak performance and may represent important areas for intervention to enhance performance.

EPIGENETICS OF STRESS

An environment of stress can have a significant impact on epigenetic modifications, which can lead to changes in gene expression and potentially contribute to the development of various diseases. Here are a few notable examples:

Childhood Trauma and DNA Methylation

Childhood trauma is known to increase the risk of developing depression, anxiety and other mental health disorders. Researchers have found that exposure to childhood trauma can cause changes in DNA methylation patterns, which can affect the expression of genes involved in stress response and emotional regulation. For example, a study published in the Journal of Child Psychology and Psychiatry found that childhood trauma was associated with increased methylation of the gene NR3C1, which encodes the glucocorticoid receptor. This can lead to a decreased ability to regulate the stress response, contributing to the development of mood disorders.

Social Stress and Histone Modifications

Social stress can also have a significant impact on epigenetic modifications. For example, a study published in the Journal of Neuroscience found that chronic social stress in mice caused histone modifications in the prefrontal cortex, a brain region involved in emotional regulation and decision-making. These histone modifications were associated with decreased expression of genes involved in synaptic plasticity and increased expression of genes involved in inflammation and oxidative stress.

Work-Related Stress and Telomere Length

Work-related stress has been shown to have an impact on telomere length, which is a marker of cellular ageing. Telomeres are protective caps on the ends of chromosomes that shorten with age and shortened telomeres have been linked to various diseases, including cancer and cardiovascular disease. A study published in PLOS ONE found that work-related stress was associated with shorter telomere length in nurses. The researchers suggested that work-related stress may lead to oxidative stress and inflammation, which can contribute to telomere shortening.

These examples demonstrate that an environment of stress can have a significant impact on epigenetic modifications, which can contribute to the development of various diseases. Understanding the mechanisms by which stress affects epigenetic modifications can help develop new interventions to prevent and treat stress-related disorders.

EPIGENETICS OF ENVIRONMENT

Epigenetics doesn't change the genetic code, it changes how that's read. Perfectly normal genes can result in cancer or death. Vice-versa, in the right environment, mutant genes won't be expressed. Genes are equivalent to blueprints; epigenetics is the contractor.

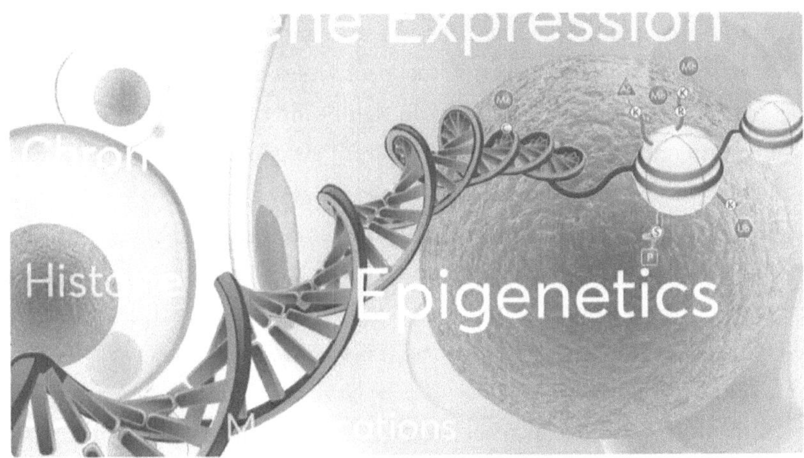

Bruce Lipton's quote highlights the importance of epigenetics in gene expression and how the environment plays a crucial role in determining the outcome of genetic expression. Our genes provide the blueprint for our body's functions, but they can be affected by environmental factors such as diet, exercise, stress and toxins.

Epigenetic modifications, such as DNA methylation and histone acetylation, affect how genes are read and expressed. These modifications can turn genes on or off, influencing various aspects of our biology, including our physical and mental health and performance.

In some cases, normal genes can result in cancer or death if epigenetic modifications turn them on or off inappropriately. For example, the BRCA1 gene, which normally helps to prevent breast cancer, can become inactive due to methylation, increasing the risk of developing breast cancer.

On the other hand, in the right environment, mutant genes may not be expressed. For example, individuals with a genetic predisposition to obesity may not develop the condition if they are in an environment that promotes healthy eating and exercise habits.

Therefore, the environment plays a critical role in determining how our genes are expressed, and we have the power to influence our gene expression by creating a favourable environment. This highlights the importance of making healthy lifestyle choices, such as eating a balanced diet, engaging in regular physical activity, managing stress and avoiding toxins, to optimise our genetic expression and achieve peak performance.

EPIGENETICS OF SOCIAL ENVIRONMENT

'A man is an average of five persons he spends most of his time with' explains the extent of the impact of the environment on a man and his success or failure. The idea that "a man is an average of five persons he spends most of his time with" suggests that the people we surround ourselves with can significantly influence our beliefs, values, behaviours and ultimately our success or failure. This quote highlights the crucial role that our environment plays in shaping who we are as individuals.

Think about it: If you spend most of your time with people who are negative, lazy and unmotivated, it's likely that you will start to adopt some of these qualities. Conversely, if you surround yourself with people who are positive, ambitious and driven, you're more likely to embody these traits as well.

Epigenetics, which is the study of how environmental factors can influence gene expression, provides further support for this idea. Research has shown that environmental factors such as diet, exercise, stress and social support can all have an impact on our epigenetic modifications and ultimately affect our performance.

For example, if you spend most of your time with people who prioritise healthy eating and regular exercise, you're more likely to adopt these habits as well. This can lead to epigenetic modifications such as DNA methylation and histone acetylation, which can positively impact your physical and mental health, cognitive function and overall performance.

On the other hand, if you surround yourself with people who engage in unhealthy behaviours such as smoking or excessive drinking, it's likely that you'll be exposed to similar environmental factors and may experience negative epigenetic modifications as a result.

In conclusion, the quote "a man is an average of five persons he spends most of his time with" highlights the importance of our environment in shaping who we are as individuals and ultimately determining our success or failure. By being mindful of the people we surround ourselves with and making conscious choices about our environment, we can positively influence our epigenetics and enhance our performance. Changing the environment one finds oneself in can drastically change a person's life.

One famous individual whose life changed drastically after being transplanted into a new environment is J.K. Rowling. Rowling had a tumultuous early life, marked by financial struggles and the tragic loss of her mother. She had always been a creative person, but it wasn't until she moved to Portugal that her life really changed.

Rowling moved to Portugal in 1990 to teach English as a foreign language. It was there that she met her future husband, and it was also there that she started writing the first Harry Potter book. The new environment was a fresh start for Rowling, away from the financial struggles and emotional turmoil of her previous life.

In Portugal, Rowling was able to focus on her writing and was inspired by the stunning landscapes and rich cultural history of the country. She wrote every spare moment she had, often in cafes and on napkins during her breaks from teaching. It was in Portugal that she also began to refine her storytelling skills, taking inspiration from the tales and legends she heard from her students and from the country's folklore.

But Rowling's life really changed when she moved back to the UK in 1993. She continued to write the Harry Potter series, but it was the new environment and the new people she met that really catapulted her to success. She joined a writing group and received feedback and encouragement from other writers, and she was also able to network with publishers and literary agents.

Rowling's life was transformed by the success of the Harry Potter series. She went from being a struggling single mother to one of the wealthiest women in the world. But it all started with a change in environment, a move to Portugal that allowed her to escape the struggles of her past and focus on her passion for writing.

Another famous individual whose life changed dramatically after being transplanted into a new environment is Steve Jobs. Jobs had a difficult upbringing, marked by family struggles and a lack of direction. But when he dropped out of college and moved to California in the 1970s, he found himself in an environment that would change his life forever.

California in the 1970s was a hotbed of innovation and creativity, particularly in the technology industry. Jobs quickly fell in love with the culture and the people, and he began to experiment with computer technology, building and selling computers out of his garage with his friend Steve Wozniak.

It was in California that Jobs found his calling as an entrepreneur and innovator. He was inspired by the counterculture movement of the time, which emphasised experimentation and creativity, and he was also surrounded by a community of like-minded individuals who were passionate about technology and pushing boundaries.

Jobs went on to co-found Apple Computer and develop some of the most revolutionary products in the technology industry, including the iPod, iPhone and iPad. His vision and leadership transformed Apple from a small startup to one of the most successful companies in history.

It's clear that Jobs' life was transformed by his move to California. The environment he found himself in allowed him to explore his passions and push the boundaries of what was possible in the technology industry. Without that move, it's hard to say whether Apple would have ever existed and whether Jobs would have become the icon he is today.

Both J.K. Rowling and Steve Jobs experienced dramatic transformations in their lives after being transplanted into new environments. For Rowling, it was the move to Portugal that allowed her to focus on her writing and refine her storytelling skills. For Jobs, it was the move to California that allowed him to explore his passion for technology and innovation. Both individuals found themselves in environments that allowed them to reach their full potential, and the world is a better place for it.

HOW EPIGENETIC INTERVENTIONS MAXIMISE PERFORMANCE

Epigenetic interventions have the potential to enhance performance by modifying gene expression and improving physiological responses. Here are a few examples:

Exercise and DNA Methylation: Exercise has been shown to modify DNA methylation patterns in skeletal muscle, which can lead to changes in gene expression and improve muscle function. For example, a study published in the Journal of Applied Physiology found that exercise training increased the methylation of the PGC-1α

gene, which encodes a transcriptional coactivator involved in energy metabolism and mitochondrial biogenesis. This increased methylation was associated with increased expression of PGC-1α and improved muscle oxidative capacity.

Nutrition and Histone Modifications: Nutrition can also affect epigenetic modifications, particularly histone modifications. For example, a study published in the Journal of Nutritional Biochemistry found that supplementation with resveratrol, a polyphenol found in grapes and red wine, increased histone acetylation in human white blood cells. Histone acetylation is associated with increased gene expression and improved immune function.

Mindfulness Meditation and Telomere Length: Mindfulness meditation has been shown to have a positive impact on telomere length, which is a marker of cellular ageing. A study published in the journal Brain, Behavior, and Immunity found that mindfulness meditation increased telomerase activity, an enzyme that adds DNA sequence repeats to telomeres, in immune cells. This increased telomerase activity was associated with increased telomere length and improved immune function.

These examples demonstrate that epigenetic interventions can enhance performance by modifying gene expression and improving physiological responses. Understanding the mechanisms by which epigenetic modifications are altered by lifestyle interventions can help develop new strategies to enhance performance and prevent disease.

SOME EPIGENETIC HACKS THAT CAN OPTIMISE YOUR PERFORMANCE

Here are 10 epigenetic interventions that can help you optimise your performance if you incorporate them into your daily routine.

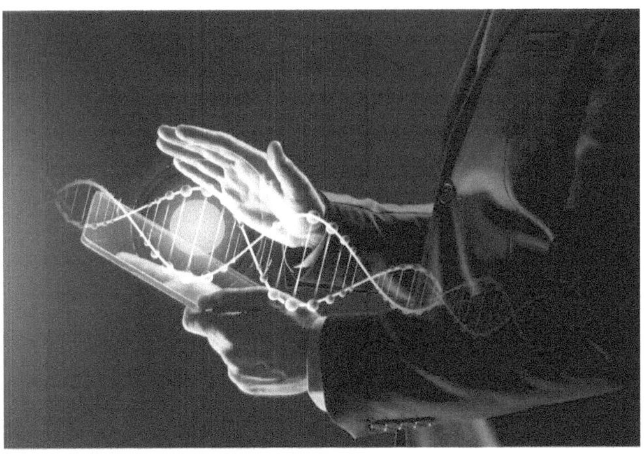

Exercise: Exercise is one of the most potent epigenetic interventions, and regular physical activity has been shown to enhance cognitive function, reduce stress and improve overall well-being. Incorporating exercise into your daily routine can be as simple as taking a brisk walk or doing a few minutes of yoga each day.

Sleep: Getting enough sleep is essential for optimal performance, as it allows our bodies to repair and regenerate. Sleep deprivation has been linked to a host of negative health outcomes, including impaired cognitive function, reduced immunity and increased stress. To optimise your sleep, try to establish a regular sleep schedule and create a sleep-friendly environment that is cool, dark and quiet.

Meditation: Meditation has been shown to have numerous health benefits, including reducing stress, improving mood and enhancing cognitive function. Incorporating a few minutes of meditation into your daily routine can help you stay focused and calm throughout the day.

Nutrition: The food we eat can influence our epigenetics and a healthy diet can enhance cognitive function, reduce inflammation and promote overall well-being. Incorporating nutrient-dense foods such as fruits, vegetables and lean proteins into your diet can help optimise your performance.

Fasting: Fasting has been shown to have numerous health benefits, including improving cognitive function, reducing inflammation and promoting longevity. Incorporating intermittent fasting into your routine can be as simple as skipping a meal (other than breakfast) a few times per week.

Cold exposure: Exposure to cold temperatures has been shown to enhance cognitive function, reduce inflammation and improve overall well-being. Incorporating cold exposure into your routine can be as simple as taking a cold shower or swimming in cold water.

Mind-body practices: Mind-body practices such as yoga, Tai Chi and Qi Gong have been shown to have numerous health benefits, including reducing stress, improving mood and enhancing cognitive function. Incorporating a few minutes of mind-body practice into your daily routine can help you stay focused and calm throughout the day.

Social connection: Social connection has been shown to have numerous health benefits, including reducing stress, improving mood and enhancing cognitive function. Incorporating social connection into your daily routine can be as simple as spending time with friends or family, or volunteering in your community.

Environmental exposure: Exposure to natural environments such as forests, beaches and mountains has been shown to have numerous health benefits, including reducing stress, improving mood and enhancing cognitive function. Incorporating regular exposure to natural environments into your routine can help you stay focused and calm throughout the day.

Mindset: Finally, our mindset can significantly influence our epigenetics and cultivating a growth mindset can help us optimise our performance. Incorporating practices such as gratitude journaling, positive self-talk and visualisation can help you cultivate a growth mindset and stay focused on your goals.

Polyphenol-rich foods: Polyphenols, found in foods such as berries, tea and dark chocolate, have been shown to promote epigenetic modifications that improve brain function and reduce inflammation.

Omega-3 fatty acids: Omega-3 fatty acids, found in fatty fish, have been shown to promote epigenetic modifications that improve brain function and reduce inflammation.

Probiotics: Probiotics have been shown to promote epigenetic modifications that improve gut health and reduce inflammation.

Prebiotics: Prebiotics, found in foods such as onions, garlic and bananas, have been shown to promote epigenetic modifications that improve gut health.

Phytochemicals: Phytochemicals, found in foods such as broccoli, kale and tomatoes, have been shown to promote epigenetic modifications that improve brain function and reduce inflammation.

Resveratrol: Resveratrol, found in red wine and grapes, has been shown to promote epigenetic modifications that improve brain function and reduce inflammation.

Vitamin D: Vitamin D has been shown to promote epigenetic modifications that improve bone health, immune function and brain function.

Curcumin: Curcumin, found in turmeric, has been shown to promote epigenetic modifications that improve brain function and reduce inflammation.

Incorporating these epigenetic interventions into your daily routine can help you optimise your performance, enhance your cognitive and physical abilities and promote overall well-being. Whether you choose to start with a few simple changes or dive in with a comprehensive lifestyle overhaul, taking control of your epigenetics can be a powerful tool for achieving your goals and living your best life. It's important to note that more research is needed to fully understand the effects of these interventions on epigenetic modifications and peak performance.

CONCLUSION

Epigenetic interventions are processes that can alter the expression of genes without actually changing the DNA sequence itself. These interventions have gained increasing attention in recent years for their potential to optimise human performance and enhance health outcomes.

The reason epigenetic interventions have an important role in achieving peak performance is that they can modulate gene expression in response to environmental cues, allowing the body to adapt and respond to stressors more effectively. This ability to adapt and respond to stressors is crucial for achieving peak performance, as it enables the body to withstand and recover from physical and mental demands.

To take full advantage of the potential of epigenetic interventions for peak performance, individuals can adopt a holistic approach that encompasses all of the aforementioned interventions. This may involve regular exercise, a healthy diet, stress management techniques and adequate sleep. It is also important to note that epigenetic interventions are not a one-size-fits-all solution, and different individuals may respond differently to different interventions based on their unique genetic makeup and environmental factors.

In summary, epigenetic interventions have an important role in achieving peak performance by modulating gene expression in response to environmental cues. To take full advantage of their potential, individuals can adopt a holistic approach that encompasses a range of interventions such as exercise, nutrition, stress management and sleep. By doing so, individuals can optimise their genetic potential and enhance their physical and mental performance.

CHAPTER 5

The Critical Role of Nutrition in Optimising Performance

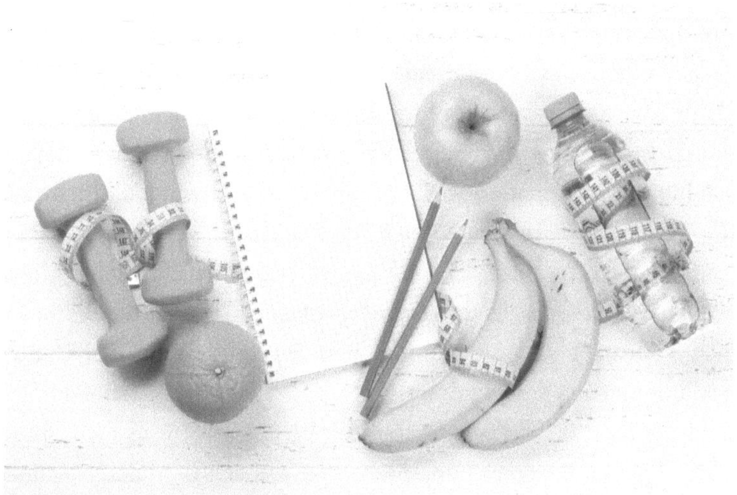

INTRODUCTION

Are you looking to take your performance to the next level? Whether you're an athlete, entrepreneur, or simply seeking to optimise your health, biohacking your nutrition could be the key to unlocking your full potential. Biohacking, the practice of using science and technology to optimise the body and mind, has gained popularity in recent years. By harnessing the power of nutrition, we can enhance our cognitive function, improve energy levels and even boost our immune system. But with so much information out there, it can be overwhelming to find out where to start. This is where a skilled biohacking nutritionist comes in. By analysing your unique biochemistry, they can create a personalised nutrition plan designed to help you achieve peak performance. So why settle for average when you can unlock your full potential through biohacking your nutrition?

Have you ever felt like your energy levels are low, your concentration is lacking, or your physical performance is not at its best? These issues can be caused by many factors, including poor nutrition. Biohacking is a way to optimise your body's performance, and it starts with the foods you eat. A few years ago, I began experiencing persistent tiredness, joint pains, dry skin and sores. After undergoing tests for my thyroid, I was diagnosed with hypothyroidism and prescribed Eltroxin. However, my symptoms persisted, and I was eventually referred to a consultant dermatologist who diagnosed me with Hashimoto's, an autoimmune condition, and prescribed medication to ease the itching. Three months ago, my doctor conducted a cholesterol test that revealed off-the-chart results for someone my age. Faced with the prospect of daily medication, I sought the advice of a nutritionist who recommended that I introduce more variety into my diet, reduce my animal fat intake, eat more vegetables and oily fish, cut out caffeine and processed foods and drink more water. I followed this advice and saw astonishing improvements, with my joint pains and dry skin disappearing and my cholesterol levels dropping dramatically. Implementing such small biohacks has made a world of difference in my life; till then my systems were wallowing in lethargy but of late they are running at full throttle like a Ferrari engine. Over the years, I have learnt several other nutritional biohacks like Bulletproof coffee for focus, energy and weight loss and the use of beet and Arginine for running, Theanine and caffeine for focus and mushrooms like Cordyceps for running and lion's mane for cognition.

One of the most effective hacks for peak performance is to focus on nutrient-dense foods. This means consuming foods that are rich in vitamins, minerals and other essential nutrients that our bodies need to function at their best. By eating a diet that is full of whole foods, such as fruits, vegetables, whole grains and lean proteins, we can provide our bodies with the fuel and nutrients they need to perform at their best.

Another important aspect of nutrition biohacking is to pay attention to our macronutrient ratios. This means balancing our intake of carbohydrates, proteins and fats to optimise our energy levels and performance. Depending on our individual needs and goals, we may need to adjust our macronutrient ratios to achieve optimal performance.

One Bollywood movie that comes to mind when discussing biohacking nutrition for phenomenal success is "Dangal" (2016), based on the true story of Indian wrestler Mahavir Singh Phogat, played by Aamir Khan. In the movie, Mahavir dreams of winning a gold medal for India in wrestling but is unable to do so himself due to family and financial constraints. Instead, he decides to train his daughters Geeta and Babita to become wrestling champions.

Mahavir takes a scientific and biohacking approach to their nutrition, training and conditioning. He feeds them a high-protein, low-fat diet and monitors their progress using a scale to measure their weight and a stopwatch to time their runs. He also hires a professional wrestling coach and creates a rigorous training regimen for them, including running in the sand, lifting weights and practising wrestling techniques for hours every day.

Despite facing societal opposition and the girls' initial reluctance, Mahavir's training pays off, and Geeta and Babita become successful wrestlers, winning numerous championships, and even representing India in the Commonwealth Games. Their success is a testament to the power of biohacking nutrition and training to achieve phenomenal success in sports and beyond.

The movie "Dangal" showcases how a determined individual can use scientific and biohacking techniques to push the limits of the human body and achieve extraordinary success.

HOW LEADING ATHLETES ARE BIOHACKING TO SUPERHUMAN PERFORMANCE

Athletes are always looking for ways to gain an edge over the competition, and many of them have turned to biohacking to do so. One popular approach is to use a high-fat, low-carb diet, also known as the ketogenic diet. By restricting carbohydrates, the body enters a state of ketosis, where it burns fat for fuel instead of glucose. This can lead to improved endurance, faster recovery times and better overall performance. Another biohacking strategy used by athletes is to use supplements to enhance their performance. Some of the most popular supplements include creatine, caffeine and beta-alanine. These supplements can improve muscle strength and endurance, increase focus and alertness and reduce fatigue.

Finally, many athletes use cryotherapy, which involves exposing the body to extremely cold temperatures, to improve their performance. Cryotherapy has been shown to reduce inflammation, speed up recovery times and improve overall well-being. Several other famous athletes have used nutrition for biohacking to achieve peak performance throughout history. Here are some examples:

Phelps: Michael Phelps is one of the most decorated Olympians in history, with 28 medals. Phelps is known to consume a high-calorie diet to fuel his training, including large quantities of carbohydrates and protein. He reportedly consumed up to 12,000 calories per day during his peak training periods.

Serena Williams: Serena Williams is considered one of the greatest tennis players of all time. Williams follows a primarily plant-based diet, with a focus on whole, nutrient-dense foods such as fruits, vegetables and whole grains. She also avoids processed foods and sugary drinks.

Tom Brady: Tom Brady is a professional football quarterback and has been known for his longevity in the sport. He follows a strict diet that focuses on whole foods, including lean protein, vegetables and whole grains. Brady also avoids processed foods, sugar and dairy.

Usain Bolt: Usain Bolt is considered the fastest man in history and has won numerous Olympic gold medals. Bolt reportedly consumes a diet high in carbohydrates, including pasta, rice and yams. He also consumes a moderate amount of protein and healthy fats.

Venus Williams: Venus Williams is also a professional tennis player and follows a raw vegan diet, which involves consuming uncooked fruits, vegetables, nuts and seeds. She credits her diet with helping her manage an autoimmune disease and improving her athletic performance.

These athletes demonstrate that nutrition can play a critical role in achieving peak performance. By consuming a diet that is high in nutrients and tailored to their individual needs, they are able to optimise their physical and mental performance. It is important to note that while these athletes follow specific diets, individual nutritional needs may vary and it is essential to consult with a qualified healthcare professional before making significant changes to one's diet or supplement regimen.

COMPONENTS OF FOOD AND THEIR IMPORTANCE IN HUMAN PERFORMANCE

As the food we eat provides the energy and nutrients needed for physical and cognitive function, recovery and growth, let's discuss the importance of macronutrients, micronutrients and phytonutrients, as well as the effects of various diets and supplements on performance. Additionally, let's explore the potential for personalised nutrition plans based on genetic and metabolic profiling.

Macronutrients

Macronutrients are nutrients required in large quantities by the body and are a critical component of a healthy diet. Each macronutrient serves a unique purpose in the body and is essential for optimising performance.

Protein

Protein is a macronutrient required for the growth and repair of tissues, making it crucial for athletes and individuals engaging in physical activity. Protein also helps to regulate metabolism, maintain immune function and aid in satiety. The recommended daily intake of protein varies depending on activity level and body weight, but generally, individuals should aim to consume 0.8 grams of protein per kilogram of body weight per day. However, athletes may require higher amounts of protein to optimise performance.

Carbohydrates

Carbohydrates are the primary fuel source for the body and are essential for maintaining energy levels during physical activity. The recommended daily intake of carbohydrates is 45-65% of total daily caloric intake, depending on activity level and individual needs. It is essential to consume high-quality, complex carbohydrates such as whole grains, fruits and vegetables, to maintain energy levels throughout the day. For example, an endurance athlete may require more carbohydrates, while a bodybuilder may need more protein.

Fats

Fats are essential for hormone production, cell membrane structure and the absorption of fat-soluble vitamins. The recommended daily intake of fat is 20-35% of the total daily caloric intake, with an emphasis on consuming healthy fats such as those found in nuts, seeds, avocados and fatty fish.

Micronutrients

Micronutrients are essential vitamins and minerals that the body needs in small amounts for optimal function. They play a crucial role in energy metabolism, immunity and cellular repair. Examples of micronutrients include vitamin C, iron and calcium. A deficiency in these nutrients can lead to poor performance, fatigue and even illness. Athletes, in particular, may have increased micronutrient needs due to increased energy expenditure and nutrient loss through sweat and urine.

Vitamins are essential for maintaining overall health and wellness, aiding in energy production and supporting immune function. Some of the critical vitamins for performance optimisation include vitamin D, vitamin B12 and vitamin C.

Minerals

Minerals play a critical role in various body functions, including muscle contraction, nerve function and bone health. Some essential minerals for performance optimisation include calcium, iron and magnesium.

Phytonutrients

Phytonutrients are plant compounds that provide health benefits beyond basic nutrition. They have anti-inflammatory and antioxidant properties and have been linked to reduced risk of chronic diseases such as cancer and heart disease. Examples of phytonutrients include polyphenols, carotenoids and flavonoids. These compounds can be found in fruits, vegetables and whole grains.

Polyphenols

Polyphenols are a type of phytonutrient found in various plant-based foods such as berries, tea and cocoa. These compounds have been shown to have anti-inflammatory properties and may aid in exercise recovery.

Carotenoids

Carotenoids are a type of phytonutrient found in various fruits and vegetables, including carrots, sweet potatoes and tomatoes. These compounds have been shown to have antioxidant properties and may improve immune function.

Diets

There are various diets that people follow to improve their performance, and each of these diets has its unique benefits and drawbacks. Some of the most popular diets and their impact on performance are discussed below:

Ketogenic Diet: A ketogenic diet is a low-carb, high-fat diet that is designed to promote weight loss and improve metabolic health. When you follow a ketogenic diet, your body enters a state of ketosis, which means that it begins to burn fat for energy instead of glucose. This can lead to improved mental clarity, increased energy levels and enhanced endurance during exercise.

Mediterranean Diet: The Mediterranean diet is a plant-based diet that is rich in fruits, vegetables, whole grains and healthy fats such as olive oil and nuts. This diet is associated with a reduced risk of heart disease, cancer and other chronic diseases. It is also believed to improve cognitive function, athletic performance and overall well-being.

Plant-Based Diet: A plant-based diet is a diet that is based primarily on foods derived from plants, such as fruits, vegetables, whole grains, legumes, nuts and seeds. This diet is associated with a reduced risk of chronic diseases, including heart disease, diabetes and cancer. It is also believed to improve athletic performance by providing a range of nutrients that are essential for energy production, muscle growth and recovery.

Paleo Diet: The paleo diet is a diet that is based on the types of foods that our ancestors would have eaten during the Palaeolithic era, such as lean meats, fish, fruits, vegetables, nuts and seeds. This diet is believed to improve athletic performance by providing a range of nutrients that are essential for muscle growth and recovery.

High-Protein Diet: A high-protein diet is a diet that is designed to promote muscle growth and improve athletic performance. This diet is typically high in lean protein sources such as chicken, fish and eggs, as well as protein supplements such as whey protein. It is also important to note that a high-protein diet can put a strain on the kidneys and lead to dehydration, so it is essential to stay hydrated and monitor kidney function.

Low-Fat Diet: A low-fat diet is a diet that is designed to reduce overall fat intake, which can help to reduce the risk of heart disease, diabetes and other chronic diseases. However, it is important to note that a low-fat diet can lead to a reduction in energy levels, which can have a negative impact on athletic performance.

In conclusion, different diets can have a significant impact on performance, depending on the individual's goals and needs. It is essential to choose a diet that is balanced and provides all the necessary nutrients for optimal health and performance. Additionally, it is important to consult with a registered dietitian or healthcare professional before making any significant dietary changes.

Probiotics and Fibre

Probiotics, prebiotics and fibre are all essential components of a healthy diet and play an important role in improving and impacting human performance.

Probiotics are live bacteria and yeasts that are good for our digestive system. They are found in certain foods like yoghurt, kefir, kimchi, sauerkraut and other fermented foods. Probiotics are important because they help to maintain a healthy balance of bacteria in the gut, which is crucial for proper digestion and absorption of nutrients. A healthy gut microbiome has been linked to improved immune function, better mental health and even better athletic performance. For example, studies have shown that athletes who consume probiotics have a reduced risk of upper respiratory tract infections, which can significantly impact their ability to train and compete.

Prebiotics, on the other hand, are a type of fibre that is found in certain foods like onions, garlic, asparagus and bananas. Prebiotics serve as food for the probiotics in our gut, helping them to thrive and maintain a healthy balance of bacteria. Prebiotics have been linked to improved digestion, better immune function and even better cognitive function. They can also help to improve nutrient absorption, which is important for athletes who need to fuel their bodies efficiently.

Fibre is also an important component of a healthy diet. It is found in plant-based foods like fruits, vegetables and whole grains. Fibre helps to promote satiety, which can help athletes to maintain a healthy body weight. It also helps to regulate blood sugar levels, which can help to prevent energy crashes and promote sustained energy levels throughout the day. Fibre is also important for gut health, as it helps to promote regular bowel movements and can help to prevent constipation.

Overall, incorporating probiotics, prebiotics and fibre into a healthy diet can have significant benefits for human performance. By promoting a healthy gut microbiome, these components can help to improve digestion and absorption of nutrients, boost immune function and promote sustained energy levels throughout the day.

Supplements

Supplements are products that are taken to supplement the diet and are often used to enhance performance. The following are some examples of popular supplements and their effects on performance.

Caffeine

Caffeine is a stimulant that has been shown to improve endurance performance by reducing fatigue and increasing alertness. It is commonly found in coffee, tea and energy drinks.

Creatine

Creatine is a compound found in muscle tissue and is commonly used by athletes to improve muscle strength and power. It has been shown to have potential benefits for high-intensity exercise performance.

Omega-3 Fatty Acids

Omega-3 fatty acids are essential fatty acids found in fatty fish and other sources. These compounds have been shown to have numerous health benefits, including reducing inflammation and improving heart health. Some studies have also suggested that omega-3 fatty acids may improve athletic performance by reducing muscle soreness and improving recovery.

Personalised Nutrition

Personalised nutrition is an emerging field that aims to tailor nutrition plans to individual needs based on genetic and metabolic profiling. Personalised nutrition plans based on genetic and metabolic profiling are becoming increasingly popular in the biohacking community. By tailoring nutrition plans to individual needs, individuals may be able to optimise their performance and overall health. This approach takes into account individual differences in nutrient metabolism and absorption, which can have a significant impact on performance optimisation.

For example, some individuals may require higher amounts of protein or specific micronutrients based on their genetic makeup. By tailoring nutrition plans to individual needs, personalised nutrition may improve athletic performance and overall health.

Nutrition plays a critical role in optimising performance, whether it be in sports, work, or daily life. The body requires a balance of macronutrients, micronutrients and phytonutrients to function at its best. Various diets and supplements may have a significant impact on performance optimisation, and personalised nutrition plans based on genetic and metabolic profiling may provide an even more effective approach to optimising performance. By paying attention to nutrition, individuals can improve their overall health and performance in various aspects of life.

Nutrition today is increasingly being used as a tool for biohacking and peak performance. Biohacking refers to the practice of using science, technology and lifestyle interventions to optimise physical and mental performance. The following are some ways nutrition is being used for biohacking and peak performance:

Tracking Macronutrients and Micronutrients

One popular biohacking strategy is to track macronutrients (protein, carbohydrates and fats) and micronutrients (vitamins and minerals) to ensure optimal intake. By tracking nutrient intake, individuals can ensure they are meeting their nutritional needs and potentially improve their performance.

Intermittent Fasting

Intermittent fasting involves alternating periods of fasting and eating. It has been shown to have potential benefits for weight loss, metabolic health and longevity. Some studies have also suggested that intermittent fasting may improve athletic performance by promoting fat utilisation during exercise.

SOME NUTRITIONAL BIOHACKING TOOLS TO IMPROVE YOUR DIET AND NUTRITION

Continuous Glucose Monitor (CGM): One of the most popular nutritional biohacking tools is the continuous glucose monitor (CGM). This device measures your blood glucose levels in real-time, allowing you to see how your body responds to different foods and drinks. It is used primarily by people with diabetes to monitor their blood sugar levels, but it can also be used by non-diabetics to optimise their diet and nutrition. By tracking your glucose levels throughout the day, you can identify which foods and meals are causing spikes and crashes in your blood sugar levels. This information can help you make more informed decisions about what to eat and when to eat it.

Personalised Nutrition Plans: Personalised nutrition plans are customised to your specific nutritional needs and goals. They take into account your age, sex, weight, height, activity level and other factors to create a diet plan that is tailored to your individual needs. By following a personalised nutrition plan, you can ensure that you are getting the nutrients you need to support your health and wellness goals.

DNA Analysis-Based Nutrition: DNA analysis-based nutrition is a relatively new field that uses genetic testing to create personalised nutrition plans. By analysing your DNA, nutritionists can identify genetic variants that impact how your body processes certain nutrients. This information can be used to create a customised nutrition plan that takes into account your unique genetic makeup.

Cryotherapy: Cryotherapy is a technique that involves exposing your body to extremely cold temperatures for a short period of time. It is believed to have a number of health benefits, including improved circulation, reduced inflammation and increased energy levels. Cryotherapy can also be used to improve athletic performance and aid in post-workout recovery.

Nanotechnology: Nanotechnology is the use of very small particles to create new materials and technologies. In the field of nutrition, nanotechnology is being used to create new supplements and functional foods that are more easily absorbed by the body. For example, some nanotechnology-based supplements are designed to improve the bioavailability of certain nutrients, such as vitamins and minerals.

Probiotics and Prebiotics: Probiotics are live bacteria that are beneficial to your digestive system. Prebiotics, on the other hand, are substances that feed the good bacteria in your gut. By incorporating probiotics and prebiotics into your diet, you can support the health of your digestive system and improve your overall health and wellness.

Finally, there are a variety of apps and websites that can help you track your nutrition and monitor your progress. These tools can provide valuable insights into your diet and help you make informed decisions about what to eat.

Overall, these nutritional biohacking tools can help you optimise your diet and nutrition for better health and performance. However, it is important to remember that each person's nutritional needs are unique, and what works for one person may not work for another. It is always a good idea to work with a qualified nutritionist or healthcare provider to create a personalised nutrition plan that is tailored to your individual needs and goals.

CONCLUSION

By incorporating nutritional biohacks into your diet, you can optimise your body's performance and achieve peak energy, cognition and even superhuman performance.

Experiment with different foods and supplements to find what works best for you. Use tools like CGMs and DNA testing kits to gain insights into your body's unique needs. Be patient and consistent. It may take time to see results, but the effort will be worth it. Don't forget about the basics. Eating a balanced diet, drinking plenty of water and getting enough sleep are all essential for optimal health and performance. Biohacking your nutrition for peak performance also involves paying attention to when and how you eat. Eating slowly and mindfully, chewing your food thoroughly and avoiding distractions while eating can help improve digestion and absorption of nutrients. Additionally, fuelling your body with the right nutrients before and after workouts can help improve performance and recovery.

In summary, nutrition is being used for biohacking and peak performance in various ways, including tracking macronutrients and micronutrients, intermittent fasting, the ketogenic diet, supplements and personalised nutrition plans. These approaches may improve athletic performance, weight loss, metabolic health and overall well-being. However, it is important to note that each individual's nutritional needs and responses may vary, and it is always best to consult with a qualified healthcare professional before making significant changes to one's diet or supplement regimen.

CHAPTER 6

The Importance of Sleep for Peak Performance

INTRODUCTION

Sleep is an essential aspect of human life, and its importance for optimal health and performance cannot be overstated. Adequate sleep is essential for physical, cognitive and emotional well-being, and its effects on performance have been studied in various fields, including sports, business and academics.

A favourite quote of mine is by Thomas Dekker that says - "Sleep is the golden chain that ties health and our bodies together." The quote beautifully captures the essence of the importance of sleep and how it is intricately connected to our physical and mental well-being. If this golden chain is disrupted our health suffers.

I have experienced firsthand the impact that sleep deprivation can have on our health and productivity. When I don't get enough sleep, I feel irritable, sluggish and unable to focus on tasks. It's almost as if my body and mind are not functioning optimally. Research has shown that even one night of sleep deprivation can cause blood sugar to surge, making a person's physiology resemble that of diabetics.

One of the most fascinating things about sleep is the way it allows our brains to undergo a thorough cleaning process. During sleep, the glymphatic system pumps cerebrospinal fluid around the brain in time with the pulsing of arteries. This liquid washes away soluble waste products before draining into the lymphatic system which clears out toxins and waste products, which otherwise could lead to a buildup of amyloid plaque. This buildup is associated with Alzheimer's disease and dementia, so getting enough sleep can help delay the onset of these debilitating conditions.

It's amazing to think about how something as simple as sleep can have such a profound impact on our health and well-being. I've come to realise that prioritising sleep is one of the most important things I can do for my overall health, and I try to make sure I'm getting enough rest every night. After all, a good night's sleep is truly priceless!

In my younger days falling asleep was never a problem. But, as I approached my mid-fifties, I began to notice that falling asleep wasn't as easy as it used to be. While I once slept soundly until 9 a.m., I started experiencing occasional bouts of restlessness in bed. However, I've since found ways to ensure a restful night's sleep.

First and foremost, I try to expose myself to natural light as soon as I wake up in the morning. This helps regulate my body's internal clock and supports healthy circadian rhythms. I've also learnt to avoid exercising too close to bedtime, as it can be too stimulating for my body.

To further promote relaxation, I've started taking Ashwagandha supplements and sipping on chamomile tea in the evenings. I make sure to avoid screens before bedtime since blue light can interfere with my body's production of melatonin. Instead, I opt for soft red lighting, which helps calm my mind and promotes a peaceful mood.

In the evenings, I spend time planning for the next day and engaging in reflective journaling. I also take a few minutes to read affirmations, which helps me stay positive and relaxed. By 10:30 p.m., I turn off all the lights in my bedroom to create a dark sleeping environment.

By following this sleep routine, I've been able to overcome occasional restlessness in bed and enjoy a more restful night's sleep. Plus, I've noticed that I'm more productive and energised the following day. Overall, prioritising healthy sleep habits is essential for our physical and mental well-being. Hence, in this chapter, we will explore the various aspects of sleep, their functions, and how they affect performance.

The Stages of Sleep

Sleep is a dynamic process that is divided into two main stages: Non-REM (NREM) sleep and REM sleep. NREM sleep is further divided into three stages, with each stage characterised by a different level of brain activity, muscle tone and eye movement.

NREM sleep

Stage 1: This is the stage of light sleep, where the person can be easily awakened. It is characterised by a decrease in muscle tone and slow eye movements.

Stage 2: This stage is marked by a decrease in heart rate, body temperature and breathing rate, and the brain produces bursts of rapid, rhythmic brain waves called sleep spindles and K-complexes.

Stage 3: This is the stage of deep sleep, also known as slow-wave sleep. It is characterised by the presence of slow, high-amplitude brain waves called delta waves. This is the stage where the body repairs and regenerates itself.

REM Sleep

REM sleep is the stage of sleep where the brain is most active and most dreaming occurs. It is characterised by rapid eye movements, increased heart rate and breathing rate and temporary paralysis of the muscles.

Tracking sleep

We can track our sleep using devices and take remedial measures to improve our sleep. There are several sleep-tracking devices available in the market for biohackers. Here are a few popular ones:

Oura Ring: The Oura Ring is a wearable device that tracks your sleep, activity and readiness levels. It uses infrared sensors to measure your body temperature, heart rate variability and respiratory rate and uses these measurements to track your sleep stages and quality. It also provides personalised feedback and guidance to help you optimise your sleep and overall health.

Fitbit: Fitbit is a popular brand of wearable devices that track sleep, activity and other health metrics. Their sleep-tracking technology uses a combination of movement sensors and heart rate monitoring to track your sleep stages and quality. They also provide personalised sleep insights and guidance to help you improve your sleep habits.

Garmin: Garmin is another brand of wearable devices that track sleep and other health metrics. Their sleep-tracking technology uses a combination of movement sensors, heart rate monitoring and pulse oximetry to track your sleep stages and quality. They also provide personalised insights and recommendations to help you optimise your sleep and overall health.

SleepScore Max: The SleepScore Max is a non-wearable device that tracks your sleep using advanced sonar technology. It measures your breathing and movement patterns to track your sleep stages and quality and provides personalised recommendations to help you improve your sleep.

Withings Sleep Analyser: The Withings Sleep Analyser is a non-wearable device that tracks your sleep using advanced sensors that slip under your mattress. It measures your movement, breathing and heart rate to track your sleep stages and quality and provides personalised insights and guidance to help you optimise your sleep.

Overall, there are many sleep-tracking devices available in the market for biohackers and choosing the right one depends on your personal preferences and needs. It's important to do your research and choose a device that is accurate, reliable and provides personalised insights and guidance to help you optimise your sleep and overall health.

FUNCTIONS OF SLEEP

Sleep serves various functions, including

Physical restoration: Sleep is essential for the restoration and repair of the body's tissues and cells, including muscle tissue, bone and skin.

Cognitive processing: Sleep plays a crucial role in consolidating memories and learning. During sleep, the brain processes and stores information, which is critical for memory retention.

Emotional regulation: Sleep is essential for emotional regulation and processing. A lack of sleep can lead to emotional instability and an increased risk of mood disorders such as depression and anxiety.

How Sleep Affects Performance

Sleep has a significant impact on performance, both physical and cognitive. Studies have shown that sleep deprivation can impair cognitive functions such as attention, memory and decision-making. It can also lead to a decline in physical performance, such as reduced reaction time, hand-eye coordination and endurance.

Impact of Sleep on Performance

There are numerous examples of how sleep affects performance in various fields, including sports, business and academics.

Sports: Professional athletes recognise the importance of sleep for peak performance. LeBron James, one of the greatest basketball players of all time, reportedly sleeps for 12 hours a day during the NBA playoffs to optimise his performance.

Business: Sleep deprivation can lead to poor decision-making, decreased productivity and an increased risk of accidents. The founder and CEO of Thrive Global, Arianna Huffington, is a strong advocate of sleep and even wrote a book on the topic called "The Sleep Revolution."

Academics: Students who get adequate sleep perform better academically than those who do not. A study conducted by Brown University found that college students who slept less than six hours a night had lower GPAs than those who slept for seven to eight hours a night.

THE IMPACT OF SLEEP DEPRIVATION AND SLEEP DISORDERS ON PERFORMANCE

Sleep deprivation and sleep disorders negatively impact performance. Here are some common sleep disorders and their symptoms.

Sleep Deprivation

Sleep deprivation is a condition where a person does not get enough sleep. This can be due to various factors, including work, school, or personal issues. Chronic sleep deprivation can have significant impacts on performance and health.

Effects of Sleep Deprivation on Performance

Sleep deprivation can cause impairments in cognitive function, including attention, memory and decision-making. It can also lead to a decline in physical performance, including reduced reaction time, hand-eye coordination and endurance.

Sleep deprivation can also affect emotional regulation and lead to irritability, mood swings and an increased risk of depression and anxiety.

Effects of Sleep Deprivation on Health

Sleep deprivation can have negative effects on overall health, including an increased risk of obesity, diabetes, heart disease and stroke. It can also weaken the immune system and increase the risk of infections.

Sleep Disorders

Sleep disorders are conditions that affect the quality or quantity of sleep. There are various sleep disorders, and their symptoms can vary depending on the disorder. Some common sleep disorders include:

Insomnia

Insomnia is a sleep disorder characterised by difficulty falling or staying asleep. Insomnia can be caused by various factors, including stress, anxiety, depression, or medications.

Sleep Apnoea

Sleep apnoea is a sleep disorder characterised by interrupted breathing during sleep. It is caused by a blockage of the airway, which can result in loud snoring, gasping for air and daytime sleepiness.

Restless Leg Syndrome

Restless leg syndrome is a sleep disorder characterised by an uncontrollable urge to move the legs during sleep. It can cause sleep disruption and daytime sleepiness.

Impact of Sleep Disorders on Performance

Sleep disorders can have a significant impact on performance in various fields.

Sports: Sleep apnoea can affect athletic performance by causing daytime sleepiness, fatigue and decreased endurance. Former NFL player Reggie White suffered from sleep apnoea, which contributed to his untimely death at the age of 43.

Business: Insomnia can affect decision-making, productivity and creativity. Media mogul Oprah Winfrey has spoken publicly about her struggles with insomnia and how it has affected her work.

Academics: Restless leg syndrome can cause sleep disruption, leading to daytime sleepiness and a decline in academic performance. Actress and singer Kristin Chenoweth has spoken about her struggles with restless leg syndrome and how it has affected her ability to learn lines and perform on stage.

SLEEP-ENHANCING STRATEGIES FOR PEAK PERFORMANCE

There are various strategies for enhancing sleep and optimising performance.

Sleep Hygiene

Sleep hygiene refers to the practices and habits that promote good sleep. Some sleep hygiene practices include:

- Establishing a regular sleep schedule
- Creating a relaxing bedtime routine
- Avoiding caffeine, alcohol and nicotine before bedtime
- Keeping the bedroom dark, quiet and cool
- Avoiding screens before bedtime

Relaxation Techniques

Relaxation techniques, such as meditation, deep breathing and progressive muscle relaxation, can help reduce stress and promote relaxation, leading to better sleep.

Sleep Aids

Sleep aids, such as prescription medications or over-the-counter supplements, can be effective in promoting sleep. However, it is essential to use these aids under the guidance of a healthcare professional.

ENHANCING BIOHACKING SLEEP

a) Examples of Sleep-Enhancing Strategies

Various individuals have adopted sleep-enhancing strategies to optimise their performance.

Sports: Tennis player Serena Williams has spoken about the importance of sleep hygiene for her athletic performance, and she reportedly sleeps for at least 10 hours a night.

Business: Jeff Bezos, founder and CEO of Amazon, has emphasised the importance of good sleep for decision-making and productivity. He reportedly gets eight hours of sleep a night and prioritises his sleep schedule.

Neuroscientist and sleep expert Matthew Walker has advocated for sleep hygiene and relaxation techniques to improve academic performance. He recommends establishing a regular sleep schedule and creating a relaxing bedtime routine to promote better sleep.

b) Some Important Athletes Who Biohacked Sleep for Peak Performance

LeBron James

LeBron James, a professional basketball player, reportedly spends around $1.5 million per year on his physical health and wellness, which includes prioritising his sleep. He aims to get at least 12 hours of sleep a night and reportedly uses a specialised bed that tracks his sleep patterns and adjusts to optimise his sleep.

Roger Federer

Tennis player Roger Federer is known for his intense training schedule, but he also prioritises his sleep to ensure he is in top form for his matches. He reportedly gets at least 10 hours of sleep a night, and when he travels for tournaments, he brings his mattress and pillows to ensure he gets a good night's rest.

Tom Brady

American football player Tom Brady is known for his strict health and wellness routine, which includes prioritising his sleep. He reportedly goes to bed by 8:30 p.m. and wakes up at 5:30 a.m. to get at least nine hours of sleep each night. He also uses blackout curtains and earplugs to create a dark and quiet sleeping environment.

Usain Bolt

Sprinter Usain Bolt, who holds multiple world records, reportedly prioritises his sleep by getting at least 8 hours of sleep a night. He also uses relaxation techniques, such as meditation, to help him fall asleep quickly and improve the quality of his sleep.

Venus Williams

Professional tennis player, Venus Williams has spoken publicly about her struggles with Sjogren's syndrome, an autoimmune disorder that can cause fatigue and joint pain. She has credited good sleep hygiene and prioritising her sleep as crucial components of her health and wellness routine.

These athletes are just a few examples of individuals who have recognised the importance of sleep in optimising their performance and have used various strategies to biohack their sleep for peak performance.

BIO HACKING TO IMPROVE SLEEP PERFORMANCE

There are various ways to "hack" sleep for better performance. Here are some strategies:

Establish a sleep routine: Set a regular sleep schedule and try to stick to it as much as possible, even on weekends. This helps regulate your body's internal clock and promotes better sleep quality.

Optimise your sleep environment: Create a sleep-conducive environment by keeping your bedroom cool, dark and quiet. Consider using earplugs, blackout curtains, or a white noise machine if necessary.

Avoid blue light exposure: Blue light from electronic devices can disrupt your sleep by suppressing melatonin production. Try to limit your exposure to electronic devices for at least an hour before bedtime, or use blue light-blocking glasses.

Manage stress: Stress can make it difficult to fall asleep and stay asleep. Incorporate relaxation techniques such as meditation, deep breathing, or progressive muscle relaxation to help manage stress levels.

Exercise regularly: Regular exercise can improve sleep quality and help regulate your body's internal clock. However, avoid exercising too close to bedtime as it can stimulate your body and make it harder to fall asleep.

Consider sleep aids: If you have trouble falling asleep or staying asleep, consider using sleep aids such as melatonin supplements, herbal remedies, or prescription medications. However, it's important to speak with a healthcare provider before using any sleep aids.

By implementing these strategies, individuals can optimise their sleep quality and quantity, leading to better performance in various aspects of their lives.

BEST SLEEP AIDS FOR SLEEPLESSNESS

There are various sleep aids available for sleeplessness, including

Melatonin: Melatonin is a hormone that regulates the sleep-wake cycle. It can be purchased over the counter as a dietary supplement and can be helpful for those who have difficulty falling asleep.

Valerian root: Valerian root is a herbal supplement that is believed to have sedative effects and can help improve sleep quality.

Chamomile: Chamomile is a plant that is commonly used as a tea and is known for its relaxing properties. It can help promote relaxation and improve sleep quality.

Lavender: Lavender is an essential oil that is believed to have calming and sedative effects. It can be used topically or aromatically to promote relaxation and improve sleep quality.

Prescription medications: In some cases, prescription medications may be necessary for treating sleep disorders such as insomnia. These medications should only be used under the guidance of a healthcare provider.

ZMA for sleep

ZMA (Zinc Magnesium Aspartate) is a dietary supplement that is marketed as a sleep aid and muscle recovery enhancer. It contains zinc, magnesium and vitamin B6, which are all essential nutrients that play a role in various bodily functions.

While some studies have suggested that ZMA may improve sleep quality, the evidence is mixed, and more research is needed to fully understand its effects. Some studies have found that ZMA supplementation improved sleep quality and duration in athletes, while others have found no significant effects on sleep.

It's important to note that ZMA is not a cure for sleep disorders, and individuals who are experiencing sleeplessness should speak with a healthcare provider to address the underlying causes of their sleep issues.

We must also keep in mind that while these sleep aids can be helpful, they should not be relied upon as a long-term solution for sleeplessness. It's essential to address the underlying causes of sleeplessness and adopt healthy sleep habits to promote long-term sleep health. If sleeplessness persists, it's important to speak with a healthcare provider to rule out any underlying medical conditions.

Use Of Barbiturates, Sedatives And Hallucinogens For Sleep

Barbiturates and sedatives are central nervous system depressants that are commonly used to treat sleep disorders such as insomnia. While these medications can help individuals fall asleep more easily, they can also disrupt the normal sleep cycle and reduce the amount of deep sleep obtained. Overuse or dependence on these medications can also lead to rebound insomnia and other negative side effects.

Hallucinogens such as LSD and psilocybin are not typically used for sleep enhancement and can have unpredictable effects on sleep. While some individuals have reported vivid and memorable dreams after using these substances, others have reported disruptions in sleep and increased wakefulness.

Overall, it's important to approach the use of any substance, whether natural or pharmaceutical, with caution when it comes to sleep. The best approach to optimising sleep quality and quantity is to focus on healthy sleep habits, such as maintaining a regular sleep schedule, creating a sleep-conducive environment and managing stress levels. If sleep problems persist, it's important to speak with a healthcare provider to rule out any underlying medical conditions and determine the most appropriate treatment plan.

SLEEP EPIDEMIC

The term "sleep epidemic" refers to the widespread problem of sleep deprivation that is affecting a large percentage of the global population. Studies suggest that the average amount of sleep that people are getting these days is around 6-7 hours per night, which is significantly less than the recommended 7-9 hours per night for adults.

There are several reasons why there may be a sleep epidemic. One major factor is the increasing demands and distractions of modern life, such as long work hours, excessive screen time and high levels of stress. These factors can interfere with the natural sleep-wake cycle and make it more difficult for individuals to obtain sufficient amounts of sleep.

Additionally, the prevalence of sleep disorders such as insomnia and sleep apnoea has increased in recent years, which can also contribute to the sleep epidemic. These disorders can disrupt the normal sleep cycle and make it more difficult for individuals to obtain restful and restorative sleep.

Another contributing factor is the cultural value placed on productivity and work, which can lead individuals to prioritise work over sleep and neglect their sleep needs. This can lead to a cycle of sleep deprivation and decreased productivity, as well as negative health consequences over the long term.

Overall, the sleep epidemic is a complex issue that requires a multifaceted approach to address. This may include education and awareness campaigns, policy changes to support work-life balance and healthy sleep habits and increased access to resources and treatments for sleep disorders.

Sleep is a critical component of overall health and performance. Sleep should be a priority in our lives. We often sacrifice sleep to meet deadlines or complete tasks, but this can have negative consequences for our health and performance. It's important to recognise that sleep is not a luxury, but a necessity for optimal health and performance. Creating a consistent sleep routine is key to ensuring that we get enough sleep and that our bodies can adjust to a regular sleep schedule. This includes going to bed and waking up at the same time every day, even on weekends.

Our sleep environment plays a crucial role in the quality of our sleep. This includes optimising factors such as temperature, noise and lighting to ensure that your bedroom is conducive to sleep. It's important to get enough sleep to ensure that our bodies have enough time to go through all the necessary sleep stages. While individual sleep needs vary, most adults require between 7-9 hours of sleep per night. Research has shown that getting enough sleep can improve cognitive function, memory and decision-making abilities. It can also improve physical performance and help with muscle recovery after exercise. During times of stress or increased workload, it's important to prioritise sleep even more. This can help reduce stress levels and improve our ability to cope with difficult situations.

CONCLUSION

In conclusion, sleep plays a critical role in optimising performance. The various stages of sleep each have unique functions that contribute to overall health and well-being. Sleep deprivation and sleep disorders can have significant impacts on performance and health, and it is essential to adopt sleep-enhancing strategies to promote better sleep. By prioritising sleep hygiene, relaxation techniques and sleep aids when necessary, individuals can optimise their performance and achieve their goals.

CHAPTER 7

The Science of Exercise for Peak Performance

INTRODUCTION

Before joining the Indian Police Service (IPS), I used to be a sedentary person, never really interested in physical activity. However, after joining the Indian Police Service, I found myself struggling with the rigorous outdoor training. My body rebelled against the intense physical demands, but I persevered. After three months of relentless training, I lost all abdominal fat and looked incredibly fit. The transformation was remarkable, and it had a significant impact on my life.

Not only did my physical fitness improve, but it also enhanced my cognition, creativity and productivity. I noticed that being fit helped me feel better both mentally and physically. As a result, my mood improved and my productivity skyrocketed. I was able to perform better at work and in other areas of my life.

However, after I joined the service and as time passed, I found myself falling into a life of comfort and lethargy. I was not doing enough to maintain my fitness level. I admired my colleagues who ran regularly, but I was reluctant to do so myself. It wasn't until one fine winter morning that I finally decided to dust off my shoes and go for a 15-minute run. Little did I know that this decision would change my life forever.

Running felt terrible at first, but as I ran consistently, it started to feel amazing. I began to enjoy the experience and soon found myself addicted to it. Running liberated me from negativity, anxiety and fear. It became my daily dose of meditation and helped me solve my life problems from a positive mental state of mind.

Running allowed me to explore new frontiers, nourished my joy and helped me be more mindful. It made fantastic things come about in my life. I felt rapturous and ecstatic beyond words, losing myself in the moment completely. I continued to run, and over time, I ran several marathons and even earned a couple of Asian records.

My story demonstrates the importance of exercise for peak performance. Physical fitness not only enhances our health but also improves our mental well-being. The benefits of exercise translate into all areas of our lives, making us more productive, creative and positive. If a couch potato like me could derive so much benefit from exercise there is so much at stake for everyone. Let's see why exercise is important for peak performance or why regular exercise is essential for maintaining a healthy body and mind. The answer lies in the science of exercise, which explores the physiological and psychological benefits of physical activity for performance.

Physiological Benefits

Regular physical activity has been shown to improve cardiovascular health, metabolic function and overall physical well-being. Let's dive into each of these areas in more detail.

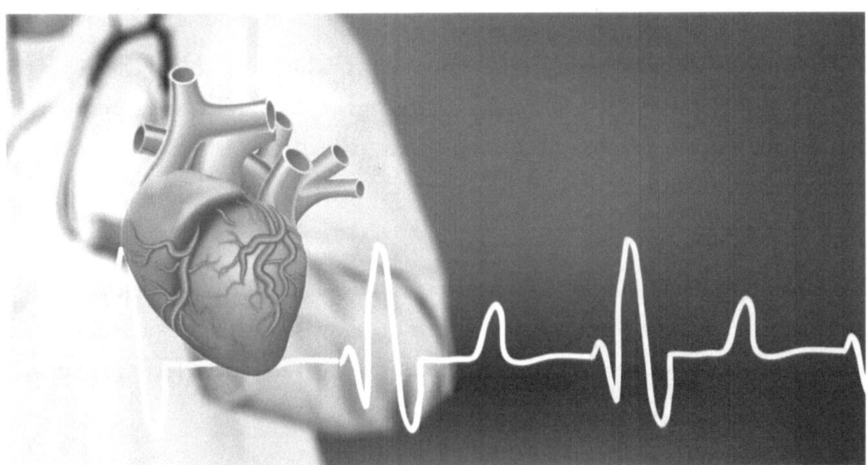

Cardiovascular Health

When you exercise, your heart pumps more blood to your muscles, increasing the efficiency of your cardiovascular system. This leads to a decreased risk of heart disease, stroke and high blood pressure. Additionally, exercise can improve the function of your blood vessels, making them more flexible and better able to regulate blood flow.

Metabolic Function

Exercise also plays a crucial role in regulating your metabolism, which is the process by which your body converts food into energy. Aerobic exercise, such as running or cycling, can increase your metabolic rate, which means that you burn more calories even when you're at rest. Resistance training, on the other hand, can increase your muscle mass, which can also help to boost your metabolism.

Physical Well-being

Physical activity has numerous benefits for your overall well-being. Regular exercise can improve your sleep quality, increase your energy levels and even improve your immune function. Additionally, exercise has been shown to be an effective tool for managing chronic conditions such as arthritis and diabetes.

Psychological Benefits

In addition to the physiological benefits, exercise also has numerous psychological benefits that can help to improve your mood, reduce stress and anxiety and boost your self-esteem.

Mood Regulation

When you exercise, your body releases endorphins, which are natural chemicals that can help to improve your mood and reduce feelings of stress and anxiety. Additionally, exercise can provide a sense of accomplishment, which can help to boost your self-esteem and confidence.

Stress Reduction

Regular exercise can also help to reduce stress levels. This is because exercise can help to reduce the levels of stress hormones in your body, such as cortisol. Additionally, exercise can provide a sense of control, which can help to reduce feelings of anxiety and helplessness.

Types of Exercise

There are many different types of exercise, each with its own unique benefits. Let's explore a few of the most common types of exercise.

Aerobic Exercise

Aerobic exercise, also known as cardio, is any type of exercise that increases your heart rate and breathing rate. This can include activities such as running, cycling, swimming and dancing. Aerobic exercise is great for improving cardiovascular health and boosting your metabolism. It has been shown to improve memory, attention and processing speed.

Resistance Training

Resistance training, also known as strength training, involves using weights or resistance bands to work your muscles. This can include exercises such as squats, lunges and bicep curls. Resistance training is great for increasing muscle mass and boosting your metabolism.

High-Intensity Interval Training (HIIT)

High-intensity interval training, or HIIT, involves alternating between periods of intense exercise and rest. This can include activities such as sprinting or jumping jacks. HIIT is great for improving cardiovascular health and boosting your metabolism. HIIT has been shown to improve cognitive function and reduce symptoms of depression and anxiety.

Yoga

Yoga combines physical exercise with mindfulness and meditation, making it an excellent choice for improving both physical and mental health.

Tailoring Exercise to Individual Needs and Goals

One of the great things about exercise is that it can be tailored to individual needs and goals. For example, if you're looking to improve your cardiovascular health, you might focus on aerobic exercise such as running or cycling. If you're looking to increase your muscle mass, you might focus on resistance training. And if you're short on time, you might opt for a HIIT workout that can be done in just a few minutes.

THE EFFECTS OF EXERCISE ON THE BRAIN

Exercise has numerous benefits for the brain, including

Increased Blood Flow: Exercise increases blood flow to the brain, which can help to nourish brain cells and improve cognitive function.

Neurogenesis: Exercise promotes the growth of new brain cells in the hippocampus, which is the part of the brain responsible for memory and learning.

Brain Plasticity: Exercise can enhance brain plasticity, which is the brain's ability to change and adapt in response to new experiences.

Neurotransmitter Release: Exercise increases the release of neurotransmitters such as dopamine and serotonin, which can improve mood and reduce stress.

Exercise offers a multitude of benefits for the body, including

Improved cardiovascular health: Exercise helps to strengthen the heart and lungs, improving their efficiency and reducing the risk of heart disease, stroke and other cardiovascular problems.

Increased muscle strength and endurance: Regular exercise helps to build and maintain strong muscles, which can improve posture, balance and overall physical function.

Weight management: Exercise can help to burn calories and reduce body fat, helping to maintain a healthy weight.

Improved bone health: Weight-bearing exercise, such as walking or jogging, can help to build and maintain strong bones, reducing the risk of osteoporosis.

Reduced risk of chronic diseases: Regular exercise has been linked to a reduced risk of chronic diseases such as type 2 diabetes, certain cancers and depression.

Better sleep: Exercise can help to improve sleep quality and reduce the risk of sleep disorders.

Increased energy and stamina: Regular exercise can help to increase energy levels and reduce feelings of fatigue.

Improved immune function: Exercise can help to boost the immune system, reducing the risk of infections and illnesses.

Overall, exercise is essential for maintaining good physical and mental health. Incorporating regular exercise into our daily routine can provide numerous benefits for our body and mind.

How Much Exercise Is Needed for Optimal Performance?

The amount of exercise needed for optimal performance can vary depending on the individual's age, health status and fitness level. However, some general guidelines include:

Cardiovascular Exercise: Adults should aim for at least 150 minutes of moderate-intensity aerobic exercise per week or 75 minutes of vigorous-intensity aerobic exercise per week.

Resistance Training: Adults should aim to do resistance training exercises at least two days per week.

Flexibility Training: Adults should aim to do flexibility training exercises, such as stretching or yoga, at least two days per week.

ROLE OF EXERCISE AS A POWERFUL BIOHACKING TOOL TO ENHANCE PERFORMANCE

Biohacking has emerged as a popular trend in recent years, with individuals looking to optimise their physical and mental performance through unconventional means. Exercise is one of the most powerful biohacking tools and several famous personalities have used it to achieve superhuman performance in various fields.

Wim Hof, also known as the "Iceman," has developed a unique method of breathing and cold exposure that he believes can boost the immune system and improve overall health. However, Hof also emphasises the importance of physical exercise in his routine. He often incorporates yoga and other forms of exercise into his routine to enhance his overall physical and mental performance.

Laird Hamilton, the American big-wave surfer, incorporates a mix of strength training, high-intensity interval training and breathing exercises into his routine. Hamilton believes that exercise is the key to achieving optimal health and performance.

He often uses unconventional training methods such as underwater weightlifting and training with large rocks to challenge his body and push his limits.

David Goggins, a retired Navy SEAL and ultramarathon runner, also emphasises the importance of exercise in his routine. Goggins has completed multiple ultramarathons, triathlons and other endurance events, often pushing himself to the brink of exhaustion. He attributes his success to his intense physical training, which includes running, weightlifting and other forms of exercise.

Tim Ferriss, an American author and entrepreneur, experiments with various biohacking techniques, including cold exposure, intermittent fasting and high-intensity interval training. However, he also emphasises the importance of exercise in his routine. Ferriss believes that exercise is one of the most powerful tools for enhancing physical and mental performance and achieving optimal health.

Joe Rogan, an American comedian and podcast host, also advocates for exercise as a biohacking tool. Rogan is an avid practitioner of Brazilian Jiu-Jitsu, a martial art that emphasises grappling and ground fighting. He also advocates for various biohacking techniques such as saunas, cold exposure and high-intensity interval training to enhance physical and mental performance.

Exercise has emerged as one of the most powerful biohacking tools for achieving superhuman performance in various fields. By incorporating physical exercise into their routine, individuals can enhance their overall physical and mental performance, push their limits and achieve their full potential.

Exercise has been depicted as a powerful tool for enhancing physical and mental performance in various movies and books. Iconic films like "Rocky" and "Creed" showcase the physical transformations of Sylvester Stallone's character, Rocky Balboa, through gruelling training regimens, demonstrating how exercise can help one achieve peak physical and mental performance. Similarly, "Unbroken," directed by Angelina Jolie, showcases the transformation of Louis Zamperini, an Olympic runner, who uses exercise to survive a gruelling internment in a Japanese prisoner of war camp.

The book, *"Can't Hurt Me"* by David Goggins, explores the power of exercise and mindset to push past perceived limits and achieve extraordinary results. In "The Rise of Superman" by Steven Kotler, we see how extreme athletes use exercise to achieve a state of flow, where their physical and mental abilities are optimised to achieve peak performance.

These movies and books illustrate the transformative power of exercise, showing how it can help individuals overcome challenges and achieve their goals.

By incorporating exercise into our daily routines, we too can harness the power of physical activity and achieve our full potential.

STUDIES CONDUCTED ON EXERCISE ON ITS ROLE IN PERFORMANCE

Numerous studies have shown that exercise can have a significant impact on an individual's physical and mental performance, leading to increased success in various aspects of life. A study published in the Journal of Applied Psychology found that employees who engaged in regular physical activity reported greater job satisfaction and overall well-being than those who did not exercise. The study also found that exercise was associated with higher levels of energy, better time management skills and improved ability to handle stress.

A meta-analysis published in the British Journal of Sports Medicine found that exercise can improve cognitive function, including attention, memory and executive function. The study concluded that regular exercise may be an effective strategy for improving cognitive performance in both healthy individuals and those with cognitive impairments. Another study published in the Journal of Clinical Psychiatry found that exercise can be as effective as medication in treating depression. The study found that individuals who engaged in regular exercise had significant reductions in symptoms of depression, and that exercise was just as effective as medication in treating mild to moderate depression.

Further, a study in the Journal of Strength and Conditioning Research has reported that regular exercise can improve athletic performance by increasing strength, power and endurance. The study found that individuals who engaged in regular resistance training saw significant improvements in their athletic performance, including increased speed, agility and vertical jump height. While a study published in the Journal of Occupational Health Psychology found that employees who engaged in regular physical activity were more productive and had lower rates of absenteeism than those who did not exercise, it also found that exercise was associated with improved job performance and job satisfaction.

These studies provide strong evidence that exercise is a powerful tool for enhancing performance and success. The findings of these studies have important implications for individuals, organisations and society as a whole.

For example, for individuals, regular exercise can be an effective strategy for improving physical health, mental well-being and cognitive function, all of which are critical for peak performance and success in various areas of life. By incorporating exercise into their daily routine, individuals can optimise their physical and mental performance and achieve their goals.

For organisations, promoting physical activity and exercise among employees can lead to higher levels of productivity, job satisfaction and overall well-being, which can ultimately benefit the bottom line. By providing opportunities for employees to engage in physical activity and exercise, organisations can create a more positive and supportive work environment that promotes peak performance and success.

For society as a whole, promoting physical activity and exercise can have numerous benefits, including reducing healthcare costs, improving public health and enhancing the overall quality of life. By investing in programmes and policies that promote physical activity and exercise, societies can create a more resilient and thriving population that is better equipped to handle the challenges of modern life.

Hence, the science of exercise provides compelling evidence that regular physical activity can have a profound impact on physical and mental performance, leading to greater success and well-being in various areas of life. Whether it's through resistance training, aerobic exercise, or high-intensity interval training, there are numerous ways to incorporate exercise into daily life and reap the benefits of this powerful biohacking tool.

CONCLUSION

In conclusion, the science of exercise is a fascinating and endlessly engrossing topic that explores the numerous benefits of physical activity for performance. By engaging in regular exercise, individuals can experience a range of physiological and psychological benefits, such as improved cardiovascular health, metabolic function and mood regulation.

Moreover, there are various types of exercises, including aerobic, resistance and high-intensity interval training, each with unique benefits. Exercise can also be tailored to individual needs and goals, making it an excellent way to improve overall physical and mental health.

By understanding the science behind exercise, individuals can make informed choices about the type of exercise they engage in, helping them to achieve their desired results. Whether you're an athlete looking to improve performance or someone looking to maintain a healthy lifestyle, incorporating exercise into your routine is a great way to achieve optimal physical and mental performance. So, let's lace up our shoes, hit the gym and start reaping the benefits of exercise for optimal performance.

CHAPTER 8

Mindfulness and Meditation for Peak Performance

INTRODUCTION

Mindfulness and meditation have gained widespread popularity in recent years, with many people practising these techniques for their numerous benefits. These practices can help individuals enhance their cognitive function, emotional regulation and stress management skills. In the present chapter, we will discuss the neuroscience of mindfulness and meditation, the various techniques and applications for enhancing performance, and how these practices have contributed to peak performance in various fields.

Many famous personalities have credited their success to the practice of mindfulness and meditation. These include George Harrison, who was a practitioner of Transcendental Meditation (TM), Steve Jobs, who famously meditated regularly and Oprah Winfrey, who is an advocate of mindfulness practices.

George Harrison was introduced to TM in the mid-1960s and became a devoted practitioner for the rest of his life. He credited the practice with helping him cope with the stress and pressure of being a member of the Beatles, as well as enhancing his creativity and productivity. In an interview with Rolling Stone magazine, he said, "It's like a key to a secret room, and the room is a better room for being there."

Steve Jobs was also a fan of mindfulness and meditation. He famously spent time at a Zen centre in India in the 1970s and continued to practise meditation throughout his life. He once said, "If you just sit and observe, you will see how restless your mind is. If you try to calm it, it only makes it worse, but over time it does calm, and when it does, there's room to hear more subtle things—that's when your intuition starts to blossom and you start to see things more clearly and be in the present more. Your mind just slows down, and you see a tremendous expanse at the moment. You see so much more than you could see before."

Oprah Winfrey is another well-known advocate of mindfulness practices. She has spoken publicly about how meditation has helped her manage stress, improve her focus and enhance her overall well-being. She has also hosted several episodes of her TV show, Super Soul Sunday, dedicated to exploring the benefits of mindfulness and meditation.

Research has consistently shown that mindfulness and meditation have numerous benefits for cognitive function, emotional regulation and stress management. For example, a study published in the journal Frontiers in Human

Neuroscience found that just four days of mindfulness meditation training improved working memory capacity and executive control. Another study published in the Journal of Personality and Social Psychology found that mindfulness meditation reduced negative effects and stress reactivity. As more research is conducted, we can expect to learn even more about how these practices can enhance peak performance in various domains.

As someone who has always been fascinated by the human mind and its vast potential, I've been exploring various techniques to enhance my performance and tap into altered states of consciousness. One approach that has captivated my attention is the use of binaural beats during meditation.

It's astonishing to think that humans have been using altered states of consciousness for ages, but our modern monophasic lifestyle has led us to forget these innate abilities. Thankfully, I stumbled upon the works of visionaries like Steven Kotler and Vishen Lakhiani, who shed light on the incredible potential of tapping into different brainwave frequencies to transform our realities.

When I slip on my headphones and listen to carefully crafted binaural beats, I'm transported to a whole new realm of consciousness. As the beats synchronise my brainwaves, I can feel a shift in my awareness. Alpha waves envelop me, and I enter a state of relaxed focus and heightened creativity. Ideas flow effortlessly, and I'm able to access insights that were once elusive in my regular waking state.

But it doesn't end there. As the beats transition to theta waves, I find myself diving into a deeper state of meditation. My mind becomes calm, and I'm able to connect with my inner self on a profound level. I experience vivid images and sensations arising from my subconscious mind, revealing hidden truths and illuminating aspects of my being that I wasn't aware of before. It's a journey of self-discovery that leaves me in awe of the vast potential of the human mind.

The binaural beats continue to guide me deeper, and I enter the realm of delta waves. I feel a profound sense of relaxation as if my body and mind are being rejuvenated at a cellular level. It's an experience of deep replenishment and revitalisation, leaving me feeling refreshed and renewed.

As I explore these altered states of consciousness with binaural beats, I can't help but envision the possibilities. I imagine effortlessly entering a flow state during my work, where my creativity and productivity soar to new heights. I see myself tapping into my subconscious mind to unlock hidden potentials and reshape my external reality. The potential for growth, insight, and transformation is awe-inspiring, and I'm left with an insatiable curiosity to continue delving into the depths of my consciousness. Everyone can unlock the hidden realms of consciousness and enhance their performance in ways they never thought possible. Please try exploring the mysteries of altered states of consciousness.

The Neuroscience of Mindfulness and Meditation:

Research has shown that mindfulness and meditation can positively impact the structure and function of the brain. Mindfulness practices such as focused attention meditation can lead to increased activity in the prefrontal cortex, which is associated with attention and cognitive control. Meditation has also been shown to increase grey matter in regions of the brain involved in emotion regulation, such as the anterior cingulate cortex and hippocampus.

Furthermore, mindfulness and meditation can also affect the default mode network, a network of brain regions that is active when we are not focused on a task. When we practise mindfulness, we are more likely to reduce activity in this network, leading to improved attention and cognitive function.

Techniques and Applications for Enhancing Performance:

There are many different techniques and applications of mindfulness and meditation for enhancing performance. One such technique is mindfulness-based stress reduction (MBSR), which is a programme that uses mindfulness practices to help individuals cope with stress and improve their overall well-being.

Another technique is loving-kindness meditation, which involves cultivating feelings of love, kindness and compassion towards oneself and others. This practice has been shown to improve empathy and reduce stress.

Mindfulness and meditation can also be used in sports and athletic training. For example, many professional athletes practise mindfulness and meditation to improve their focus and mental clarity during competitions.

There are many books, movies and celebrities that have embraced mindfulness and meditation as a way to enhance their performance. One notable example is the book *"10% Happier"* by Dan Harris, which chronicles the author's journey from scepticism to embracing mindfulness meditation.

Another example is the movie "The Mindful Athlete," which explores how mindfulness practices can be used to enhance performance in sports. The movie features interviews with many professional athletes who practise mindfulness, including NBA player George Mumford.

Celebrities such as Katy Perry and Hugh Jackman have also spoken publicly about their meditation practices and how it has helped them improve their mental well-being and performance in their respective fields.

How the Practice of Meditation Contributes to Peak Performance:

The practice of meditation has been shown to contribute to peak performance in various fields. For example, studies have shown that mindfulness practices can improve cognitive function, including attention and memory. This can be particularly helpful for students and professionals who need to maintain focus and concentration for long periods.

Furthermore, mindfulness practices can also help individuals regulate their emotions and reduce stress. This can be helpful for individuals in high-pressure jobs or in situations where they need to remain calm under pressure, such as athletes competing in high-stakes competitions.

Finally, mindfulness and meditation practices can also improve overall well-being, which can contribute to peak performance in all areas of life. By reducing stress and improving emotional regulation, individuals are better able to focus on their goals and perform at their best.

KEY BENEFITS OF MINDFULNESS AND MEDITATION FOR PEAK PERFORMANCE

Improved Focus and Concentration:

One of the most widely recognised benefits of mindfulness and meditation is improved focus and concentration. These practices can help us train our minds to stay present at the moment, rather than getting lost in distractions and multitasking. By learning to stay focused and attentive, we can achieve greater productivity and efficiency in our work and personal lives.

Reduced Stress and Anxiety

Stress and anxiety can be significant barriers to peak performance, as they can interfere with our ability to think clearly and make decisions. Mindfulness and meditation can help us manage stress and anxiety by teaching us how to respond to challenging situations with calm and equanimity. By learning to stay centred and grounded, we can approach challenges with a clear head and make better decisions.

Increased Emotional Intelligence

Emotional intelligence is the ability to understand and manage our own emotions, as well as to perceive and respond to the emotions of others. Mindfulness and meditation can help us develop greater emotional intelligence by teaching us how to observe our thoughts and feelings without judgement. By cultivating a non-judgemental awareness of our inner world, we can develop greater empathy and compassion for others.

Improved Creativity

Another benefit of mindfulness and meditation is increased creativity. These practices can help us access the deeper parts of our minds, where creative ideas often originate. By learning to quiet our busy minds and listen to our intuition, we can tap into our innate creativity and generate new and innovative ideas.

Greater Resilience

Finally, mindfulness and meditation can help us develop greater resilience in the face of challenges and setbacks. By teaching us how to stay present in the moment and accept things as they are, these practices can help us bounce back from adversity and stay focused on our goals. Here are a few examples of how these practices are being used in different fields:

Professional Sports

Many professional athletes have embraced mindfulness and meditation as ways to improve their performance on the field or court. For example, LeBron James, Kobe Bryant and Michael Jordan are all known to have practised meditation to help them stay focused and calm during high-pressure situations. In addition, many professional sports teams now incorporate mindfulness and meditation into their training programmes to help athletes manage stress and improve mental resilience.

Education

In recent years, mindfulness and meditation have also become popular tools in the education field. Teachers and students alike are using these practices to help manage stress and anxiety, improve focus and attention and enhance overall well-being. For example, a study of a mindfulness programme in schools found that students who participated in the programme had better executive function and emotional regulation than those who did not.

Business

Mindfulness and meditation are also being used in the business world to help leaders and employees manage stress and improve productivity. Many companies now offer mindfulness and meditation programmes as part of their wellness initiatives, recognising that these practices can lead to better job performance and overall job satisfaction.

SOME WAYS OF BIOHACKING MEDITATION FOR PEAK PERFORMANCE

Binaural Beats

Binaural beats are a type of sound therapy that involves playing two different frequencies in each ear. This creates a third frequency that the brain perceives as a rhythmic beat. Studies have shown that listening to binaural beats can enhance relaxation, reduce anxiety and improve focus during meditation. By using binaural beats during meditation, you can enhance the benefits of the practice and potentially achieve deeper states of relaxation and focus.

Neurofeedback

Neurofeedback is a type of biofeedback that uses real-time brain activity data to train the brain to regulate its activity. This can be particularly useful for enhancing the benefits of meditation and mindfulness, as it can help you learn to control your brainwaves and enter deeper states of relaxation and focus.

Wearable Technology

There are now several wearable technologies available that can help enhance the benefits of meditation and mindfulness. For example, the Muse headband uses EEG sensors to measure brain activity and provide feedback on your meditation practice. This can help you stay focused and engaged during meditation and track your progress over time.

Supplementation

Certain supplements have been shown to enhance the benefits of meditation and mindfulness. For example, omega-3 fatty acids have been shown to reduce inflammation and enhance brain function, while magnesium can help reduce stress and promote relaxation. By supplementing your diet with these and other nutrients, you can enhance the benefits of your meditation practice and achieve peak performance.

Mindfulness-based Cognitive Therapy (MBCT)

MBCT is a type of therapy that combines mindfulness practices with cognitive therapy techniques. It is effective for reducing symptoms of depression and anxiety, as well as enhancing overall well-being. By integrating MBCT into your meditation practice, you can enhance the cognitive benefits of mindfulness and potentially achieve peak performance in various areas of your life.

These are just a few examples of the many ways to hack meditation and mindfulness for peak performance. By experimenting with different techniques and technologies, you can discover what works best for you and unlock the full potential of these practices.

DEVICES THAT CAN BE USED TO ENHANCE THE BENEFITS OF MINDFULNESS AND MEDITATION

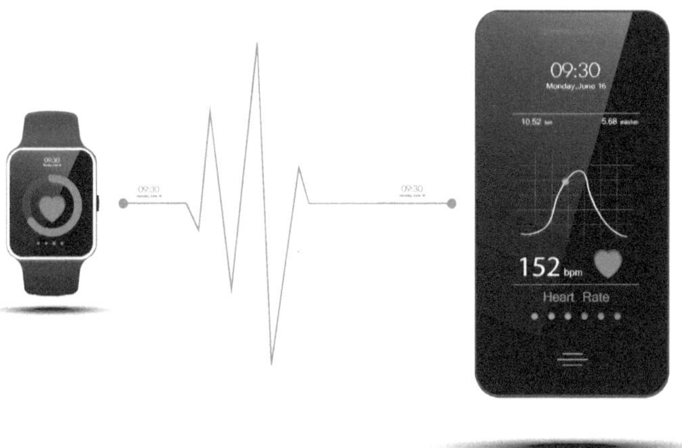

Heart Rate Variability (HRV) Monitors

HRV monitors measure the variation in time between successive heartbeats, which is an indicator of overall heart health and stress levels. By using an HRV monitor during meditation, you can track your stress levels and see how they change in response to different techniques and practices.

Light Therapy Devices

Light therapy devices use special lights to simulate natural sunlight and promote relaxation and mood enhancement. By using a light therapy device during meditation, you can enhance the relaxation and mood-enhancing benefits of the practice.

Essential Oil Diffusers

Essential oils are plant extracts that have been shown to have various health benefits, including promoting relaxation and reducing stress. By using an essential oil diffuser during meditation, you can enhance the relaxation and stress-reducing benefits of the practice.

Biofeedback Devices

Biofeedback devices use sensors to monitor physiological data, such as heart rate, blood pressure and muscle tension. By using a biofeedback device during meditation, you can receive real-time feedback on your physiological responses and learn to control them through mindfulness practices.

Mindfulness Apps

There are many mindfulness apps available that provide guided meditations and other tools to enhance your practice. Examples include Headspace, Calm and Insight Timer. By using a mindfulness app, you can receive guidance and support for your meditation practice and potentially enhance the benefits of the practice.

Neuralink

Neuralink is a company co-founded by Elon Musk that is working on developing brain-machine interfaces (BMIs). The goal of these BMIs is to create a direct connection between the human brain and computers, which could potentially revolutionise the way we interact with technology and even enhance human performance.

One potential application of Neuralink's technology is to enhance the benefits of meditation and mindfulness. By creating a direct link between the brain and a computer, Neuralink could potentially monitor brain activity during meditation and provide real-time feedback to help the meditator enter deeper states of relaxation and focus.

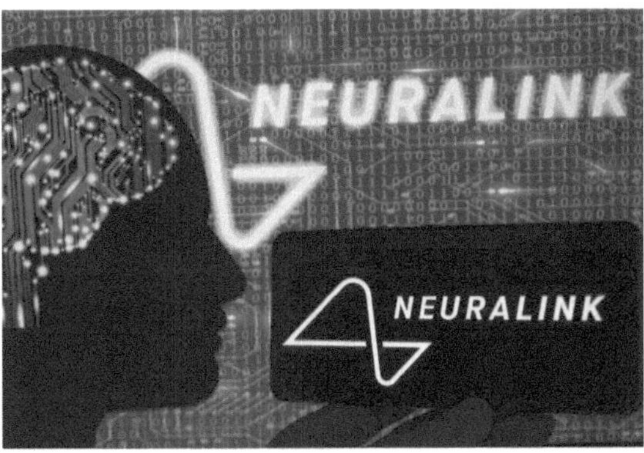

Another potential application is to use BMIs to enhance cognitive function and memory. By creating a direct connection between the brain and a computer, it may be possible to enhance memory recall and cognitive function by augmenting the brain's natural abilities.

While these are exciting possibilities, it's important to note that Neuralink's technology is still in the early stages of development, and many ethical and safety concerns need to be addressed. It's also unclear how these technologies will be regulated and how they will impact society as a whole. Neuralink has the potential to revolutionise the way we interact with technology and potentially enhance human performance, including the benefits of meditation and mindfulness. However, it's important to approach these developments with caution and ensure that ethical and safety concerns are carefully addressed.

These are just a few examples of the many devices and technologies available to enhance the benefits of meditation and mindfulness. By experimenting with different tools and techniques, you can find what works best for you and potentially achieve peak performance in various areas of your life.

CONCLUSION

In conclusion, mindfulness and meditation are powerful tools for enhancing performance in all areas of life. By improving focus and concentration, reducing stress and anxiety, increasing emotional intelligence, promoting creativity and enhancing resilience, these practices can help us achieve our goals and reach our full potential. Whether you're an athlete, a student, a business professional, or simply someone who wants to improve their mental and emotional well-being, mindfulness and meditation can be an invaluable addition to your arsenal of peak performance tools.

CHAPTER 9

Nootropics: Cognitive Enhancers for Peak Performance

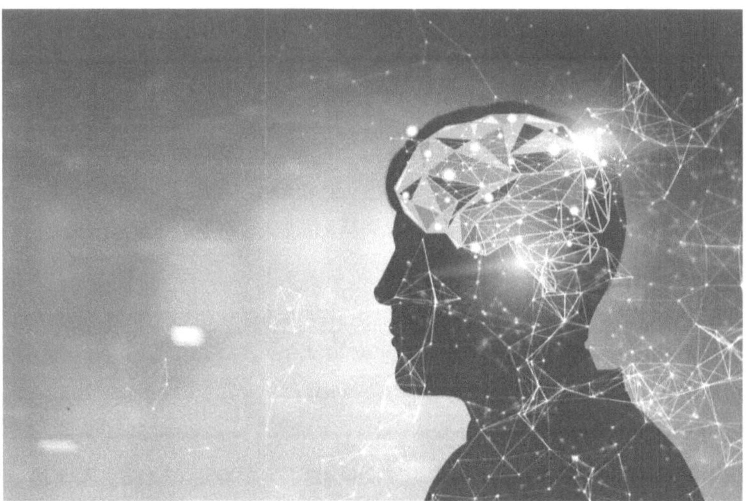

INTRODUCTION

In today's fast-paced world, people are always looking for ways to improve their cognitive performance. Nootropics, also known as cognitive enhancers, are substances that can enhance cognitive function, such as memory, attention and creativity. They can help individuals achieve peak performance, especially in high-stress situations, such as exams, work presentations, or sports competitions. I dabbled a bit with some nootropics like caffeine, nicotine, phenibut, Alpha Brain, etc. to enhance my cognition, focus and productivity. I shall here share my experience before I explore the concept of nootropics, their types, benefits and risks, ethical and safety considerations and examples of compounds, methods and celebrities who have hacked their performance.

As far as my story is concerned, I was raised as a child in a household where consuming tea or coffee was considered a bad habit, and I was discouraged from indulging in them. However, as I entered college, I became curious about the energy-boosting effects that many of my peers claimed to experience from caffeine. So, I decided to give tea and coffee a try, and I was amazed by the enhanced productivity and focus they provided me.

Gradually, I developed a habit of consuming coffee and tea to kickstart my day and keep me alert during long study sessions. However, over time, I noticed that my tolerance to caffeine increased, and the same amount of coffee or tea no longer had the same impact on my cognitive performance. I knew I needed to find an alternative that could help me maintain my productivity levels without developing a tolerance.

That's when I stumbled upon the world of nootropics: cognitive-enhancing supplements that could potentially provide me with the mental edge I was seeking. I started experimenting with different options and found that a combination of coffee and Theanine in a 1:2 ratio worked wonders for me.

Theanine, an amino acid naturally found in tea, helped to counteract the jittery effects of caffeine, promoting a state of calm and relaxation without causing drowsiness. This perfect synergy of coffee and Theanine provided me with a smooth, focused and sustained cognitive boost, allowing me to excel in my studies and other cognitive tasks.

Not only did this nootropic stack improve my focus and cognition, but it also enhanced my productivity, enabling me to accomplish more in less time. I was able to breeze through my assignments, exams and other academic tasks with clarity of thought and heightened mental acuity.

In addition to my coffee and Theanine combo, I also occasionally incorporated Alpha Brain into my nootropic regimen. Alpha Brain is a well-formulated nootropic supplement that contains a blend of ingredients like Tyrosine, Theanine and Huperzine, which are known for their cognitive-enhancing properties. I found Alpha Brain to be effective in combating anxiety, boosting my mood and further enhancing my productivity during times of increased stress or high-pressure situations.

I did experiment with other nootropics as well, such as Phenyl Ethylamine (PEA), which is known for its mood-enhancing effects. However, I found that the effects of PEA were short-lived and not sustainable, as it caused spikes in blood pressure and heart rate, which I deemed to be harmful in the long run.

Through careful experimentation and observation, I have developed a strategic approach to using nootropics to enhance my cognition, focus and productivity. My nootropic stack consisting of coffee and Theanine, along with the occasional use of Alpha Brain, has become an invaluable tool in my quest for optimal mental performance. With this regimen, I am able to tackle my academic, professional and personal tasks with heightened cognitive abilities, allowing me to achieve my goals and excel in various areas of my life.

My journey with nootropics has been an exciting one from initially exploring tea and coffee for their energy-boosting effects, to discovering the benefits of Theanine, Alpha Brain and other cognitive-enhancing supplements, I have strategically incorporated these nootropics into my routine to optimise my cognitive performance, focus and productivity. Nootropics have become an invaluable ally in my pursuit of peak mental performance, helping me unlock my full potential and achieve success in various aspects of my life. We will now take a look at various types of nootropics.

Types of Nootropics

There are various types of nootropics, each with its unique mechanism of action and potential benefits and risks. Some of the most common types include:

Stimulants: These include caffeine, amphetamines and Modafinil, which can enhance wakefulness, alertness and concentration. They work by increasing the levels of dopamine and norepinephrine in the brain, which are neurotransmitters that regulate mood, motivation and attention.

Herbal remedies: These include Ginkgo Biloba, Bacopa Monnieri and Ashwagandha, which are natural extracts that can improve cognitive function, reduce stress and boost memory. They work by increasing blood flow to the brain, reducing inflammation and regulating stress hormones.

Synthetic compounds: These include racetams, choline and phosphatidylserine, which are synthetic molecules that can enhance memory, learning and focus. They work by modulating neurotransmitter activity, increasing brain cell communication and reducing oxidative stress.

Benefits and Risks of Nootropics

The potential benefits of nootropics are numerous, including enhanced memory, learning, focus, creativity and motivation. They can also reduce stress, anxiety and depression, improve mood and sleep quality and protect the brain from age-related decline and neurodegenerative diseases. However, they also carry potential risks, such as addiction, tolerance, side effects and long-term harm to the brain and body. Some nootropics can also interact with other medications, supplements, or health conditions, leading to adverse effects.

Ethical and Safety Considerations

The use of nootropics raises ethical and safety considerations, such as fairness, cheating and harm to oneself and others. Some people may argue that using nootropics to enhance cognitive performance is cheating or unfair to those who do not use them. Others may argue that using nootropics is a personal choice that does not harm anyone else and can help individuals achieve their goals. However, it is important to consider the potential harm to oneself and others when using nootropics, such as addiction, tolerance, side effects and long-term harm to the brain and body.

Nootropics and Biohacking

Nootropics work through different mechanisms of action, which may include improving blood flow to the brain, enhancing neurotransmitter function, reducing inflammation and protecting against oxidative stress. Some of the most commonly used nootropics include:

Caffeine: Caffeine is one of the most well-known and widely used stimulants that can improve cognitive function, including alertness, focus and attention. It works by blocking the action of adenosine, a neurotransmitter that promotes sleep and relaxation and thereby increases the release of dopamine and norepinephrine, neurotransmitters associated with wakefulness and arousal. Caffeine is found in coffee, tea, energy drinks and certain supplements and its effects can vary depending on individual tolerance and sensitivity.

Modafinil: Modafinil is a prescription medication that is FDA-approved for the treatment of narcolepsy, a sleep disorder characterised by excessive daytime sleepiness. It is also commonly used off-label as a nootropic due to its ability to enhance wakefulness, alertness and cognitive function. Modafinil is believed to work by increasing the release of dopamine in the brain, which can improve motivation, concentration and cognitive performance.

Piracetam: Piracetam is one of the original nootropics discovered by Dr. Giurgea and is a member of the racetam family of compounds. It is believed to work by improving blood flow to the brain, enhancing the function of neurotransmitters and protecting against oxidative stress. Piracetam is commonly used to improve memory, concentration and learning, although its exact mechanisms of action are still not fully understood.

Omega-3 fatty acids: Omega-3 fatty acids, found in fatty fish, flaxseed and chia seeds, are essential fats that are important for brain health. They are known to have anti-inflammatory properties, improve blood flow to the brain and support the structure and function of cell membranes. Omega-3 fatty acids are believed to play a role in cognitive function, including memory, mood and attention.

Bacopa Monnieri: Bacopa Monnieri, also known as Brahmi, is a herbal supplement commonly used in Ayurvedic medicine for its purported cognitive-enhancing properties. It is believed to work by enhancing the function of neurotransmitters, reducing inflammation and protecting against oxidative stress. Bacopa Monnieri has been studied for its potential benefits in improving memory, attention and cognitive performance, particularly in older adults.

Rhodiola Rosea: Rhodiola Rosea is an adaptogenic herb that has been used for centuries in traditional medicine for its ability to improve physical and mental performance under stress. It is believed to work by reducing fatigue, improving blood flow to the brain and enhancing neurotransmitter function. Rhodiola Rosea has been studied for its potential benefits in improving cognitive function, mood and mental performance, particularly during periods of stress or fatigue.

Ginseng: Ginseng is a herbal supplement that has been used in traditional Chinese medicine for its purported cognitive-enhancing properties. It is believed to work by improving blood flow to the brain, enhancing neurotransmitter function and reducing inflammation. Ginseng has been studied for its potential benefits in improving cognitive function, mood and mental performance, although more research is needed to fully understand its mechanisms of action.

L-theanine: L-theanine is an amino acid found in green tea that is believed to have calming and relaxing effects on the brain. It is believed to work by increasing alpha brainwave activity, which is associated with a relaxed but alert mental state. L-theanine has been studied for its potential benefits in improving focus, attention and cognitive performance, particularly when combined with caffeine in a synergistic manner.

Creatine: Creatine is a naturally-occurring compound found in small amounts in certain foods, such as meat and fish and is also available in supplement form. It is well-known for its benefits in improving physical performance and muscle strength, but emerging research suggests that it may also have cognitive-enhancing properties. Creatine is believed to work by enhancing the production of ATP, which is the primary source of energy for cells, including brain cells. It has been studied for its potential benefits in improving cognitive function, memory and mental performance, particularly in tasks requiring short-term memory and quick thinking.

Phenylpiracetam: Phenylpiracetam is a synthetic racetam compound that is believed to have cognitive-enhancing properties. It is believed to work by improving blood flow to the brain, enhancing neurotransmitter function and reducing inflammation. Phenylpiracetam has been studied for its potential benefits in improving cognitive function, memory and mental performance, particularly in tasks requiring focus, attention and motivation.

Nicotine: Nicotine is a stimulant that can enhance focus, attention and memory. It can also increase dopamine release in the brain, which can enhance motivation and pleasure. Some studies suggest that nicotine can also enhance creativity by improving divergent thinking and idea generation. However, nicotine is highly addictive and can have negative health effects, so it should be used with caution and under medical supervision.

Phenibut: Phenibut is a nootropic that can reduce anxiety and enhance mood and sociability. It can also improve cognitive function, memory and creativity by reducing stress and promoting relaxation. However, phenibut can also be addictive and cause withdrawal symptoms, so it should be used sparingly and under medical supervision.

Lucid Dreaming Nootropics: Some nootropics, such as Galantamine and Choline, can enhance lucid dreaming by promoting Acetylcholine production in the brain. Lucid dreaming can enhance creativity by allowing people to explore their subconscious and generate new ideas and perspectives.

Anxiety-reducing nootropics: Some nootropics, such as Ashwagandha and Rhodiola Rosea, can reduce anxiety and stress, which can enhance cognitive function, creativity and productivity. By reducing the negative effects of stress on the brain, these nootropics can promote relaxation, focus and mental clarity.

While nootropics offer promising potential benefits for cognitive enhancement, it's important to note that the field is still relatively young, and more research is needed to fully understand their mechanisms of action, efficacy and long-term safety. Additionally, the effects of nootropics can vary greatly among individuals and some may experience side effects.

NOOTROPICS AND BIOHACKING

There are numerous examples of celebrities/biohackers who have used nootropics to enhance their cognitive performance. One such biohacker is Dave Asprey, the founder of Bulletproof Coffee, who used Modafinil to boost his energy and focus during long workdays. Asprey also developed the Bulletproof Diet, which involves consuming healthy fats, such as butter and coconut oil, to enhance cognitive function and reduce inflammation. Many other celebrities, including Joe Rogan, Tim Ferriss, Elon Musk and Gwyneth Paltrow, have openly shared their experiences with using nootropics to achieve peak cognitive performance. Rogan, a comedian and podcast host, has spoken about his use of Alpha Brain and its benefits in improving focus and mental clarity. Ferriss, an author and podcast host, has written about his experiences with Modafinil and other cognitive enhancers. He has also used transcranial direct current stimulation (tDCS), a non-invasive brain stimulation technique, to improve his learning and memory. Musk, a billionaire entrepreneur, has openly discussed his use of nootropics like Adderall and caffeine to enhance his cognitive function and work longer hours. Paltrow, an actress and entrepreneur, has shared her use of racetams to improve memory and cognitive function. It's worth noting that everyone's body and brain chemistry is different, and what works for these celebrities may not work for everyone. It's important to approach biohacking, including the use of nootropics, with caution and informed consent.

The popular movie "Limitless" (2011), features a protagonist achieving superhuman performance through the use of a nootropic. Starring Bradley Cooper, in the movie, Cooper takes a fictional drug called NZT-48, which enhances his cognitive abilities to the point where he is able to learn new languages, solve complex equations and make millions in the stock market. However, as he becomes more dependent on the drug, he experiences negative side effects and risks his health and well-being.

In the book *"The Rise of Superman"* by Steven Kotler, the author explores the concept of "flow", or the state of optimal performance and creativity. He argues that achieving flow is the key to unlocking human potential and achieving peak performance in any field, whether it's sports, music, or entrepreneurship.

Kotler discusses how nootropics and other biohacking techniques can be used to enhance the flow state and achieve peak performance. He describes how some extreme athletes, such as big-wave surfers and snowboarders, have used nootropics like Modafinil and caffeine to enhance focus and reaction times and how musicians have used substances like LSD and marijuana to enhance creativity and reduce inhibitions.

However, Kotler also acknowledges the risks and potential downsides of using nootropics and other substances to achieve flow. He warns that these substances can have negative side effects and can be addictive and that they should only be used under the guidance of a healthcare professional.

Instead of relying solely on nootropics, Kotler suggests that a holistic approach to biohacking can be more effective for achieving flow and peak performance. This includes strategies like meditation, mindfulness and exercise, which can enhance cognitive function and promote a state of mental clarity and focus.

Overall, "The Rise of Superman" explores the potential benefits and risks of using nootropics and other biohacking techniques for achieving flow and peak performance, and provides a comprehensive guide to achieving these states through a holistic approach to biohacking. Nootropics should be used with caution. Let us now take a look at the downsides and the precautions one should take while using them.

THE DOWNSIDES OF NOOTROPICS

While nootropics can offer potential benefits for cognitive enhancement and productivity, it is important to recognise that they also carry risks and potential downsides. Here are some of the common downsides of nootropics and precautions that new initiates should take:

Adverse Side Effects: Some nootropics can cause adverse side effects, such as headaches, insomnia, gastrointestinal distress, or increased anxiety. It is important to carefully monitor your response to nootropics and start with lower dosages to minimise the risk of side effects.

Addiction and Dependence: Certain nootropics, such as Modafinil or Phenibut, can be habit-forming and lead to dependence or withdrawal symptoms. It is important to use nootropics responsibly and avoid using them on a daily basis to reduce the risk of addiction.

Interactions with Medications: Nootropics can interact with other medications, including prescription drugs and supplements, which can cause unintended side effects or reduce the effectiveness of medications. It is important to consult with a healthcare professional before starting any new nootropic regimen if you are taking any medications.

Quality Control and Purity: Because the nootropic industry is not regulated, there is a risk of purchasing contaminated or impure substances that can lead to adverse effects or unexpected interactions. It is important to purchase nootropics from reputable sources and verify the purity and quality of the substances before use.

Lack of Long-Term Research: While some nootropics have been studied extensively, there is a lack of long-term research on the safety and effectiveness of many substances. It is important to weigh the potential benefits and risks of using nootropics and to be cautious with untested or experimental substances.

As a new initiate to nootropics, it is important to start with lower dosages, carefully monitor your response to the substances, and consult with a healthcare professional before starting any new regimen. It is also important to research the substances thoroughly and understand the potential benefits and risks of each nootropic before use. Additionally, it is important to maintain a healthy lifestyle with good nutrition, exercise, and sleep habits, as these can have a significant impact on cognitive function and productivity.

CONCLUSION

In conclusion, nootropics can enhance cognitive function and improve performance, but they also carry potential risks and ethical and safety considerations. It is important to research the potential benefits and risks of each nootropic, consult with a healthcare provider and use them responsibly and ethically. Some nootropics, such as caffeine and omega-3 fatty acids, are natural and safe, while others, such as Modafinil and Aniracetam, may have more potential risks and side effects. Biohacking can be a powerful tool for self-improvement, but it should be done with caution and informed consent.

CHAPTER 10

The Impact of Stress on Performance and How to Manage It

INTRODUCTION

Stress is a natural and inevitable part of life, and it affects individuals in different ways. Stress is a response to any physical, mental, or emotional challenge or threat. While a certain amount of stress can be beneficial and prolonged and intense stress can have negative effects on an individual's performance, productivity and overall well-being.

Throughout my illustrious career in the Police department, spanning over 30 years, I have walked the thin blue line and witnessed firsthand the toll that stress can take on both myself and my fellow officers. From holding critical positions in the Government of India and Tamil Nadu, including Chief of Crime Branch CID,

Director of Vigilance and Anti-Corruption, Additional Director General of Police, Law and Order, to commanding a massive team of 30,000 as Inspector General in the paramilitary, overseeing the security of 55 critical national installations—I have been at the forefront of high-pressure situations, making critical decisions and managing teams during times of crisis. But amidst the chaos and challenges, I have learnt the art of stress management through the power of biohacking.

As a firm believer in leading by example, I have made it my mission to prioritise my well-being and combat stress through various cutting-edge techniques. One of my pillars of stress management is physical fitness. I lace up my running shoes and hit the pavement every day, clocking in at least 10 kilometres. My unwavering dedication to running has even earned me two prestigious entries in the Asian Book of Records for marathon running. The rush of endorphins and the sense of accomplishment that comes with pushing my body to its limits not only helps me stay physically fit but also provides a much-needed release of stress.

But that's not all—I have delved deep into the world of mindfulness and meditation to further enhance my stress-busting arsenal. I make it a daily practice to meditate using various techniques like mantra meditation and binaural beats for at least half an hour. The stillness and tranquillity that I cultivate during these sessions help me calm my mind, centre my thoughts and keep stress at bay.

In addition to physical fitness and mindfulness, I have also made significant changes to my nutrition to optimise my stress resilience. Embracing a plant-based diet and moderating my alcohol intake has helped me fuel my body with the nutrients it needs to thrive while avoiding the pitfalls of stress-induced emotional eating or unhealthy habits. I have even dabbled in the ketogenic diet, experimenting with different approaches to find what works best for my body and mind.

As a firm believer in the power of rest and recovery, I also prioritise my sleep. I track my sleep patterns religiously and make sure to get a minimum of six to seven hours of quality sleep each night. This allows me to wake up rejuvenated and ready to tackle the challenges of the day with a clear mind and a well-rested body.

To further support my body's ability to manage stress, I have incorporated adaptogens like Ashwagandha and Ginseng into my routine. These natural herbs have been proven to help the body adapt to stress and promote overall well-being, providing me with an added layer of resilience in the face of stressors.

Through my unwavering commitment to biohacking my way out of stress, I have been able to maintain peak productivity, stay focused and lead my team with unwavering resolve, even in the most demanding of situations. I firmly believe that these techniques are not limited to my profession or life circumstances—anyone can learn and implement them to effectively manage their stress levels and optimise their performance in any walk of life.

So, whether you are a police officer, a busy professional, or simply someone looking to conquer stress and elevate your performance, I am living proof that biohacking your way out of stress is not only possible but also immensely beneficial. Remember, with the right tools and techniques, you too can conquer stress and emerge.

The fight or flight response is a physiological reaction to stress that evolved as a survival mechanism in primitive times. It allowed individuals to respond to acute stressors, such as a predator, by either fighting or fleeing. However, in modern times, individuals are experiencing prolonged stress from a variety of sources, including work, family, financial concerns and technology. The prevalence of stress in modern life can have significant negative effects on an individual's physical and mental health.

One of the most significant contributors to modern-day stress is technology. With the constant connectivity and fast-paced nature of modern life, individuals may feel like they are always "on" and never have a chance to truly disconnect. This can lead to burnout, exhaustion and an inability to manage stress effectively.

To combat this, individuals need to take intentional breaks from technology and prioritise self-care. This can involve mindfulness practices such as meditation or deep breathing exercises, as well as physical activity such as exercise or spending time outdoors. Finding ways to disconnect from technology and reduce exposure to stressors can help individuals manage stress and improve overall well-being.

In addition to technology-related stress, individuals may also face financial stress, loneliness and social media-related stress, among other types of stress. Stress affects the body and impacts it physiologically and psychologically. Let's take a look at how it impacts.

Physiological Effects of Stress

Stress triggers the release of hormones such as cortisol and adrenaline, which activate the body's "fight or flight" response. These hormones increase heart rate, blood pressure and breathing rate, preparing the body to respond to a perceived threat. While this response can be helpful in short bursts, chronic stress can lead to elevated cortisol levels, which can result in numerous negative physiological effects such as headaches, digestive problems and a weakened immune system.

Psychological Effects of Stress

Stress can also have a significant impact on an individual's psychological well-being. Chronic stress can lead to impaired attention, decreased memory and cognitive function and negative emotions such as anxiety and depression. The impact of stress on mental health is a growing concern, with numerous studies linking stress to an increased risk of developing mental health conditions.

Scientific studies have extensively researched the impact of stress on individuals, both physiologically and psychologically. Here are a few key findings:

Increased cortisol levels: Cortisol is a hormone that is released in response to stress. Studies have found that prolonged stress can lead to elevated cortisol levels, which can contribute to a variety of negative health effects, including impaired immune function, weight gain and cardiovascular disease.

Impaired attention: Chronic stress has been shown to impair attention and cognitive function, making it harder for individuals to focus and concentrate on tasks.

Negative emotions: Stress can also lead to negative emotions, including anxiety, depression and irritability. These emotions can further exacerbate stress and create a vicious cycle.

Physical health: Chronic stress has been linked to a variety of physical health problems, including high blood pressure, heart disease and digestive issues.

Mental health: Stress has been linked to a variety of mental health issues, including anxiety, depression and post-traumatic stress disorder (PTSD).

It's important to note that not all stress is bad. Short-term stress, known as acute stress, can be beneficial and can help individuals respond to challenges and perform better in certain situations. However, chronic stress is a different story and can have serious negative impacts on both physical and mental health.

Famous personalities, including athletes, actors and politicians, often face immense pressure and stress. Despite this, they have developed various coping mechanisms to manage stress and optimise their performance. For example, Olympic swimmer Michael Phelps, who won 28 medals, including 23 gold medals, has used visualisation techniques to prepare for races and reduce stress. Similarly, actor Emma Stone practises mindfulness meditation to manage stress and anxiety.

MANAGING STRESS TO ENHANCE PERFORMANCE

Relaxation Techniques

Relaxation techniques such as deep breathing, progressive muscle relaxation and yoga have been shown to reduce stress and improve overall well-being. These techniques promote relaxation and decrease the physiological and psychological effects of stress. For example, research has shown that regular practice of yoga can reduce stress, anxiety and depression.

Mindfulness

Mindfulness is a mental state characterised by present-moment awareness and non-judgemental acceptance. Mindfulness-based stress reduction (MBSR) is effective in reducing stress and improving mental health outcomes. Practising mindfulness can enhance performance by increasing attention and focus.

Cognitive-Behavioural Therapy

Cognitive-behavioural therapy (CBT) is a form of talk therapy that helps individuals identify and change negative thought patterns and behaviours. CBT is effective in reducing stress, anxiety and depression. By changing negative thought patterns, individuals can reduce the psychological effects of stress and enhance their performance.

Resilience and Adaptability

Resilience is the ability to bounce back from adversity and adapt to change. Developing resilience can help individuals manage stress and enhance their performance by promoting positive coping strategies. Adaptability is the ability to adjust to new situations and challenges. By developing adaptability, individuals can better manage stress and maintain their performance in challenging situations.

SOME WAYS OF BIOHACKING STRESS

Biohacking is the practice of using science and technology to optimise physical and mental performance. Here are a few ways you can use biohacking to manage stress and become more productive:

Meditation: Meditation has been shown to reduce stress, increase focus and improve overall well-being. By incorporating a daily meditation practice into your routine, you can better manage stress and improve productivity.

Exercise: Regular exercise has been shown to reduce stress and anxiety, improve mood and boost cognitive function. Incorporating exercise into your daily routine can be a powerful tool for reducing stress and improving productivity.

Sleep: Getting adequate sleep is essential for both physical and mental health. Poor sleep can increase stress and impair cognitive function, while adequate sleep has been shown to reduce stress and improve productivity.

Nutrition: Eating a healthy diet can help reduce stress and improve mental and physical performance. Focus on eating whole, nutrient-dense foods and avoiding processed foods and added sugars.

Supplements: Certain supplements, such as adaptogens, can help the body better cope with stress. Ashwagandha, Rhodiola and holy basil are a few examples of adaptogenic herbs that have been shown to reduce stress and improve cognitive function.

Breathing techniques: Various breathing techniques, such as the Wim Hof breathing method, can help reduce stress and improve mental and physical performance.

There are many resources available to help individuals manage stress, including apps such as Calm and Headspace, which offer guided meditation and other mindfulness practices.

By incorporating these biohacking strategies into your daily routine, you can better manage stress and become more productive. However, it's important to note that everyone is different and what works for one person may not work for another. It's important to experiment and find the biohacking strategies that work best for you

STRESS ADAPTOGENS

Stress adaptogens are natural substances that help the body adapt to and cope with stress. They work by regulating the body's response to stressors, including physical, emotional and environmental stressors. Adaptogens are found in a variety of herbs and plants and have been used for centuries in traditional medicine to promote overall health and well-being.

One of the primary benefits of stress adaptogens is their ability to regulate the body's stress response by reducing cortisol levels. Cortisol is a hormone that is released in response to stress and elevated cortisol levels can lead to a variety of negative health effects, including impaired immune function, weight gain and cardiovascular disease.

By reducing cortisol levels, stress adaptogens can help mitigate the negative effects of stress on the body. They can also help improve mental clarity and cognitive function, reduce fatigue and boost energy levels. This can help individuals manage stress more effectively and perform better in their daily lives.

Some of the most commonly used stress adaptogens include:

Ashwagandha: This herb has been used for centuries in Ayurvedic medicine to promote overall health and well-being. Ashwagandha has been shown to reduce cortisol levels and improve symptoms of anxiety and depression.

Rhodiola: This herb is native to the Arctic regions of Europe and Asia and has been used in traditional medicine to boost energy levels and reduce fatigue. Rhodiola has been shown to improve mental clarity, reduce stress levels and improve physical endurance.

Ginseng: Ginseng is a popular adaptogen that has been used in traditional Chinese medicine for centuries to promote overall health and well-being. Ginseng has been shown to improve mental function, reduce stress levels and boost energy levels.

Incorporating stress adaptogens into one's daily routine can be an effective way to manage stress and promote overall health and well-being. However, it is important to note that adaptogens are not a substitute for medical treatment and should be used in conjunction with other stress management techniques as needed.

In today's fast-paced world, stress has become a ubiquitous part of modern life. It can affect individuals from all walks of life, regardless of age, gender, or occupation. The good news is that there are effective ways to combat and overcome stress, allowing individuals to lead healthier, happier and more fulfilling lives. Here are some key strategies:

Recognise and acknowledge stress: The first step in overcoming stress is to recognise and acknowledge its presence in your life. Take the time to reflect on the sources of stress in your life, whether it's work-related deadlines, financial pressures, relationship issues, or other factors. Acknowledging stress allows you to take ownership of it and take proactive steps to manage it.

Practice self-care: Taking care of yourself is crucial in managing stress. Make sure to prioritise self-care activities. Taking care of your physical and mental well-being can help you build resilience and better cope with stress.

Develop coping mechanisms: Everyone has different ways of coping with stress. Find healthy coping mechanisms that work for you, such as deep breathing, meditation, journaling, talking to a trusted friend or family member, or seeking professional help from a therapist. Experiment with different techniques and incorporate them into your daily routine to effectively manage stress.

Manage time and prioritise tasks: Time management is crucial in reducing stress. Make a to-do list, set realistic deadlines and prioritise tasks based on their importance and urgency. Avoid overloading yourself with too many responsibilities and learn to say no when necessary. Managing your time effectively can help you feel more in control and reduce stress levels.

Build a support system: Surround yourself with a strong support system of family, friends, or colleagues who can provide emotional support and encouragement during stressful times. Sharing your concerns with others can help alleviate stress and provide different perspectives and solutions.

Take breaks and practise relaxation techniques: Taking regular breaks throughout the day and practising relaxation techniques, such as progressive muscle relaxation or meditation, or guided imagery, can help you relax and recharge. These techniques can also help you release tension and reduce stress levels.

Overcoming stress requires proactive efforts to recognise, acknowledge and effectively manage stressors in your life. Remember, stress is a natural part of life, but with the right strategies, you can minimise its impact and lead a more balanced and fulfilling life.

CONCLUSION

In conclusion, biohacking offers innovative and effective ways to manage stress and optimise productivity in the modern world. From sleep optimisation to exercise and movement, meditation and mindfulness, nutrition and supplements and cold exposure, there are numerous biohacking techniques that individuals can incorporate into their daily routines to achieve their goals. By leveraging science and technology, individuals can take control of their physical and mental well-being, improve their ability to handle stress and increase productivity. As we continue to navigate the demands of modern life, biohacking provides a promising avenue for individuals to optimise their performance and thrive in an increasingly fast-paced and stressful world. So, why not explore the world of biohacking and unlock your full potential today? Start implementing these techniques and reap the benefits of improved stress management and increased productivity. Remember, the power to optimise your performance and well-being lies within you and biohacking can be a valuable tool on that journey.

CHAPTER 11

Critical Role of Mindset in Peak Performance

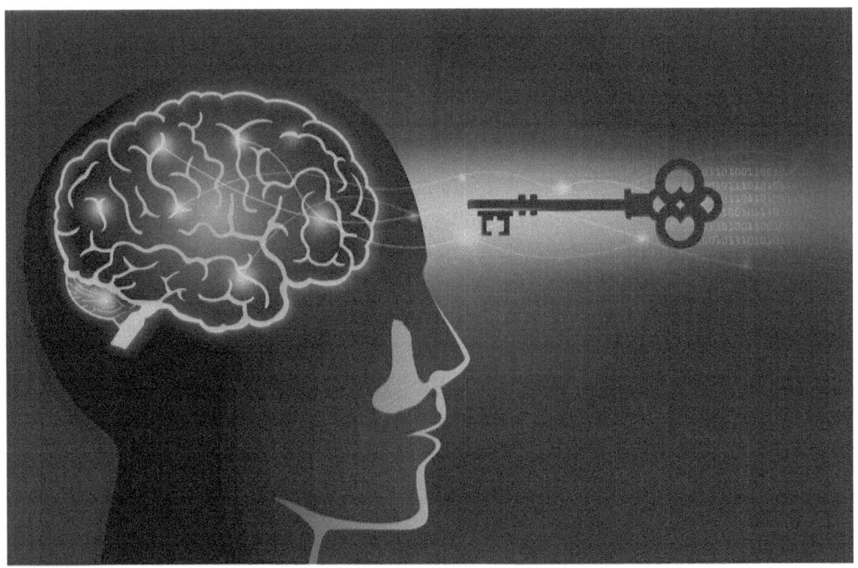

INTRODUCTION

Mindset plays a critical role in achieving peak performance. A person's mindset is the lens through which one views the world, influencing how one interprets events and responds to challenges. As a result, many experts believe that mindset is one of the essential factors in achieving success.

For instance, John, a 30-year-old man, had been struggling with his career and personal life. John had always been a negative thinker, constantly doubting his abilities and fearing failure. He habitually blamed others for his problems and never took responsibility for his actions.

One day, John met an old friend who had turned his life around and had become a successful entrepreneur. The friend shared his story with John and how he had changed his mindset to cultivate positivity and a can-do attitude. His friend's story inspired John, and he changed his life.

John started by setting small achievable goals for himself and celebrating every little success. He learnt to be grateful for what he had and stopped comparing himself to others. Instead of complaining about his problems, he started focusing on finding solutions to them.

John also started surrounding himself with positive people who supported him and encouraged him to keep going. He began to read self-help books, listen to motivational speakers and attend personal development workshops.

With his new mindset, John could land a job in his desired field, and within a few months, he was promoted to a managerial position. He also met the love of his life and they got married.

John's success story did not stop there. He started his own business, which became a huge success. He attributed his success to changing his mindset and cultivating a positive attitude.

John's journey teaches us that changing our mindset and cultivating a positive attitude can lead to great success in our personal and professional lives. It takes time and effort, but it is worth it. We can achieve anything we set our minds to with a positive mindset.

Henry Ford's famous quote, "Whether you think you can, or you think you can't—you're right," highlights the importance of mindset in achieving success. It suggests that our beliefs and attitudes have a powerful impact on our ability to achieve our goals and realise our potential.

In the context of mindset, this quote emphasises the power of self-belief. If we believe in our ability to succeed, we are more likely to act towards our goals, persist in facing challenges and ultimately achieve success. Conversely, if we doubt our abilities or believe we cannot achieve our goals, we are more likely to give up or not even try.

This quote also suggests that our mindset can be a self-fulfilling prophecy. If we believe we can succeed, we are more likely to put in the effort and take the necessary actions to achieve our goals. On the other hand, if we believe that we can't succeed, we are more likely to hold back, make excuses and ultimately fail.

This quote highlights the importance of cultivating a positive and growth-oriented mindset. By believing in ourselves and our ability to achieve our goals, we can overcome obstacles, push past our limits and reach our full potential. Our mindset is critical in determining our success, and we can shape it through our thoughts, beliefs and attitudes.

The power of mindset cannot be underestimated when it comes to achieving peak performance. One's mindset and belief system significantly impact sports, academics, or business performance. In this article, we will explore the concept of mindset and how it influences performance, the difference between fixed and growth mindsets, and how to cultivate a growth mindset to achieve peak performance.

Mindset refers to individuals' beliefs and attitudes about their abilities and potential. It is a fundamental aspect of human psychology that can determine how we approach challenges and obstacles.

One Bollywood movie that comes to my mind where the hero achieves success by changing his mindset is the 2008 film "Rock On.". The movie stars Farhan Akhtar as Aditya Shroff, a former rockstar who gave up music after a bitter fallout with his bandmates. Aditya now leads a mundane life as a banker, but he is still haunted by his past and the unfinished dreams of his band, Magik.

One day, Aditya meets an old friend, Joe Mascarenhas (played by Arjun Rampal), who is still a successful musician. Joe encourages Aditya to revive Magik and fulfil their dream of winning a music competition. At first, Aditya is reluctant, but after a series of events, he realises he cannot let go of his passion for music and decides to give it another shot. However, Aditya faces several challenges as he tries to reunite with his bandmates, who have moved on with their lives. He also must confront his inner demons, including his fear of failure and inability to forgive his bandmates for betraying him in the past.

Throughout the movie, Aditya transforms as he learns to let go of his past and embrace his passion for music. He changes his mindset from defeated and bitter to determined and optimistic, driven by his love for music. With the support of his bandmates and his wife, played by Prachi Desai, Aditya works hard to prepare for the music competition. They face tough competition, but ultimately, they win and achieve their dream of making a successful comeback as a band. "Rock On." is a movie that showcases the power of changing one's mindset and following one's passion. Aditya's journey from a disillusioned and bitter person to a confident and optimistic musician inspires anyone who wants to achieve their dreams.

HERE ARE SOME REASONS WHY MINDSET IS ESSENTIAL FOR PEAK PERFORMANCE:

Motivation: A positive mindset can help you stay motivated and focused on your goals. It can also help you overcome obstacles and setbacks, inevitable in any pursuit of excellence. With a growth mindset, you are more likely to see challenges as opportunities for growth and learning rather than as threats or barriers.

Confidence: Confidence is a critical component of peak performance. A strong mindset can help you build confidence in your abilities, essential for taking risks, pushing past your comfort zone and achieving your goals. Believing in yourself makes you more likely to take on challenges and perform at your best.

Resilience: Resilience is the ability to bounce back from setbacks and keep moving forward. A resilient mindset can help you weather the ups and downs of life and stay focused on your goals. With a growth mindset, you are more likely to see setbacks as temporary and learn from them rather than giving up or becoming discouraged.

Focus: A positive mindset can help you stay focused and avoid distractions. When you have a clear vision of what you want to achieve and believe you can do it, you are less likely to be sidetracked by negative thoughts or external distractions. A focused mindset is essential for achieving peak performance in any area of life.

Carol S. Dweck's book, *"Mindset: The New Psychology of Success,"* is a groundbreaking work that explores the impact of mindset on success. The book is based on years of research and provides insights into how our mindset can help or hinder our ability to achieve our goals.

Dweck identifies two types of mindsets: fixed mindset and growth mindset. Fixed mindset individuals believe that their abilities and intelligence are predetermined and cannot be changed. They tend to avoid challenges, give up quickly and feel threatened by the success of others. In contrast, growth mindset individuals believe that their abilities and intelligence can be developed through hard work and dedication. They embrace challenges, persist in the face of setbacks and view the success of others as inspiration for their growth and development.

Dweck's book explores how mindset impacts different areas of our lives, including relationships, parenting, business and education. She provides real-world examples and practical advice on cultivating a growth mindset and overcoming the limitations of a fixed mindset.

Changing one's mindset is challenging, as it requires a conscious effort to shift one's perspective and thought patterns. However, changing your mindset and developing a more positive and growth-oriented outlook is possible with dedication and persistence.

HERE ARE SOME STEPS YOU CAN TAKE TO CHANGE YOUR MINDSET

Identify limiting beliefs: The first step in changing your mindset is identifying the beliefs and thought patterns holding you back. These may be negative self-talk, limiting beliefs, or fixed mindsets that prevent you from seeing opportunities and growth.

Challenge negative thoughts: Once you have identified your limiting beliefs, challenge them by asking yourself if they are true. Are they based on facts, or are they assumptions or fears? Replace negative thoughts with positive affirmations and focus on solutions instead of problems.

Cultivate a growth mindset: A growth mindset believes one's abilities can be developed through hard work and dedication. Focus on your strengths and seek out opportunities to learn and grow. Embrace challenges as opportunities for growth and view failures as learning experiences.

Practise mindfulness: Mindfulness is the practice of being present and fully engaged in the current moment. Focusing on the present can reduce anxiety and negative thoughts and develop a more positive and grateful outlook.

Surround yourself with positive influences: Surround yourself with people who support and encourage your growth and a positive mindset. Seek mentors and role models who embody the mindset you want to develop.

Take action: Finally, take action towards your goals and practise your new mindset daily. Set small achievable goals and celebrate your progress along the way. Remember that changing your mindset is a process, and it takes time and effort to develop new habits and ways of thinking.

In conclusion, changing your mindset requires a conscious effort and a commitment to developing a more positive and growth-oriented outlook. By identifying limiting beliefs, challenging negative thoughts, cultivating a growth mindset, practising mindfulness, surrounding yourself with positive influences, and taking action, you can shift your perspective and achieve your full potential.

Peter Diamandis is an entrepreneur, author and futurist who is known for his work in the fields of innovation and technology. He has developed several mindsets that he believes are crucial for success in these fields, including the abundance mindset, exponential mindset, moonshot mindset and longevity mindset. Let's take a closer look at each of these mindsets:

Abundance Mindset: This mindset is based on the belief that there is enough abundance in the world for everyone to succeed. Rather than operating from a scarcity mentality, where we believe that resources are limited and must be hoarded, the abundance mindset encourages us to embrace collaboration and seek win-win opportunities. This mindset can be constructive for entrepreneurs and innovators looking to create new solutions and disrupt existing industries.

Exponential Mindset: The exponential mindset is based on recognising that technology is advancing at an accelerating pace and that this change will continue to increase. Those who embrace the exponential mindset can see opportunities where others see challenges, and they are willing to take risks and pursue ambitious goals.

This mindset is particularly relevant in artificial intelligence, biotechnology and robotics.

Moonshot Mindset: The moonshot mindset is about setting ambitious, audacious goals that inspire and motivate us to work towards a better future. Moonshots are typically big, bold ideas that must still be feasible with current technology or knowledge. By pursuing moonshots, we can drive innovation and create solutions that have a transformative impact on society. This mindset can be seen in companies like Google, which has pursued moonshots like self-driving cars and smart contact lenses.

Longevity Mindset: The longevity mindset is based on the belief that we can use technology to increase our lifespan and improve our healthspan. Those who embrace this mindset are focused on creating solutions that help us live longer, healthier lives. This mindset is particularly relevant in regenerative medicine, anti-ageing and personalised health.

Overall, these mindsets developed by Peter Diamandis are designed to help entrepreneurs and innovators navigate the rapidly changing world of technology and create solutions that have a transformative impact on society. By embracing these mindsets, we can shift our perspective, take risks and pursue ambitious goals that drive innovation and create a better future.

CONCLUSION

In conclusion, mindset is a crucial factor in achieving peak performance. A positive and growth-oriented mindset can help you stay motivated, build confidence, develop resilience and focus on your goals. By cultivating a strong mindset, you can overcome obstacles, push past your limits and achieve your full potential.

CHAPTER 12

How to Cultivate a Growth Mindset for Peak Performance

INTRODUCTION

In the picturesque town of Ooty, nestled in the scenic Nilgiri Hills of Tamil Nadu, India, two twins were born on a stormy night. They were separated soon after birth and given up for adoption to two different families. Little did anyone know that the beliefs and mindset instilled in them during their formative years would shape their destinies in dramatically different ways.

The first twin, Arjun, grew up with adoptive parents who believed in the power of hard work, dedication and the idea that abilities and intelligence can be developed through perseverance and learning. They encouraged him to embrace challenges, see them as opportunities for growth and persist in the face of obstacles. Arjun imbibed these values from a young age and grew up with a growth mindset.

The second twin, Rohit, was adopted by a family that believed abilities and intelligence are predetermined and cannot be changed. They discouraged him from taking risks or embracing challenges, and he grew up with a fixed mindset. Rohit often gave up easily when faced with obstacles and felt threatened by the success of others, leading to jealousy and a lack of motivation. He languished, doing odd jobs and living in abject poverty.

As the years passed, Arjun and Rohit took divergent paths in life, shaped by their respective mindsets. Arjun pursued higher education, excelled in academics and sports and eventually became a successful entrepreneur and athlete. He embraced challenges, saw failure as an opportunity for growth and persevered despite setbacks. On the other hand, Rohit struggled to find his footing in life, plagued by self-doubt and a fixed mindset that limited his potential.

Arjun's success story became a beacon of inspiration for many and people marvelled at his ability to overcome challenges and achieve peak performance. But what set him apart? How did he develop a growth mindset that propelled him to success? Let's explore the concepts in depth.

Embracing Challenges

Arjun learnt early in life that challenges are not obstacles to be feared, but opportunities for growth and learning. He understood that facing challenges head-on can lead to personal and professional development. Instead of shying away from challenges, he embraced them with enthusiasm and a positive attitude.

Arjun's adoptive parents encouraged him to try new things, take calculated risks and step out of his comfort zone. They taught him that challenges are not roadblocks, but stepping stones towards success. Arjun took up various challenges in academics, sports and personal life, and approached them with a mindset that viewed challenges as opportunities to learn, grow and expand his horizons.

For example, in school, Arjun struggled with math, but instead of giving up, he sought help, practised diligently and eventually mastered the subject. He participated in sports competitions, knowing that he might not always win, but he saw every competition as a chance to improve his skills and learn from his mistakes. This mindset of embracing challenges and seeing them as opportunities for growth became deeply ingrained in Arjun's personality and propelled him to achieve peak performance. Therefore, parents have a role in inculcating a growth mindset in their children, and such children are likely to succeed in their life because of the growth mindset.

Seeing Failure as an Opportunity for Growth

Arjun also learnt that failure is not something to be feared or avoided, but a valuable learning experience. He understood that failure does not define one's abilities or intelligence, but it provides an opportunity to reflect, learn and make adjustments for future success.

When Arjun faced failures or setbacks, he did not dwell on them or succumb to self-doubt. Instead, he embraced a "fail forward" mentality, where he saw failure as a stepping stone towards success. He analysed his mistakes, learnt from them and made necessary improvements. He did not let failure deter him from pursuing his goals but rather used it as a catalyst for growth and improvement.

For example, in his entrepreneurial journey, Arjun faced multiple failures and setbacks. Some of his business ventures failed, and he made mistakes along the way. However, he did not view these failures as the end of the road, but as valuable lessons that helped him refine his approach, learn from his mistakes and come back stronger.

Arjun's adoptive parents also played a crucial role in shaping his mindset towards failure. They taught him that failure is a natural part of the learning process and should not be feared or avoided. They emphasised that mistakes and failures are opportunities to learn and grow, and encouraged him to persevere in the face of setbacks.

Resilience and Perseverance

Another important aspect of cultivating a growth mindset is developing resilience and perseverance. Arjun learnt that success does not come easy, and setbacks are inevitable on the path to peak performance. However, what sets apart those who achieve peak performance is their ability to bounce back from failures and persevere despite challenges.

Arjun developed resilience through consistent practice and effort. He learnt to view setbacks as temporary hurdles that can be overcome with determination and perseverance. He did not give up easily, but instead, he persisted in the face of challenges and kept pushing forward towards his goals. He understood that success is a journey, not a destination, and it requires resilience and perseverance to overcome obstacles along the way.

Arjun's adoptive parents also instilled in him a positive attitude towards challenges and failures. They taught him to see setbacks as opportunities to learn and grow and to never give up on his dreams. They encouraged him to stay resilient, persevere in the face of challenges and keep striving for excellence.

Positive Attitude

A positive attitude is another essential element in cultivating a growth mindset for peak performance. Arjun learnt that having a positive attitude towards challenges, failures, and setbacks can greatly impact his ability to achieve success. He understood that a positive attitude enables him to approach challenges with optimism, learn from failures without getting discouraged and maintain a mindset of continuous improvement.

Arjun developed a positive attitude through self-awareness and self-reflection. He learnt to manage his thoughts and emotions and to cultivate a positive outlook towards life. He practised gratitude, focused on his strengths and reframed challenges as opportunities for growth. He surrounded himself with positive influences and learnt from successful individuals who had a growth mindset.

Arjun's positive attitude also extended to how he viewed others' success. He did not feel threatened by the success of others, but instead, he celebrated their achievements and saw them as inspiration for his own growth. He understood that everyone has their unique strengths and talents, and their success does not diminish their own potential.

Arjun's story exemplifies how cultivating a growth mindset can lead to peak performance. By embracing challenges, seeing failure as an opportunity for growth, developing resilience and perseverance and maintaining a positive attitude, Arjun was able to overcome obstacles and achieve success in his entrepreneurial and athletic endeavours.

The journey towards peak performance requires a mindset that embraces challenges, sees failures as opportunities for growth, and maintains a positive attitude towards oneself and others. It requires self-awareness, self-reflection and consistent effort to develop a growth mindset that propels one towards excellence.

As you embark on your own journey towards peak performance, remember Arjun's story and the power of a growth mindset. Embrace challenges, learn from failures, develop resilience and perseverance and cultivate a positive attitude. With a growth mindset, you can unlock your true potential and achieve peak performance in any area of your life.

PRACTICAL STRATEGIES TO CULTIVATE A GROWTH MINDSET FOR PEAK PERFORMANCE

Embrace Challenges: Challenge yourself to step out of your comfort zone and take on new tasks or projects that push your boundaries. Embrace challenges as opportunities for growth and learning, rather than as threats or obstacles. Approach challenges with a positive attitude and see them as a chance to develop new skills, gain experience and expand your capabilities.

For example, if you are working on a project at work that seems daunting, instead of feeling overwhelmed, view it as a chance to learn and improve your skills. Break the project down into smaller, manageable tasks and tackle them one by one. Celebrate your progress and the skills you acquire along the way, rather than focusing on the difficulties.

Embrace Failure as a Learning Opportunity: Shift your mindset towards failure from being a negative outcome to being a valuable learning opportunity. Understand that failure is a natural part of the learning process and does not define your worth or potential. When you encounter failure, reflect on what went wrong, what you can learn from it and how you can improve in the future.

For instance, if you fail to achieve a goal or make a mistake, instead of dwelling on the failure or feeling discouraged, take it as a chance to learn and grow. Ask yourself what you could have done differently, what you learnt from the experience and how you can apply those lessons to future situations.

Develop Resilience and Perseverance: Cultivate resilience and perseverance in the face of challenges and setbacks. Recognise that success does not come overnight and that setbacks are inevitable on the path to peak performance. When faced with obstacles or failures, do not give up easily, but rather, persist with determination and a positive attitude.

For example, if you encounter a setback, such as not getting a promotion or facing rejection in a job application, do not let it discourage you. Instead, use it as a motivation to improve your skills, seek feedback and keep working towards your goal. Cultivate a mindset of resilience that views setbacks as temporary hurdles that can be overcome with perseverance and effort.

Maintain a Positive Attitude: Cultivate a positive attitude towards yourself, others and life in general. Practise gratitude, focus on your strengths and reframe challenges as opportunities for growth. Surround yourself with positive influences, such as mentors or supportive peers, who can encourage and inspire you to maintain a positive mindset.

For instance, when facing challenges or setbacks, avoid negative self-talk or self-blame. Instead, practise self-compassion and kindness towards yourself. Celebrate your achievements and progress, no matter how small and focus on your strengths and capabilities. Maintain a positive outlook towards life and see the potential for growth and improvement in every situation.

Embrace a Love for Learning: Cultivate a curiosity and eagerness to learn throughout your life. Embrace a love for learning and see it as a lifelong journey, rather than a destination. Seek out new knowledge, skills and experiences that can help you grow and improve.

For example, make it a habit to read books, articles, or research papers related to your field of expertise or areas of interest. Take courses, attend workshops or seminars and engage in continuous learning opportunities. Stay open to new ideas, perspectives and feedback and be willing to adapt and update your knowledge and skills as needed.

Practise Self-Reflection and Self-Awareness: Develop self-reflection and self-awareness as essential tools for personal and professional growth. Regularly reflect on your thoughts, emotions and behaviours and how they impact your mindset and performance. Be honest with yourself and identify any limiting beliefs or negative thought patterns that may be hindering your growth mindset.

For instance, if you notice that you tend to doubt your abilities or have a fear of failure, take a moment to reflect on the underlying beliefs or emotions that may be driving those thoughts. Challenge and reframe them to align with a growth mindset. Practise self-awareness to recognise when you may be falling into a fixed mindset and consciously shift towards a growth mindset.

Cultivate a Supportive Environment: Surround yourself with a supportive environment that fosters a growth mindset. Surround yourself with people who believe in your potential, encourage your growth and provide constructive feedback. Avoid negative influences or toxic environments that may hinder your progress or reinforce a fixed mindset.

For example, seek out mentors or coaches who can provide guidance and support in your personal and professional development. Collaborate with colleagues or peers who are also committed to growth and learning. Create a positive and inclusive work culture that promotes continuous improvement, innovation and collaboration.

Set Meaningful Goals: Set meaningful goals that align with your values, strengths and aspirations. Goals can provide direction, motivation and a sense of purpose, which are essential for cultivating a growth mindset. Set realistic and achievable goals that challenge you to stretch beyond your comfort zone, but are also within your capabilities.

For instance, set short-term and long-term goals that are specific, measurable, attainable, relevant and time-bound (SMART). Break down larger goals into smaller, manageable steps and track your progress along the way. Celebrate your achievements and learn from any setbacks or obstacles that you may encounter.

Practise Mindfulness: Cultivate mindfulness as a practice to develop a growth mindset. Mindfulness involves paying attention to the present moment with non-judgemental awareness. It can help you become more aware of your thoughts, emotions and behaviours and enable you to respond to challenges or setbacks with clarity and intention.

For example, practise mindfulness techniques such as deep breathing, meditation, or body scan exercises to cultivate present-moment awareness. When faced with challenges or setbacks, pause and observe your thoughts and emotions without judgement. This can help you respond to the situation with a growth mindset, rather than reacting impulsively or emotionally.

Practise Positive Affirmations: Practise positive affirmations to reinforce a growth mindset. Use positive and empowering language to affirm your abilities, potential and worth. Repeat affirmations that align with a growth mindset regularly to rewire your subconscious mind and reinforce positive beliefs about yourself and your abilities.

For example, use affirmations such as "I am capable of overcoming challenges and growing stronger," "I embrace failure as a learning opportunity," "I am resilient and persevere in the face of obstacles," or "I am constantly learning and improving." Say these affirmations to reinforce a growth mindset.

I personally believe that developing a growth mindset is one of the most essential steps to achieving success and living a fulfilling life. I've personally experienced the power of a growth mindset in my own life. When I first started writing, I struggled with self-doubt and fear of failure. However, I made a conscious effort to shift my perspective and view mistakes as opportunities for growth. I began seeking out feedback and critiques, rather than avoiding them and worked to continuously improve my craft. As a result, I've been able to publish multiple books and build a successful writing career.

Famous individuals like Michael Jordan, Oprah Winfrey and J.K. Rowling are great examples of individuals who have embraced a growth mindset. Michael Jordan, widely considered one of the greatest basketball players of all time, was initially cut from his high school basketball team. Rather than viewing this as a failure, he used it as motivation to work harder and eventually became a star player. Oprah Winfrey, a media mogul and philanthropist, grew up in poverty and faced numerous challenges throughout her life. However, she used these obstacles as opportunities for personal growth and worked tirelessly to build her career. J.K. Rowling, the author of the Harry Potter series, faced rejection from multiple publishers before finally finding success. Rather than giving up, she persisted and continued to improve her writing skills, eventually becoming one of the most successful authors in history.

Carol S. Dweck's book, *"Mindset: The New Psychology of Success"* is a groundbreaking work that explores the impact of mindset on success. The book is based on years of research and provides insights into how our mindset can either help or hinder our ability to achieve our goals.

Dweck identifies two types of mindsets: fixed mindset and growth mindset. Dweck's book goes on to explore how mindset impacts different areas of our lives, including relationships, parenting, business and education. She provides real-world examples and practical advice on how to cultivate a growth mindset and overcome the limitations of a fixed mindset.

Other good books on mindset include *"Grit: The Power of Passion and Perseverance"* by Angela Duckworth, *"The Mindset Makeover: Tame Your Fears, Change Your Self-Sabotaging Thoughts, and Learn from Your Mistakes"* by Anne Marie McQuaid and "Peak: Secrets from the New Science of Expertise" by Anders Ericsson and Robert Pool.

CONCLUSION

Cultivating a growth mindset is a lifelong journey that requires awareness, effort and practice. Embrace challenges, failures and setbacks as opportunities for growth and learning. Develop resilience, perseverance and a positive attitude towards yourself and others. Practise self-reflection, self-awareness and mindfulness to become aware of your thoughts, emotions and behaviours and consciously align them with a growth mindset. Surround yourself with a supportive environment that fosters growth and learning, and set meaningful goals that challenge you to stretch beyond your comfort zone. With a growth mindset, you can unlock your full potential, achieve peak performance and thrive in all areas of your life.

Remember the story of the twins from Ooty? While one twin with a growth mindset embraced challenges, persisted in the face of obstacles and achieved great success, the other twin with a fixed mindset gave up easily, felt threatened by the success of others and struggled with poverty and odd jobs. The power of a growth mindset cannot be overstated and by cultivating it, you can unlock your own potential and achieve peak performance in whatever you set your mind to.

So, go ahead and embrace a growth mindset, and let it be the driving force behind your pursuit of excellence and success. Believe in your abilities, embrace challenges as opportunities for growth and keep learning, growing and improving. With a growth mindset, you can achieve peak performance and fulfil your highest potential.

CHAPTER 13

Developing Mental Toughness for Peak Performance

INTRODUCTION

When I'm running a marathon, there comes a point where I feel like I've hit a wall. My body is aching, my legs feel like lead, and it seems like there's no energy left in me to take the next step. In those moments, I remember the powerful quote from Rafael Nadal: 'Mental toughness is when you can find fuel in an empty tank.'

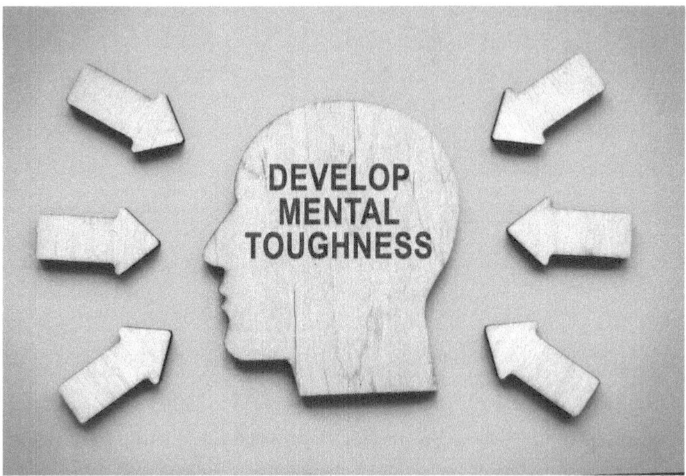

These words resonate with me deeply because they remind me that my mind is my most powerful tool. Despite feeling physically drained, I can tap into a well of mental strength that allows me to push through the pain and keep going. When I make the decision not to give up, something shifts within me, and I find reserves of energy that I never knew existed.

In those moments, I realise that mental toughness isn't just about physical endurance; it's about the power of the mind to overcome the limits of the body.

By finding the strength to keep going when everything in me is screaming to stop, I am tapping into the true essence of mental toughness—"resilience and determination that can overcome any obstacle."

Similarly, as a young student pursuing my PhD in Microbiology at the prestigious Indian Agricultural Research Institute (IARI) in New Delhi, I often found myself daydreaming about a different kind of future for myself. I had always been fascinated by the idea of public service and dreamed of one day becoming an Indian Police Service (IPS) officer.

Determined to make my dreams a reality, I began to study for the Civil Services examination. The process was long and arduous, and there were many moments when I felt overwhelmed and discouraged. But I refused to give up. I knew that if I wanted to succeed, I needed to cultivate a deep sense of mental toughness and resilience.

That's when I turned to yoga nidra, a powerful technique of deep relaxation that can help calm the mind and increase focus. Every day, I would spend an hour in deep trance, visualising myself acing the UPSC exams and becoming an IPS officer. I imagined myself walking confidently into the exam hall, answering every question with ease and grace. I saw myself standing tall and proud in my uniform, serving my country with honour and distinction.

At first, it was difficult to quiet my mind and focus on my visualisation practice. But over time, I found that it became easier and easier to slip into a deep state of relaxation and mental clarity. I began to feel more confident and focused than ever before.

And then, one day, it happened. I received the news that I had passed the UPSC exams with flying colours. Eventually, I was selected to join the prestigious Indian Police Service. I was overjoyed and overwhelmed with emotion. I knew that all of my hard work and dedication had paid off and that my visualisation practice had played a key role in helping me achieve my dreams

Today, as an IPS officer having served my country with pride and honour, I often think back on those early days at IARI and smile. I know that I never would have made it this far without the mental toughness and resilience that I developed through my daily visualisation practice. It just goes to show that with hard work, dedication and a little bit of visualisation, anything is possible.

What Is Mental Toughness?

Mental toughness is a term used to describe a person's ability to overcome adversity, push through challenges and maintain a strong and resilient mindset in the face of obstacles. It involves having a strong sense of purpose, perseverance and resilience in the face of difficult circumstances.

Mentally tough individuals are able to stay focused and motivated, even in the face of setbacks, and they are able to maintain a positive attitude and outlook, even when things are tough. They are able to manage stress, regulate their emotions and stay calm under pressure, allowing them to perform at their best even in high-stress situations.

Ultimately, mental toughness is about having the inner strength to push through difficulties and achieve their goals, even when the odds are against them. It's an essential quality for success in many areas of life, including sports, business and personal relationships. Mental toughness requires the development of specific skills and strategies that help individuals overcome adversity and perform at their best. Here, we will explore various techniques for developing mental toughness, including visualisation, goal-setting, positive self-talk, mindfulness and self-awareness.

Developing Mental Toughness

The science of developing mental toughness is a complex and multidisciplinary field that draws from psychology, neuroscience and sports science, among other areas of study. Here are some key insights from this field:

Practice: Mental toughness, like any skill, can be developed and strengthened with practice. Consistent exposure to challenging situations and deliberate practice of mental toughness skills can help to build resilience and improve performance.

Cognitive restructuring: One of the key strategies for developing mental toughness is cognitive restructuring. This involves changing the way we think about challenging situations and reframing them in a more positive light. For example, instead of viewing a setback as a failure, we can see it as an opportunity for growth and learning.

Visualisation: Visualisation is a powerful tool for developing mental toughness. It involves creating vivid mental images of success, which can help athletes or individuals visualise themselves performing at their best. Visualisation helps develop mental toughness by allowing individuals to focus on their goals and envision themselves overcoming obstacles. For example, a tennis player may visualise himself/herself hitting perfect shots or winning important matches. Similarly, a public speaker may visualise himself/herself delivering a flawless speech or presentation. When it comes to visualisation and mental toughness there can't be a better example than the retired US Navy SEAL David Goggins.

David Goggins is widely regarded as one of the toughest human beings on the planet. But his path to greatness was far from easy. Growing up in rural Indiana, Goggins faced numerous challenges, including poverty, racism and abuse. He struggled in school and dropped out of college, and for a time, he worked as a pest control technician to make ends meet.

But Goggins refused to let his circumstances define him. In his mid-twenties, he decided to join the United States Navy, where he became a Navy SEAL. And that was just the beginning.

Over the years, Goggins has pushed his body and mind to the limit, setting records in some of the most gruelling endurance events in the world. He's run ultramarathons, completed Ironman triathlons and even set the Guinness World Record for the most pull-ups in 24 hours.

But what sets Goggins apart is not just his physical prowess, but his mental toughness. He has repeatedly demonstrated the ability to push past pain, discomfort and fear to achieve his goals.

One of the techniques that Goggins used to develop this mental toughness was visualisation. He would imagine himself overcoming his fears and pushing past his limits, even when his body was screaming for him to stop.

This visualisation practice allowed Goggins to develop the mental resilience that he needed to conquer his fears and push himself to new heights. It helped him to stay focused and motivated, even in the face of seemingly insurmountable challenges.

Today, Goggins is an inspiration to millions of people around the world. His story is a testament to the power of hard work, determination and visualisation. It's proof that with the right mindset and attitude, anything is possible.

Goal-Setting

Setting goals is a crucial aspect of developing mental toughness. Goals help individuals to focus their energy and efforts towards achieving specific outcomes. By setting realistic and achievable goals, individuals can build confidence and self-belief, which are essential for mental toughness. For instance, a salesperson may set a goal of achieving a certain number of sales each month. In the book *"Grit: The Power of Passion and Perseverance"* by Angela Duckworth, the author explores the concept of grit, which Duckworth defines as "a combination of passion and perseverance for long-term goals." Through research and real-life examples, she shows how mental toughness and a growth mindset can help individuals achieve success in any field. By consistently meeting or exceeding these goals, the individual builds resilience and mental toughness.

In 2022, I set myself a daunting goal of running four marathons in four successive weeks to raise funds for the Tanker Foundation. The foundation had planned to equip all the police stations in Tamil Nādu with BP monitoring machines to prevent kidney disease among police personnel. Initially, I knew this goal would require a significant amount of physical and mental endurance, but I was driven by the cause and meaning behind it.

My motivation came from knowing that my efforts would make a meaningful contribution to a cause that I believed in. This purpose and meaning gave me the mental toughness needed to push through the challenges I faced during my training and the actual marathons.

Throughout the four weeks, I encountered various obstacles, such as muscle fatigue, blisters and mental exhaustion. However, knowing the reason why I was doing this gave me the motivation to persevere. I remained focused and resilient in the face of adversity, which helped me complete all four marathons.

In summary, my story highlights the importance of setting meaningful goals that align with one's values and beliefs. When a goal has a higher purpose and meaning, it can help individuals develop the mental toughness needed to overcome obstacles and achieve success.

Positive Self-Talk

Positive self-talk is another powerful tool for developing mental toughness. It involves using positive affirmations and self-talk to build confidence, motivation and resilience. Positive self-talk can help individuals overcome negative thoughts or doubts and maintain a positive mindset. By using positive and empowering self-talk, individuals can overcome self-doubt, boost their confidence and stay focused on their goals even in the face of adversity.

One great example of the power of self-talk can be seen in the story of Muhammad Ali, one of the greatest boxers of all time. Ali was known for his confident and often brash personality, but behind his words was a deep belief in himself and his abilities. He used positive self-talk to build up his confidence and maintain his focus, even in the midst of intense pressure and competition.

One famous example of Ali's use of self-talk came before his 1974 fight against George Foreman, known as the "Rumble in the Jungle." Ali was considered the underdog going into the fight, and many doubted his ability to win against the powerful Foreman. However, Ali used positive self-talk to build up his confidence and maintain his focus.

In an interview before the fight, Ali famously declared, "I am the greatest! I said that even before I knew I was. I figured that if I said it enough, I would convince the world that I really was the greatest." He repeated this phrase over and over again in the weeks leading up to the fight, using it to build his self-belief and drown out any doubts or fears.

During the fight itself, Ali employed a strategy known as the "rope-a-dope," in which he leaned against the ropes and absorbed Foreman's punches while conserving his energy. Despite taking a beating in the early rounds, Ali remained calm and focused, using positive self-talk to stay confident and maintain his composure.

In the eighth round, Ali saw an opening and delivered a series of devastating punches that knocked Foreman out and secured his victory. His use of positive self-talk and mental toughness allowed him to overcome his doubts and fears and achieve one of the greatest upsets in boxing history.

This example shows how self-talk can be a game-changer for mental toughness, allowing individuals to build their confidence and maintain their focus even in the face of intense pressure and competition. By using positive and empowering self-talk, individuals can overcome self-doubt, boost their resilience and achieve their goals.

Mindfulness

Mindfulness is a technique that involves focusing on the present moment and paying attention to one's thoughts and feelings without judgement. Mindfulness can help individuals develop mental toughness by increasing self-awareness and improving focus. By being more aware of their thoughts and feelings, individuals can identify and overcome negative thinking patterns and distractions. For instance, a business leader may use mindfulness techniques to stay focused during a critical meeting or negotiation.

Self-Awareness

Self-awareness is an essential aspect of developing mental toughness. It involves understanding one's strengths, weaknesses and emotions. By being aware of their limitations and emotions, individuals can develop strategies to overcome challenges and maintain focus. Self-awareness can also help individuals identify and address potential obstacles before they arise. For example, a student may be aware of their tendency to procrastinate and develop strategies to overcome this behaviour.

Physical fitness

Physical fitness and exercise have been shown to have a positive impact on mental toughness. Regular exercise can help to reduce stress and anxiety, improve cognitive function and increase resilience.

Overall, developing mental toughness involves a combination of psychological, cognitive and physical strategies. By practising these techniques and exposing ourselves to challenging situations, we can build resilience, improve performance and achieve our goals.

Mental toughness can be developed by following the "7 Cs" framework. The 7 Cs framework for developing mental toughness was developed by Dr Jim Loehr, a world-renowned performance psychologist and author. Loehr is known for his work with top athletes, executives and organisations, helping them to achieve high levels of performance and success through the development of mental toughness. The 7 Cs framework is based on Loehr's extensive research and experience working with individuals and teams in a variety of settings and has been widely adopted as a framework for developing mental toughness in both personal and professional contexts. Here's what each "C" stands for:

Control: Mental toughness requires a sense of control over oneself and one's environment. This means taking responsibility for one's thoughts and emotions and focusing on what can be controlled rather than what cannot.

Commitment: Mental toughness requires a strong commitment to one's goals and values. This involves setting clear goals, creating a plan of action and staying the course even when faced with obstacles or setbacks.

Challenge: Mental toughness requires embracing challenges and viewing them as opportunities for growth and learning. This involves stepping out of one's comfort zone and pushing oneself to new levels of performance.

Confidence: Mental toughness requires a sense of self-confidence and belief in one's abilities. This involves developing a positive mindset and cultivating a strong sense of self-efficacy.

Composure: Mental toughness requires the ability to stay calm and composed in the face of adversity. This involves developing emotional regulation skills, such as mindfulness and deep breathing and maintaining mental clarity and focus under pressure.

Consistency: Mental toughness requires a consistent and disciplined approach to one's goals and values. This involves developing a strong work ethic, setting and maintaining daily habits and staying focused on long-term objectives.

Courage: Mental toughness requires courage to take risks, confront fears and overcome obstacles. This involves developing a sense of bravery and determination to face challenges head-on and persevere in the face of adversity.

I think, William Wallace in the movie Braveheart embodies the 7 Cs framework for developing mental toughness. Here is why I think so.

Control: William Wallace demonstrates a sense of control over his emotions and actions, even in the face of great personal loss and injustice. He remains focused on his goals and values and uses his emotions to fuel his determination rather than letting them control him.

Commitment: William Wallace is deeply committed to his cause of fighting for Scottish independence from English rule. He sets clear goals for himself and his fellow Scots and stays the course even when faced with immense challenges and setbacks.

Challenge: William Wallace embraces challenges and sees them as opportunities for growth and learning. He is willing to take on the formidable English army, even though he and his fellow Scots are vastly outnumbered and outmatched.

Confidence: William Wallace has a strong sense of self-confidence and belief in his abilities. He inspires his fellow Scots to believe in themselves and their cause and leads them into battle with a sense of conviction and purpose.

Composure: William Wallace maintains composure and mental clarity even in the heat of battle. He stays calm under pressure and can think clearly and strategically even in the midst of chaos and danger.

Consistency: William Wallace demonstrates consistency and discipline in his approach to his goals and values. He is steadfast in his commitment to Scottish independence and is willing to make sacrifices and endure hardships to achieve it.

Courage: William Wallace displays great courage and bravery in the face of his opponents. He is willing to take on the might of the English army and is prepared to put his own life on the line for the sake of his cause and his fellow Scots.

Overall, William Wallace is a powerful example of how the 7 Cs framework for developing mental toughness can be applied in a variety of contexts, from sports to politics to personal struggles. By cultivating these qualities, individuals can build the resilience and determination needed to overcome obstacles and achieve their goals.

By following the 7 Cs framework, individuals can develop the qualities needed to build mental toughness and achieve their goals, both in their personal and professional lives.

KEY CHARACTERISTICS OF MENTALLY TOUGH PEOPLE

Mental toughness is a combination of attitudes, behaviours and traits that enable a person to cope effectively with challenges, stress and adversity. To become mentally tough, it's important to hack some key characteristics of mentally tough people such as:

Resilience: Mentally tough individuals are able to bounce back from setbacks and failures. They see challenges as opportunities for growth and learning, rather than as insurmountable obstacles.

Positive attitude: Mentally tough individuals tend to have a positive outlook on life. They are optimistic and believe in their ability to overcome challenges and achieve their goals.

Persistence: Mentally tough individuals are persistent in the face of difficulty. They don't give up easily, and they keep pushing themselves to achieve their objectives.

Emotional control: Mentally tough individuals are able to manage their emotions effectively. They don't let negative emotions like anger, fear, or anxiety get the better of them.

Focus: Mentally tough individuals are able to maintain focus and concentrate on the task at hand, even in the midst of distractions or obstacles.

Adaptability: Mentally tough individuals are able to adapt to changing circumstances and situations. They are flexible and open to new ideas and approaches.

Self-confidence: Mentally tough individuals have a strong sense of self-confidence and belief in their abilities. They trust themselves to succeed, even in challenging situations.

Discipline: Mentally tough individuals are disciplined in their approach to life. They have a strong work ethic and are willing to put in the time and effort required to achieve their goals.

Courage: Mentally tough individuals have the courage to face their fears and take risks. They are not afraid of failure, and they are willing to step outside of their comfort zones to achieve success.

Overall, mentally tough individuals have a combination of inner strength, resilience and a positive mindset that enable them to overcome challenges and achieve their goals.

How does mental toughness translate to peak performance?

Mental toughness is a key factor in achieving peak performance, as it helps individuals to overcome challenges, maintain focus and motivation and perform at their best under pressure. Here are a few ways in which mental toughness can translate to peak performance:

Increased Resilience: Mentally tough individuals are able to bounce back quickly from setbacks, using their strength and determination to overcome obstacles and keep moving forward. This resilience helps them to stay focused on their goals, even when faced with difficult circumstances.

Improved Focus and Concentration: Mental toughness allows individuals to stay focused on the task at hand, even in the face of distractions or challenges. This helps them to maintain their concentration, avoid errors and perform at their best.

Enhanced Motivation: Mentally tough individuals are driven by a strong sense of purpose and motivation, which helps them to push through difficulties and stay committed to their goals. This motivation translates into peak performance, as they are able to maintain their intensity and drive even in the face of adversity.

Better Stress Management: Mental toughness helps individuals to manage stress and anxiety, allowing them to stay calm and focused even in high-pressure situations. This enables them to perform at their best, without succumbing to stress-related distractions or performance anxiety.

Overall, mental toughness is a crucial component of peak performance, as it helps individuals to overcome obstacles, stay focused and motivated and achieve their goals even in the face of adversity.

Biohacking mental toughness for peak performance

Biohacking is the process of using science, technology and personal experimentation to optimise the human body and mind. Here are some ways to biohack mental toughness for peak performance:

Meditation: Practising meditation has been shown to increase mental toughness by improving focus, reducing stress and anxiety and enhancing self-awareness. Start with a few minutes of meditation each day and gradually increase the duration.

Breathing Techniques: Breathing exercises, such as deep breathing or Box Breathing, can help to calm the mind, reduce stress and improve focus. Incorporate breathing techniques into your daily routine or use them as a tool to manage stress during high-pressure situations.

Cold Exposure: Exposure to cold temperatures has been shown to improve mental toughness by increasing resilience to stress and enhancing focus and concentration. Try taking cold showers or incorporating cold exposure into your workout routine.

Nutrition: Eating a healthy diet rich in nutrients and antioxidants can help to improve brain function and mental toughness. Incorporate foods such as leafy greens, nuts and berries into your diet and avoid processed foods and sugar.

Exercise: Regular exercise has been shown to increase mental toughness by improving mood, reducing stress and enhancing focus and concentration. Incorporate both aerobic and strength training exercises into your routine for optimal benefits.

Positive Self-Talk: Positive self-talk can help to improve mental toughness by building confidence, reducing stress and enhancing focus. Use positive affirmations and visualisation techniques to reframe negative thoughts and improve your mindset.

Overall, biohacking mental toughness involves experimenting with different techniques and practices to optimise your mental and emotional well-being and improve your performance in all areas of life.

CONCLUSION

Developing mental toughness is essential for achieving peak performance in any field. It requires the cultivation of specific skills and strategies, including visualisation, goal-setting, positive self-talk, mindfulness and self-awareness. By practising these techniques, individuals can overcome adversity, maintain focus and achieve their goals. Examples of some of the world's mentally toughest individuals highlight the importance of developing mental toughness and provide inspiration for those looking to cultivate this trait.

CHAPTER 14

The Role of Emotion in Peak Performance and How to Regulate It

"Emotions are the fuel that powers peak performance." - Hal Elrod.

INTRODUCTION

The quote of Hal Elrod on emotions fully resonates with me. I truly believe that emotions are a powerful tool that can be harnessed to fuel peak performance. After the elections and the change of the government, I was transferred from my position as ADGP-L&O to ADGP-Armed Police. This belief was put to the test when I was unexpectedly transferred again after I had only spent less than a year as ADGP-AP and posted as the ADGP-Idol Wing. I felt insulted and punished for no apparent reason. However, instead of dwelling on my negative emotions, I decided to channel them positively towards my new assignment.

I knew that the Idol Wing had a reputation for not being very successful in recovering stolen artefacts, and I was determined to change that. I turned my anger and frustration into a motivation to excel in my new position. I made the decision to give it my all and make the Idol Wing one of the best-performing units in the state.

I focused on the task at hand and set clear goals for myself and the Wing. I wanted to recover as many stolen artefacts as possible and bring in innovative measures that had not been implemented before. I believed that my positive attitude and determination would rub off on my team, and we would all work together to achieve our goals.

Despite the initial frustration, with determination and hard work, we achieved a record of retrieving 10 stolen antique idols from countries like the USA and Australia. In addition, we registered the highest number of cases (81) and arrested 56 accused while recovering 298 idols—a feat that had never been accomplished in the history of the Idol Wing or anywhere in India. I am proud to say that we were able to achieve these milestones because of the positive emotions that we channelled towards our work.

As we continued to work, I brought in several innovative measures, such as launching a virtual museum, introducing Blockchain technology and introducing NFTs and Soulbound Tokens as a reward for the staff of the Idol Wing for doing good work. With my team's hard work and dedication, we uploaded 3D images of the idols to the Virtual Museum to help the connoisseurs of art and culture and the general public view and appreciate the ancient cultural treasures of Tamil Nadu.

The Virtual Museum was a collection of digital Virtual Reality / Augmented Reality images, of stolen antique idols recovered by the team which the viewers could access through the tnidols.com website. One of the most significant benefits of virtual museums is that visitors can immerse themselves in the uploaded antique idols in the Virtual Museum regardless of location and geographical boundaries. Eventually, my team and I envisioned curating and transforming the Virtual Museum into a Metaverse of tomorrow where visitors could interact in 3D Cyberspace and have the experience of visiting a museum in physical space, with separate galleries having exhibits for different categories bringing on a total experience of the Metaverse.

Additionally, we launched an initiative that was the first of its kind in the state and country of receiving information from informants and enabling our staff to submit grievances on the Block Chain. The public could also launch complaints on the Blockchain. Using the Blockchain's immutable nature, the Idol Wing now had an efficient and secure way to track and store data, providing a digital trail and allowing for easier identification of any issues or concerns regarding the handling of complaints. Overall, using the Blockchain by Idol Wing would help create a more reliable and secure system for tracking and resolving complaints. These initiatives helped to motivate my team and fostered a sense of pride in their work.

My experience in Idol Wing clearly reveals how emotions can be powerful tools for achieving peak performance. By channelling my negative emotions positively towards my new assignment, I was able to achieve mind-boggling work in the Wing, which was never before achieved in the history of the Tamil Nādu Police. My experience perfectly captures the essence of Hal Elrod's quote about how emotions can be harnessed to achieve peak performance.

Emotions, therefore, play a crucial role in our lives, affecting our thoughts, behaviours and physiological responses. Emotions can be positive, such as happiness, excitement and enthusiasm, or negative, such as anger, fear and anxiety. In the context of performance, emotions can either enhance or impair performance. Emotions can be powerful motivators, energising performers to achieve their goals. However, emotions can also be distracting and overwhelming, hindering performance. Here, we will discuss the role of emotions in performance and provide strategies for regulating emotions to optimise performance.

The Role of Emotions in Performance

Emotions can have a significant impact on performance. Positive emotions such as happiness, joy and excitement can enhance performance by improving motivation, increasing focus and promoting creativity. For example, athletes who feel confident and excited before a competition may perform better than those who feel anxious or nervous. Similarly, musicians who feel joyful and passionate about their music may give a more inspired performance.

Negative emotions such as anxiety, fear and anger can impair performance by causing distraction, reducing focus and increasing physiological arousal. For example, a student who feels anxious about an upcoming exam may have difficulty concentrating and remembering information, leading to poor performance. Similarly, a public speaker who feels nervous and intimidated may stumble over their words and appear unconfident.

Emotional Intelligence and Self-Awareness

To regulate emotions effectively, it is essential to develop emotional intelligence and self-awareness. Emotional intelligence is the ability to recognise and manage one's emotions and the emotions of others. Self-awareness is the ability to recognise one's own emotions, thoughts and behaviours and understand how they affect oneself and others.

Developing emotional intelligence and self-awareness can help individuals regulate their emotions, leading to better performance. For example, a performer who is aware of his emotions and the impact they have on his performance can use strategies to regulate their emotions, such as deep breathing, visualisation, or positive self-talk.

Strategies for Regulating Emotions

There are several strategies that individuals can use to regulate their emotions and optimise performance. Strategies such as deep breathing, visualisation, positive self-talk, mindfulness and exercise have been discussed in detail in other chapters of this book.

HARNESSING EMOTIONS FOR PEAK PERFORMANCE

Emotions can be powerful motivators that can help individuals achieve peak performance in various domains. Harnessing emotions for peak performance involves recognising and managing one's emotions to achieve optimal performance levels.

"Whiplash" (2014), directed by Damien Chazelle beautifully brings out how emotions can be harnessed for peak performance. The movie follows the story of a young jazz drummer named Andrew Neiman, played by Miles Teller, who dreams of becoming a great musician. Andrew enrols in a prestigious music conservatory and catches the attention of Terence Fletcher, played by J.K. Simmons, a demanding and abusive music teacher who believes in pushing his students to their limits to achieve greatness.

Throughout the movie, emotions play a significant role in Andrew's journey towards peak performance. At first, he struggles with anxiety and self-doubt, but as he becomes more confident in his abilities, he starts to channel his emotions into his drumming. When Fletcher pushes him to the brink of exhaustion and frustration, Andrew uses his anger and determination to fuel his performance.

The scene in which Andrew performs a solo during a music competition is a prime example of how emotions are used for peak performance. The tension and intensity build as Andrew's drumming becomes faster and more complex, culminating in a breathtaking finale that leaves the audience and judges in awe. Andrew's emotions drive him to push beyond his limits and deliver a performance that earns him the respect and admiration of his peers.

Overall, "Whiplash" illustrates how emotions can be harnessed for peak performance, but it also shows the darker side of this approach, including the toll it can take on one's mental and physical health. The movie raises important questions about the relationship between emotions, perfectionism and creativity and how they can both drive and hinder success.

STRATEGIES FOR HARNESSING EMOTIONS FOR PEAK PERFORMANCE

Recognise and Label Emotions:

The first step in harnessing emotions for peak performance is to recognise and label them. Emotions are complex, and it can be challenging to identify them accurately. However, by recognising and labelling emotions, individuals can gain greater self-awareness and manage their emotions more effectively. For example, an athlete who feels anxious before a competition can label their emotions as anxiety and use strategies to manage it, such as deep breathing or visualisation.

Understand the Relationship Between Emotions and Performance:

To harness emotions for peak performance, individuals must understand the relationship between emotions and performance. Emotions can either enhance or impair performance, depending on the situation. Positive emotions such as excitement, joy and passion can enhance performance by increasing motivation, focus and creativity. Negative emotions such as anxiety, fear and anger can impair performance by causing distraction, reducing focus and increasing physiological arousal. By understanding this relationship, individuals can use their emotions to achieve peak performance.

Use Emotions as Motivators:

Emotions can be powerful motivators that can help individuals achieve peak performance. By using emotions as motivators, individuals can channel their energy and focus towards achieving their goals. For example, an athlete who feels motivated and passionate about their sport can train harder and perform better during competitions.

Channel Emotions Towards the Task at Hand:

To achieve peak performance, individuals must learn to channel their emotions towards the task at hand. This involves focusing on the present moment and using emotions to enhance performance. For example, a public speaker who feels nervous before a presentation can use their nervous energy to deliver an enthusiastic and engaging speech.

Develop Emotional Resilience:

Developing emotional resilience is crucial for harnessing emotions for peak performance. Emotional resilience involves the ability to adapt to and cope with stress, adversity and setbacks. By developing emotional resilience, individuals can manage their emotions effectively and overcome obstacles that may hinder their performance. For example, a student who receives a poor grade on an exam can use their emotional resilience to bounce back and perform better on future exams.

Some great celebrities, who harnessed emotions for peak performance are Oprah Winfrey, a media mogul and philanthropist, known for her empathetic nature and emotional intelligence. She used her own struggles and experiences to connect with her audience and inspire them to overcome their own challenges. Winfrey's ability to connect emotionally with her viewers made her one of the most influential and successful personalities in the entertainment industry. Similarly, Albert Einstein, the renowned physicist who developed the theory of relativity, was known for his creativity and intuition. He used his emotions to inspire his scientific discoveries, often relying on his "gut feeling" to guide his research. Einstein believed that emotions were a crucial part of the creative process and that they could help him see patterns and connections that others might miss.

Harnessing emotions for peak performance involves recognising and labelling emotions, understanding the relationship between emotions and performance, using emotions as motivators, channelling emotions towards the task at hand and developing emotional resilience. By incorporating these strategies into their daily routine, individuals can use their emotions to achieve peak performance in various domains of life.

Connection Between Emotional Regulation and Peak Performance

Emotional regulation and peak performance are closely connected. Emotional regulation refers to the ability to recognise, understand and manage one's emotions effectively, while peak performance refers to achieving optimal levels of performance in a particular domain. In this section, we will discuss the connection between emotional regulation and peak performance.

Emotional Regulation Enhances Focus:

Emotional regulation can enhance focus, which is essential for achieving peak performance. By managing their emotions effectively, individuals can reduce distractions and concentrate on the task at hand. For example, an athlete who experiences anxiety before a competition can use emotional regulation techniques, such as deep breathing or positive self-talk, to calm their nerves and focus on their performance.

Emotional Regulation Reduces Stress

Stress can hinder performance, making it difficult to achieve peak performance. Emotional regulation can reduce stress levels and promote a state of relaxation, allowing individuals to perform at their best. For example, a student who experiences stress before an exam can use emotional regulation techniques, such as mindfulness or visualisation, to reduce their stress levels and perform better on the exam.

Emotional Regulation Improves Decision-Making

Emotional regulation can improve decision-making, which is crucial for achieving peak performance. By managing their emotions effectively, individuals can make more rational and logical decisions. For example, a business executive who experiences anger during a negotiation can use emotional regulation techniques, such as taking a break or practising empathy, to make more informed decisions.

Emotional Regulation Enhances Resilience

Emotional regulation can enhance resilience, which is essential for achieving peak performance. By managing their emotions effectively, individuals can adapt to and cope with stress, setbacks and obstacles that may hinder their performance. For example, an athlete who experiences a setback during training can use emotional regulation techniques, such as reframing or positive self-talk, to bounce back and perform at their best.

Emotional Regulation Promotes Positive Emotions

Emotional regulation can promote positive emotions, such as joy, passion and excitement, which can enhance performance and promote a sense of well-being. For example, a musician who experiences joy while performing can use emotional regulation techniques, such as mindfulness or visualisation, to enhance their performance and promote a sense of fulfilment.

In conclusion, emotional regulation and peak performance are closely connected. Emotional regulation can enhance focus, reduce stress, improve decision-making, enhance resilience and promote positive emotions, all of which are crucial for achieving peak performance. By incorporating emotional regulation techniques into their daily routine, individuals can manage their emotions effectively and achieve optimal levels of performance in various domains of life.

Importance of Emotional Intelligence for Peak Performance

Emotional intelligence is the ability to recognise, understand and manage one's own emotions, as well as the emotions of others. It is an important factor in achieving peak performance in any domain, including sports, business and creative fields. Here are some reasons why emotional intelligence is essential for peak performance:

Self-awareness: Emotional intelligence helps individuals develop self-awareness, which is the foundation of peak performance. By understanding their own emotions, strengths and weaknesses, individuals can identify areas for improvement and work to overcome challenges. Self-awareness also helps individuals set realistic goals and focus their efforts on achieving them.

Self-regulation: Emotionally intelligent individuals are able to regulate their emotions effectively, which is crucial for maintaining focus and staying calm under pressure. This skill helps individuals avoid becoming overwhelmed by stress or negative emotions and enables them to make rational decisions even in high-pressure situations.

Empathy: Emotional intelligence involves the ability to understand and connect with others' emotions. This skill is essential for building strong relationships and collaborating effectively with others. Empathy helps individuals anticipate others' needs and respond to them in a supportive and constructive manner.

Adaptability: Emotionally intelligent individuals are better equipped to adapt to changing circumstances and new challenges. They are more open to feedback and are able to adjust their approach based on the situation. This flexibility is crucial for achieving peak performance in dynamic environments.

Leadership: Emotional intelligence is a key component of effective leadership. Leaders who are emotionally intelligent are able to inspire and motivate their teams, build trust and loyalty and create a positive and productive work environment. They are also able to handle conflicts and difficult conversations in a constructive manner.

Gandhi who practised emotional intelligence is widely regarded as one of the most influential figures in Indian history, known for his leadership in the Indian independence movement and his philosophy of nonviolent resistance. He was able to bring together diverse groups of people and unite them towards a common goal through his exceptional emotional intelligence.

Gandhi's emotional intelligence helped him connect with people on a deeper level and understand their motivations, fears and aspirations. He was able to communicate effectively with people from all walks of life, whether they were peasants, intellectuals, or political leaders. Gandhi's ability to empathise with others helped him to build trust and credibility, which in turn enabled him to inspire and motivate people to take action towards their shared goals.

Additionally, Gandhi had a strong sense of self-awareness and was able to manage his emotions effectively. He was known for his calm and composed demeanour, even in the face of adversity. This enabled him to remain focused and resilient in the face of challenges, which was critical to his success in leading the Indian independence movement.

Overall, Gandhi's emotional intelligence played a crucial role in his ability to achieve peak performance and lead India towards independence. His ability to connect with people, build trust and manage his emotions effectively enabled him to inspire and mobilise millions of people towards a shared vision of a free and independent India.

Hence, Emotional intelligence is a crucial factor in achieving peak performance. By developing self-awareness, self-regulation, empathy, adaptability and leadership skills, individuals can harness their emotions to drive success in any domain.

CONCLUSION

Emotions play a crucial role in performance. Positive emotions can enhance performance by increasing motivation, focus and creativity, while negative emotions can impair performance by causing distraction, reducing focus and increasing physiological arousal. To regulate emotions effectively, individuals must develop emotional intelligence and self-awareness, which involves recognising and managing one's emotions and the emotions of others.

There are several strategies that individuals can use to regulate their emotions and optimise performance, such as deep breathing, visualisation, positive self-talk, mindfulness and exercise. By incorporating these strategies into their daily routine, individuals can reduce stress, improve focus and enhance performance.

In summary, emotions are an essential aspect of human life and learning to regulate them is crucial for optimal performance in various areas of life. By developing emotional intelligence and self-awareness and using effective strategies to regulate emotions, individuals can achieve their goals and lead a fulfilling life.

CHAPTER 15

The Role of Visualisation and Mental Rehearsal for Peak Performance

INTRODUCTION

It was the winter of 1990, and I had just got married and moved to the Indian Agricultural Research Institute in New Delhi. I was a PhD scholar in Microbiology, and I had my sights set on a bigger goal—cracking the Civil Services exam.

But things weren't easy. The Mandal Agitation was in full swing, and the main exams had been postponed. The winter in Delhi was getting harsher by the day, but I couldn't let go of my dreams. As fate would have it, one day I stumbled upon an advertisement by the Alpha Mind Institute of Mumbai in an English daily. The ad boasted success for people practising their method by programming the subconscious. The cost of it was a whopping rupees 300, a big sum for a student in those days.

But I wasn't one to let go of an opportunity. I ordered the book and cassette tape, eager to try out this new method. The book spoke about the subconscious mind and how it could be programmed by using the audio tape. I was required to progressively relax my mind and listen to the tape and visualise whatever outcome I desired out of my life. This was basically a self-hypnosis exercise with visualisation thrown in at the end.

Without any second thoughts, I began practising it twice a day, visualising myself passing the Civil Services exams and seeing myself in uniform receiving salutes. I had never used visualisation before, but I had a gut feeling that it would work.

The main exams were finally conducted after a delay, and I continued with my visualisation exercises even as I prepared for the interview. The day finally arrived when the results were announced. I passed the exams with flying colours and was later allotted to the Indian Police Service according to my rank. It was a dream come true for me and my wife.

That was my first experiment with visualisation, and it turned out to be a huge success. Since then, I have used visualisation to achieve desired outcomes in life. I realised the power of the subconscious mind and the importance of programming it with positive thoughts and visualisations. And that, my friends, is the story of how my belief in the power of visualisation changed my life forever.

WHAT ARE VISUALISATION AND MENTAL REHEARSAL?

Visualisation and mental rehearsal are powerful techniques that can be used to improve performance in various areas of life, including sports, academics and business. Visualisation involves using mental imagery to create a clear picture of a desired outcome, while mental rehearsal involves practising and rehearsing a desired outcome in the mind. Both techniques have been studied extensively by researchers and have been shown to be effective in enhancing performance. In this chapter, we will explore the science behind visualisation and mental rehearsal and provide practical techniques for using them to improve performance. We will also discuss the importance of goal-setting and creating a clear mental image of success in visualisation and mental rehearsal.

The Science Behind Visualisation and Mental Rehearsal

The brain is a powerful tool that can be trained to improve performance through visualisation and mental rehearsal. When we visualise something, our brain creates a mental image of the desired outcome, and this mental image activates the same neural pathways as if we were actually performing the task. In other words, our brain cannot differentiate between a real experience and a vividly imagined one. This phenomenon is called the "mental simulation theory" and has been supported by numerous studies.

Similarly, mental rehearsal involves practising a desired outcome in the mind, and this practice helps to strengthen the neural pathways associated with the desired behaviour. Mental rehearsal has been shown to improve physical performance, such as in sports, by enhancing motor skills and reducing anxiety.

Both visualisation and mental rehearsal can also be used to improve cognitive performance, such as in academics and business. Visualising success in a specific task or project can help to increase motivation, reduce anxiety and improve focus and concentration.

VISUALISATION IS A POWERFUL PEAK PERFORMANCE TOOL

Visualisation is a powerful peak performance tool that can help individuals achieve their goals and reach their full potential. By creating a mental image of success and rehearsing that image repeatedly in the mind, individuals can improve their focus, confidence and motivation, leading to better performance in various areas of life.

Visualisation has been used by athletes, performers, business professionals and even students to enhance their performance and achieve success. By visualising themselves performing at their best, individuals can build the mental skills and habits necessary to perform at that level in real life.

Research has shown that visualisation can have a positive impact on physical performance, such as improving motor skills, strength and endurance. It can also improve cognitive performance, such as enhancing memory, attention and problem-solving skills.

Visualisation is not just a mental exercise, but it also has a physiological effect on the body. Studies have shown that when individuals visualise a movement or activity, the same neural pathways are activated in the brain as when actually performing that movement or activity. This means that visualisation can help to strengthen the neural connections in the brain that are necessary for performing at a high level.

Overall, visualisation is a powerful tool that can help individuals to achieve their goals, reach their full potential and perform at their best in various areas of life.

Ways of Using Visualisation and Mental Rehearsal

Visualisation and mental rehearsal can be used in various ways to improve performance. Here are some practical techniques:

Create a Clear Mental Image of Success: The first step in visualisation and mental rehearsal is to create a clear mental image of success. This involves setting a specific goal and visualising yourself achieving that goal. For example, if your goal is to win a race, visualise yourself crossing the finish line first, hearing the cheers of the crowd and feeling a sense of accomplishment.

Use All Your Senses: When visualising or mentally rehearsing, use all your senses to create a vivid and realistic mental image. For example, if you are visualising yourself giving a presentation, imagine the sound of your voice, the feel of the podium and the expressions of your audience.

Practice Regularly: Visualisation and mental rehearsal are skills that can be developed with practice. Set aside time each day to visualise or mentally rehearse your desired outcome. This can be done in a quiet space or during a downtime activity, such as before going to bed.

Use Positive Self-Talk: During visualisation and mental rehearsal, use positive self-talk to reinforce your mental image of success. For example, tell yourself that you are capable of achieving your goal and that you have the skills and knowledge to do so.

Visualise the Process, Not Just the Outcome: When visualising or mentally rehearsing, focus on the process of achieving your goal, not just the outcome. For example, if your goal is to ace an exam, visualise yourself studying effectively, being focused and productive and feeling confident during the exam.

Visualisation and Mental Rehearsal in Performance

Visualisation and mental rehearsal have been used by athletes, musicians and business executives to enhance performance.

Athletes: Athletes use visualisation and mental rehearsal to improve physical performance, reduce anxiety and increase motivation. For example, Olympic skier Lindsey Vonn used visualisation to overcome a knee injury and win a gold medal in the 2010 Winter Olympics. She would visualise herself skiing the course in her mind, focusing on her technique and form and imagining herself successfully completing the race. This mental rehearsal helped her build confidence and overcome her injury.

Musicians: Musicians use visualisation and mental rehearsal to improve their performance by practising in their minds. For example, classical pianist Vladimir Horowitz would often mentally rehearse a piece of music before performing it in front of an audience. He would visualise himself playing the piece perfectly, focusing on his technique, phrasing and musical expression.

Business Executives: Business executives use visualisation and mental rehearsal to improve their performance in high-pressure situations, such as presentations, negotiations and public speaking. For example, Steve Jobs, the co-founder of Apple, was known for his use of visualisation and mental rehearsal. Before presenting a new product or idea, he would spend hours visualising the presentation in his mind, imagining himself on stage, delivering the message with confidence and clarity.

Movie stars: Jim Carrey is a famous comedian, actor and writer who used visualisation to achieve his dreams. Before he became famous, he was a struggling actor living in Los Angeles. To stay motivated, he wrote himself a cheque for $10 million and kept it in his wallet. He would look at the cheque every day and visualise himself receiving it. He believed that one day he would be paid that amount for his work. Years later, when he starred in the movie "Dumb and Dumber," he was paid $10 million, the exact amount he had written on the cheque years before. Carrey believes that visualisation played a big role in his success, and he continues to use it to this day.

Sports persons: Jack Nicklaus, also known as "The Golden Bear," is one of the most successful golfers of all time, with 18 major championship wins. He is also a strong advocate of visualisation, which he credits for much of his success on the course.

Nicklaus would often visualise the perfect shot before hitting it, imagining the trajectory of the ball, the swing and the follow-through. He believed that visualisation helped him to stay focused and calm under pressure and to make more accurate shots. In his book *"Golf My Way,"* Nicklaus wrote, "I never hit a shot, not even in practice, without having a very sharp, in-focus picture of it in my head. First, I see the ball where I want it to finish, nice and white and sitting up high on the bright green grass. Then the scene quickly changes, and I see the ball going there: its path, trajectory, shape, even its behaviour on landing." Nicklaus' use of visualisation is a testament to its effectiveness in golf and other sports and to the importance of mental preparation in achieving success.

CONCLUSION

Visualisation and mental rehearsal are powerful techniques that can be used to improve performance in various areas of life. By creating a clear mental image of success, using all your senses, practising regularly, using positive self-talk and focusing on the process, not just the outcome, you can develop these skills and enhance your performance. Visualisation and mental rehearsal have been used successfully by athletes, musicians and business executives and can be applied in any area of life where performance improvement is desired. By incorporating these techniques into your daily routine, you can achieve your goals and reach your full potential.

CHAPTER 16

The Role of Hormones in Performance

INTRODUCTION

In the realm of my professional life as an IPS officer, I found myself facing a personal battle that threatened to overshadow my aspirations. The uniform may have symbolised strength and authority, but deep within, I struggled with an unexpected obstacle—weight gain. Determined to reclaim my vitality, I embarked on a running regimen alongside my striking force in the scenic landscapes of Tanjore.

Every evening, we explored the beauty of a newly-laid bypass road, its serene green paddies and majestic wooded areas offering solace and inspiration. Our consistent dedication to our runs turned our endeavour into a town legend, but my excess weight persisted despite the hours spent on the road. Perplexed and concerned, a fateful evening brought forth an excruciating pain that altered the course of my journey.

My legs, swollen and aching, impeded my usual stride, yet I persisted, driven by sheer willpower. Eventually, the agony became unbearable, forcing me to surrender to the undeniable truth—I needed medical attention. Hospitalised and awaiting test results, my world turned on its axis when I discovered the cause behind my struggles—hypothyroidism, a hormonal imbalance. The diagnosis revealed high TSH levels, necessitating the introduction of synthetic thyroxine to restore equilibrium.

This revelation illuminated the profound impact hormones have on our overall well-being. These biochemical messengers, secreted by our endocrine glands, orchestrate our physical and mental health in ways we often overlook. Reflecting, I recalled an encounter at the Presidency College gym that left an indelible mark on my understanding of hormones.

A gym companion, whose sculpted physique was a testament to dedication, imparted wisdom that would later prove invaluable. He recommended the herb Ashwagandha, known for its ability to boost endogenous testosterone and aid in muscle development. Alongside, other herbal supplements like Mucuna and Tribulus were advised. With the guidance of an Ayurveda doctor, I procured these herbs and incorporated them into my regimen, experiencing moderate gains in muscle mass without resorting to drastic measures like anabolic steroids.

It became clear to me that maintaining hormonal balance is paramount for optimal health and performance. Several key hormones play a significant role in an athlete's journey:

1. **Growth Hormone (GH):** The catalyst for growth, repair and regeneration of cells, promoting muscle development and recovery.
2. **Thyroxine (T4):** Regulating metabolism, this hormone influences energy levels, weight management and overall vitality.
3. **Oestrogen:** Crucial for female athletes, this hormone impacts bone health, muscle strength and performance.
4. **Testosterone:** The cornerstone of male athleticism, testosterone fuels muscle growth, strength and endurance.
5. **Cortisol:** Known as the stress hormone, it can impede performance if not managed properly, affecting recovery and overall well-being.

The Role of Hormones in Performance and Optimising Hormone Levels

In the pursuit of peak performance, athletes often focus on training, nutrition and recovery. However, one crucial aspect that is frequently overlooked is the role of hormones in optimising performance. Hormones act as powerful messengers within our bodies, influencing various physiological processes and ultimately impacting our athletic abilities. In this chapter, we will delve into the significance of hormones in performance and explore strategies for optimising hormone levels to unlock our true potential.

The Key Hormones and Their Impact on Performance

A. Growth Hormone (GH)

Growth hormone, or GH, plays a vital role in muscle growth, repair and regeneration. It acts as a catalyst for cellular development, promoting muscle development and enhancing recovery. GH is particularly important for athletes seeking to improve their strength, power and overall athletic performance. By understanding how GH affects our bodies and implementing strategies to naturally stimulate its production, athletes can optimise their training results.

B. Thyroxine (T4)

Thyroxine, or T4, is a hormone produced by the thyroid gland that regulates metabolism. T4 influences energy levels, weight management and overall vitality.

Achieving a balanced T4 level is crucial for athletes as it directly impacts their endurance, stamina and body composition. By ensuring optimal thyroid function through proper nutrition and lifestyle choices, athletes can maximise their athletic potential.

C. Oestrogen

While oestrogen is typically associated with female athletes, it also plays a significant role in male athletes. In females, oestrogen is crucial for bone health, muscle strength and overall performance. For male athletes, maintaining an appropriate balance of oestrogen is essential for optimal muscle growth and body composition. Understanding the influence of oestrogen and implementing strategies to support its balance can enhance performance and prevent potential hormonal imbalances.

D. Testosterone

Testosterone is often recognised as the cornerstone of male athleticism, but it also plays a vital role in female athletes. Testosterone is responsible for promoting muscle growth, strength and endurance. In males, optimal testosterone levels are crucial for achieving peak athletic performance. In females, maintaining an appropriate balance of testosterone supports muscle development and overall athletic capabilities. Strategies to naturally support testosterone levels can help athletes reach their full potential.

E. Cortisol

Cortisol, known as the stress hormone, can either enhance or hinder athletic performance depending on its levels and management. In small amounts, cortisol is beneficial for providing energy during exercise and promoting recovery.

However, excessive or prolonged cortisol release can lead to muscle breakdown, fatigue and impaired performance. Managing stress levels through proper training, recovery and stress-reducing techniques can help maintain cortisol within an optimal range for improved performance.

Optimising Hormone Levels for Peak Performance

A. Nutrition and Hormonal Balance

Proper nutrition plays a fundamental role in optimising hormone levels. Macronutrients such as carbohydrates, proteins and fats, along with micronutrients like vitamins and minerals, impact hormone production and regulation. A well-balanced diet rich in whole foods, with an emphasis on nutrient timing and specific dietary choices, can support hormonal balance and enhance athletic performance.

B. Exercise and Hormonal Regulation

Exercise intensity, duration and type can significantly impact hormone secretion. Implementing a well-designed training programme that includes a combination of strength training, cardiovascular exercise and targeted workouts can optimise hormone release. High-intensity interval training (HIIT), resistance training and specific exercises targeting hormone-stimulating muscle groups can be particularly effective in promoting favourable hormonal responses. Remember, finding the right balance is crucial. Overtraining and excessive exercise can lead to hormonal imbalances and negatively impact performance. Rest and recovery are just as important as the exercise itself. Listen to your body, incorporate rest days into your routine and prioritise adequate sleep to allow your hormones to reset and optimise.

C. Sleep and Hormonal Restoration

Adequate sleep and proper sleep quality are vital for hormonal restoration and optimal performance. During the sleep cycle, our bodies undergo important hormonal processes that support recovery, muscle growth and overall well-being. By prioritising sufficient sleep duration, creating a conducive sleep environment and practising good sleep hygiene, athletes can optimise hormone secretion and maximise their athletic potential.

D. Stress Management and Hormonal Equilibrium

Chronic stress can disrupt hormonal balance and hinder athletic performance. Stress reduction techniques such as mindfulness meditation, deep breathing exercises and engaging in activities that promote relaxation can help regulate stress hormone levels. Managing stress through adequate recovery, maintaining a healthy work-life balance and seeking support when needed are crucial for maintaining hormonal equilibrium and achieving peak performance.

E. Herbal Remedies and Adaptogens

Nature offers a treasure trove of herbs and adaptogens that have been used for centuries to support hormonal balance and enhance performance. Let's explore some popular herbs and adaptogens known for their potential benefits and delve into the scientific evidence supporting their use.

Ashwagandha, an adaptogenic herb, takes centre stage when it comes to hormonal balance. It has been traditionally used in Ayurvedic medicine to reduce stress, enhance vitality and improve sexual function. Scientific studies have shown that Ashwagandha supplementation can lead to significant increases in testosterone levels, sperm quality and reproductive hormone profiles in males. It is believed that Ashwagandha works by reducing stress hormone levels, promoting antioxidant activity and supporting healthy inflammatory responses.

Maca, a root vegetable native to the high-altitude regions of Peru, is another herb gaining popularity for its potential benefits in hormone regulation. Maca has long been recognised as an aphrodisiac and is believed to support hormonal balance in both men and women. It has been associated with increased libido, improved energy levels and enhanced mood. While more research is needed to fully understand its mechanisms, anecdotal evidence and traditional use suggest its effectiveness.

Rhodiola, an adaptogenic herb found in mountainous regions, is renowned for its ability to combat stress and enhance mental performance. It has been shown to improve cognitive function, reduce mental fatigue and support the body's stress response. While not directly targeting hormonal balance, the positive effects of Rhodiola on stress management can indirectly contribute to optimising hormone levels.

When considering herbal remedies and adaptogens, it's important to remember that individual responses may vary. It's advisable to consult with healthcare professionals or qualified practitioners to determine the appropriate dosage and ensure safety, especially if you have any underlying health conditions or are taking medications.

F. Supplements: Navigating the Terrain

Supplements such as vitamin D, Omega-3 fatty acids and zinc, can be a valuable tool in optimising hormone levels, but it's essential to navigate the supplement terrain with caution. Vitamin D, often referred to as the "sunshine vitamin," plays a crucial role in hormone regulation. It is involved in the production and function of various hormones, including testosterone. Adequate vitamin D levels have been associated with improved testosterone production and overall well-being. Omega-3 fatty acids, commonly found in fatty fish like salmon and in certain plant sources like flaxseed and chia seeds, have been linked to hormone balance and performance. Incorporating natural food sources of Omega-3s into your diet is generally recommended, but supplementation may be considered if dietary intake is insufficient. Zinc, a vital mineral, is involved in numerous enzymatic reactions, including those related to hormone synthesis and regulation. Zinc deficiency has been associated with impaired hormone production and function. Supplementation with zinc has shown potential benefits in boosting testosterone levels, enhancing immune function and supporting overall hormonal balance. Supplements should not replace a healthy lifestyle but rather complement it. It's advisable to seek professional guidance, conduct regular blood tests to assess your hormone levels and make informed decisions based on your individual needs and circumstances.

Testing and Monitoring Hormonal Status

A. Importance of Baseline Testing

Before embarking on an intense training regimen, it is crucial to establish a baseline of hormonal and nutritional status. Baseline testing provides valuable insights into an individual's current hormone levels, allowing for targeted interventions and adjustments throughout the training process. By understanding their baseline, athletes can identify potential areas of improvement and prevent imbalances or deficiencies that may hinder performance.

B. Hormone Testing Options

Various non-invasive methods are available for hormone testing. Saliva testing provides a comprehensive view of steroid hormones, offering insights into what the cells are experiencing. Dried blood spot testing can assess thyroid hormone levels. Laboratories like ZRT offer comprehensive testing panels that cover a wide range of hormones, providing athletes with a thorough analysis of their hormonal status.

C. Interpreting Test Results and Making Adjustments

Interpreting hormone test results can be complex, requiring the expertise of healthcare professionals. Upon receiving test results, athletes should work closely with qualified practitioners to understand the implications and identify appropriate interventions. Adjustments to training, nutrition and supplementation can be made based on the specific hormone levels, aiming to restore balance and optimise performance.

TRT or HRT for Women: Supporting Hormonal Balance

Testosterone Replacement Therapy (TRT) and Hormone Replacement Therapy (HRT) can play a vital role in supporting hormonal balance in women. TRT is primarily used for women with testosterone deficiencies, while HRT involves the replacement of various hormones, including oestrogen and progesterone, to address imbalances. These therapies are carefully prescribed and monitored by healthcare professionals to ensure safety and efficacy.

Role of Each Hormone in Peak Performance for Women

Understanding the significance of hormones like testosterone, oestrogen and progesterone in female athletes is essential. Testosterone contributes to muscle development, strength and athletic performance in women. Oestrogen plays a crucial role in bone health, muscle strength and overall performance. Progesterone influences energy levels, recovery and mood. By working with healthcare professionals, female athletes can determine the appropriate hormone replacement therapy and optimise their hormone levels for peak performance.

TRT IN MEN

Some men may experience a decline in testosterone levels due to factors such as ageing or certain medical conditions. This decline can lead to a variety of symptoms, including fatigue, reduced muscle mass, decreased libido and diminished cognitive abilities. To address these concerns and optimise performance, Testosterone Replacement Therapy (TRT) has emerged as a potential solution.

TRT involves the administration of testosterone through various methods, such as injections, patches, gels, or pellets, to supplement the body's natural testosterone production. By restoring testosterone levels to an optimal range, TRT aims to alleviate the symptoms associated with low testosterone and enhance overall performance.

While TRT/ HRT can provide significant benefits for individuals with clinically diagnosed hormone deficiencies, it is essential to approach it under the guidance of a qualified medical professional. Hormone levels should be carefully monitored to ensure appropriate dosing and minimise potential side effects. Additionally, TRT/ HRT should be considered within a comprehensive approach that includes lifestyle modifications, exercise and proper nutrition to maximise its effectiveness.

CONCLUSION

In conclusion, optimising hormone levels is a critical aspect of achieving peak performance. Understanding the role of key hormones such as growth hormone, thyroxine, oestrogen, testosterone and cortisol is crucial for those seeking to unlock their full potential. By implementing strategies for hormone optimisation, including proper nutrition, exercise, sleep, stress management and regular testing, athletes can create an environment conducive to hormonal balance and elevate their performance to new heights. Embracing the power of hormones is not only transformative for athletic endeavours but also promotes overall well-being and vitality. However, it's important to approach hormone optimisation holistically, considering factors like nutrition, sleep, stress management and individualised approaches. Striving for hormone balance can contribute to enhanced performance, improved well-being and a greater sense of vitality. Remember, hormones are complex and achieving optimal balance may require patience, consistency and the support of healthcare professionals. Embrace the journey of hormone optimisation and unleash your full potential in the pursuit of peak performance.

CHAPTER 17

The Power of Breathwork on Peak Performance

INTRODUCTION

Once upon a time, in the depths of my quest for self-improvement, I stumbled upon the captivating world of breathwork. Little did I know that this discovery would become a transformative journey, altering the course of my life and unlocking a new level of performance and vitality within me. It all began when I eagerly tuned in to Tim Ferriss's podcast on that fateful day.

As I listened intently to his interview with the incredible Wim Hof, I was immediately captivated by the tales of extraordinary feats achieved through the power of breath. Intrigued and inspired, I embarked on a journey to explore this realm of possibility.

With a heart full of curiosity, I delved into the teachings of renowned spiritual leaders and masters of breathwork. Sri Shri's So Hum breathing, Sadhguru's Inner Engineering, and Ramdev's yogic pranayama techniques became my guides in this newfound exploration. I immersed myself in the wisdom of ancient practices such as Anulom Vilom and Kapalabhati, weaving their magic into the fabric of my daily life.

As the days turned into weeks, I began to witness the subtle yet profound shifts within me. Energy surged through my veins like a mighty river, infusing every cell of my being with renewed vitality. The fog of lethargy lifted, replaced by a vibrant zest for life that I had not experienced in years.

But it wasn't just my physical energy that underwent a remarkable transformation. The layers of anxiety that had once weighed heavily upon my shoulders began to dissipate like morning mist. As I engaged in intentional, deep breathing, my parasympathetic nervous system responded, weaving a tapestry of calm and serenity. Stressors that once seemed insurmountable now appeared manageable, allowing me to navigate life's challenges with newfound grace.

With this newfound sense of tranquillity came a remarkable surge in mental clarity and focus. The once-scattered fragments of my mind began to align, creating a symphony of lucidity and creativity. Tasks that once felt overwhelming became conquerable, and I discovered a renewed ability to channel my efforts into productive endeavours.

But perhaps the most profound change of all was the elevation of my mood and overall well-being. Like a phoenix rising from the ashes, I emerged from the shadows of negativity and self-doubt. Each breath became a mantra, weaving a tapestry of joy and contentment into the fabric of my existence. The world around me shimmered with vibrant hues, and the mundane became an opportunity for wonder and gratitude.

Embracing breathwork had not only enhanced my physical health but had become a catalyst for personal growth. It had propelled me towards a version of myself that was capable of achieving more, dreaming bigger and transcending limitations. The power of my breath had become a symphony, orchestrating a life filled with boundless possibilities.

In the end, it wasn't just the techniques themselves that brought about this profound transformation. It was the dedication, the commitment to exploring the depths of my being and the unwavering belief in the power of the breath that set my soul ablaze. Breathwork had become my faithful companion, guiding me towards a life brimming with vitality, clarity and purpose.

In today's fast-paced world, individuals from various walks of life are seeking ways to enhance their performance and unlock their full potential. Amidst this pursuit, the power of breathwork has emerged as a transformative tool, offering profound benefits for peak performance. So when you embark on your journey of breathwork, may you too uncover the magnificent treasures that lie within the cadence of each inhale and exhale.

Embrace the power of your breath, for it holds the key to unlocking the vast reservoirs of your potential. With every breath, you have the opportunity to soar to new heights, breathe life into your aspirations, and become the embodiment of your most extraordinary self. So let's delve into the intricacies of breathwork and explore its tremendous impact on physical, mental and emotional well-being, providing practical guidance on harnessing its potential.

UNDERSTANDING THE BREATH-MIND-BODY CONNECTION

The Breath-Mind-Body Trinity

To understand the power of breathwork for peak performance, it is essential to recognise the profound link between breath, mind and body. Breath is not only a physiological function but also a gateway to our mental and emotional states. By exploring this connection, we can tap into our full potential and achieve optimal performance in various aspects of life.

The breath-mind-body trinity signifies that our breath is intricately connected to our thoughts, emotions and physical sensations. When we consciously regulate our breath, we can influence our mental and emotional states, as well as our physiological responses. This connection is at the core of breathwork practices.

Conscious breathing acts as a bridge between the physical and mental realms. It allows us to bring awareness to our breath, harness its power and use it as a tool to navigate our inner landscape. By cultivating a deeper connection with our breath, we gain greater control over our thoughts, emotions and physical sensations, enabling us to achieve a state of peak performance.

The Science Behind Conscious Breathing

Scientific research has provided valuable insights into the mechanisms behind the impact of conscious breathing on our physiology and cognitive function. The autonomic nervous system, which regulates our involuntary bodily functions, plays a crucial role in this process.

When we engage in conscious breathing, particularly slow and deep breaths, we activate the parasympathetic branch of the autonomic nervous system, often referred to as the "rest and digest" response. This activation leads to a decrease in heart rate, blood pressure and the release of stress hormones like cortisol.

Conversely, shallow and rapid breathing, which is commonly associated with stress and anxiety, triggers the sympathetic branch of the autonomic nervous system, known as the "fight or flight" response. This response increases heart rate, blood pressure and the release of stress hormones, preparing the body for immediate action.

By understanding these mechanisms, we can intentionally modulate our breath to elicit specific physiological responses. By practising conscious breathing techniques, such as deep diaphragmatic breathing, alternate nostril breathing, or coherent breathing, we can activate the relaxation response, reduce stress and enhance overall well-being.

Moreover, conscious breathing also affects cognitive function. Research has shown that controlled breathing patterns can influence brain activity, improving attention, focus and cognitive performance. By regulating our breath, we can optimise the balance between alertness and relaxation, leading to heightened mental clarity and cognitive abilities. The science behind conscious breathing validates its profound impact on our physiology and cognitive function. By harnessing the power of breath, we can regulate our autonomic nervous system, manage stress responses and optimise our mental and physical states for peak performance.

BREATHWORK TECHNIQUES FOR PHYSICAL PERFORMANCE

Enhancing Physical Endurance and Stamina

Breathwork techniques play a crucial role in optimising oxygenation, energy utilisation and muscular efficiency, thereby enhancing physical performance. By focusing on specific breathing patterns, individuals can improve their oxygen intake, increase endurance and sustain energy levels during demanding activities. These techniques involve deep diaphragmatic breathing, where the breath is directed towards the lower abdomen, allowing for efficient oxygen exchange and improved stamina.

One notable breathwork technique that has gained recognition is the Win Hof breathing method. Developed by Wim Hof also known as "The Iceman," this technique involves a combination of controlled hyperventilation and breath retention. By consciously altering their breathing pattern, individuals can increase oxygen saturation in the blood, improve circulation and enhance their athletic endurance and resilience. This method has found applications in various sports disciplines and has proven beneficial in extreme environments.

Cultivating Focus and Mental Resilience

Breathwork techniques are instrumental in cultivating focus, reducing stress and enhancing mental resilience, enabling individuals to perform optimally in high-pressure situations. Certain breathwork practices help individuals calm the mind, regulate emotions and stay present, despite external distractions.

Yogic pranayama techniques, such as Kapalabhati (skull-shining breath) and Anulom Vilom (alternate nostril breathing), have been extensively studied for their impact on mental clarity, concentration and overall performance. Kapalabhati involves forceful exhalations followed by passive inhalations, activating the body's energy centres and promoting mental alertness. Anulom Vilom, on the other hand, balances the flow of breath through alternate nostrils, harmonising the left and right hemispheres of the brain and enhancing focus and mental balance.

By incorporating these breathwork techniques into their routines, individuals can better manage stress and anxiety, sharpen their focus and cultivate the mental resilience necessary for peak performance in athletic and business endeavours.

Recovery and Regeneration

Breathwork also plays a vital role in post-exercise recovery, facilitating relaxation, reducing fatigue and enhancing overall well-being. After intense physical activity, the body requires adequate rest and recovery to repair muscles and restore energy levels. Certain breathwork techniques can aid in this process.

Sudarshan Kriya, a specific breathing technique introduced by Sri Sri Ravi Shankar, has gained recognition for its ability to support athletes' recovery processes. This rhythmic and cyclical breathing pattern helps release accumulated stress and tension, promoting deep relaxation and rejuvenation. By engaging in Sudarshan Kriya and other similar techniques, individuals can enhance their recovery from physical exertion, reduce fatigue and optimise their overall well-being.

Incorporating breathwork techniques for physical recovery not only supports the body's natural healing processes but also contributes to maintaining a balanced and sustainable approach to peak performance.

In summary, breathwork techniques for physical performance encompass optimising oxygenation, energy utilisation and muscular efficiency, cultivating focus and mental resilience and facilitating recovery and regeneration. By integrating these techniques into training routines and daily life, individuals can unlock their physical and mental potential, achieve peak performance and experience a holistic sense of well-being.

BREATHWORK FOR COGNITIVE PERFORMANCE

Enhancing Cognitive Function and Mental Agility

Breathwork techniques not only impact physical performance but also have a profound influence on cognitive processes, memory, creativity and decision-making abilities. By consciously regulating the breath, individuals can optimise oxygenation and blood flow to the brain, thereby enhancing cognitive function and mental agility.

Techniques like coherent breathing, where the inhalation and exhalation are equal in duration, have shown promising results in improving cognitive performance. This balanced breathing pattern synchronises brain activity, promotes a state of mental coherence and enhances focus, concentration and information processing. Similarly, alternate nostril breathing, where the breath is directed through alternate nostrils, balances the left and right brain hemispheres, promoting cognitive balance and enhancing mental clarity.

Managing Stress and Emotional Regulation

Breathwork techniques play a vital role in managing stress and anxiety and promoting emotional balance, which in turn positively impacts cognitive performance. Stress can impair cognitive function and hinder decision-making abilities, while emotional regulation supports cognitive flexibility and adaptability.

Practices such as Soma Breath and Box Breathing are effective tools for managing stress and promoting emotional regulation. Soma Breath combines rhythmic breathing patterns, conscious connected breathing and meditation techniques. It activates the parasympathetic nervous system, facilitating relaxation and reducing stress levels. Box Breathing, characterised by inhaling, holding the breath, exhaling and holding again in a four-count cycle, calms the mind, balances emotions and promotes mental clarity.

By incorporating these breathwork techniques into daily routines, individuals can effectively manage stress, enhance emotional regulation and optimise their cognitive performance. By practising techniques like coherent breathing, alternate nostril breathing, Soma Breath and Box Breathing, individuals can optimise their cognitive abilities, improve decision-making and experience greater mental well-being.

BREATHWORK FOR EMOTIONAL INTELLIGENCE AND MENTAL WELL-BEING

Cultivating Emotional Intelligence

Breathwork is a powerful tool for developing emotional intelligence, enhancing empathy and fostering self-awareness. By bringing conscious attention to the breath, individuals can access the wisdom of their emotions, understand and regulate them effectively and cultivate meaningful connections with others.

Practices like loving-kindness meditation, also known as Metta meditation, involve directing positive intentions and well-wishes towards oneself and others. Through focused breathwork, individuals develop a sense of compassion, empathy and emotional resilience, leading to improved emotional well-being and performance. This practice finds its roots in ancient Indian traditions, emphasising the importance of cultivating loving-kindness towards all beings.

Heart-focused breathing is another technique that contributes to emotional intelligence. By shifting the focus of the breath towards the heart centre and consciously breathing in a way that connects the heart and mind, individuals can develop greater emotional coherence, fostering self-awareness, emotional balance and authentic connections with others.

Mindfulness and Presence

Breathwork serves as a gateway to mindfulness and presence, enabling individuals to fully engage in the present moment and optimise their performance. By anchoring attention to the breath, individuals can cultivate a state of heightened awareness, clarity and focus.

Mindful breathing involves consciously observing the breath without judgement, anchoring oneself in the present moment. This practice allows individuals to develop greater mindfulness skills such as non-reactivity and non-judgement, leading to improved concentration, decision-making and overall well-being. By incorporating mindful breathing into daily life, individuals can experience the transformative power of being fully present.

Body scan meditation is another technique that promotes mindfulness and presence. It involves systematically directing attention to different parts of the body, observing physical sensations and the breath. This practice enhances body awareness, relaxation and the ability to notice subtle cues and signals from the body, contributing to peak performance and overall mental well-being.

In India, ancient practices like Vipassana meditation, which emphasises mindful observation of bodily sensations and the breath, have been instrumental in cultivating mindfulness and presence. These practices have been passed down through generations and continue to be widely embraced for their profound impact on mental and emotional well-being.

CONCLUSION

In conclusion, the power of breathwork for peak performance is undeniable. Through a comprehensive exploration of the breath-mind-body connection, breathwork techniques for physical and cognitive performance and their impact on emotional intelligence and well-being, this chapter has shed light on the transformative potential of conscious breathing. By integrating breathwork practices into daily routines, individuals can unlock their full potential, experience enhanced performance and embark on a journey of holistic growth and fulfilment.

Remember, the greatest power lies within us, waiting to be awakened through the simple act of conscious breathing. Embrace the power of breathwork and witness your life being transformed.

CHAPTER 18

The Impact of Environment on Performance

As Jim Rohn famously said, "You are the average of the five people you spend the most time with." And looking back on my life, I can say with certainty that this rings true.

During my school days at St. John's Church High School in Secunderabad, I was fortunate to be surrounded by the best and brightest in my class. These were exceptional individuals with a drive to succeed that inspired me to do better. Their academic prowess and exceptional upbringing left an indelible mark on me, and I was able to excel both in my studies and in life.

However, my undergraduate years were spent in the company of brilliant but wayward peers. It was during this time that I learnt the vices of smoking and drinking, and as a result, my academic performance suffered, and my personal life spiralled out of control. I was left with a mountain of debt and no direction in life.

This experience taught me a powerful lesson—the company we keep has a profound impact on our lives. The saying "birds of a feather flock together" holds true, and we must be mindful of the people we surround ourselves with. If we wish to be successful, we must seek out those who are already succeeding in their chosen fields, for it is only in their company that we can hope to elevate our own performance.

Indeed, the environment we find ourselves in can make all the difference in the world. It is up to us to choose wisely and to surround ourselves with people who inspire and motivate us to be the best versions of ourselves. So let us be mindful of the company we keep, for it is they who will shape the trajectory of our lives.

INTRODUCTION

The environment we perform in can have a significant impact on our performance, whether it's at work, school or in sports. Factors such as lighting, noise, temperature, and ergonomics can all affect our ability to focus, concentrate and perform at our best. In this module, we will explore each of these environmental factors in detail and provide strategies for optimising one's environment for peak performance.

Lighting

Lighting is one of the most important environmental factors that can impact our performance. The right lighting can improve our mood, reduce eye strain and fatigue and help us to concentrate better. On the other hand, poor lighting can cause headaches and eye strain and affect our ability to focus.

In a study conducted by the American Society of Interior Designers, it was found that the quality of lighting in an office environment has a significant impact on employee productivity and satisfaction. In a well-lit environment, employees were found to be more productive, have fewer errors and experience less eye strain.

In order to optimise one's environment for peak performance, it's important to ensure that the lighting is adequate and appropriate for the task at hand. For example, bright overhead lighting may be appropriate for a busy office environment, while softer, dimmer lighting may be more appropriate for a relaxed, creative environment.

Noise

Noise is another environmental factor that can impact our performance. Loud or distracting noises can cause stress, reduce concentration and affect our ability to perform well. On the other hand, certain types of background noise, such as music, can improve our mood and increase our productivity.

In a study conducted by the University of British Columbia, it was found that moderate noise levels can enhance creativity, while high noise levels can impair it. The study found that a moderate level of noise, such as the background noise in a coffee shop, can increase creativity by stimulating the brain's processing power.

To optimise one's environment for peak performance, it's important to consider the type and level of noise in the environment. For example, playing calming music or white noise may help to reduce distracting noises in a busy office environment and improve concentration.

Temperature

Temperature is another important environmental factor that can impact our performance. Extreme temperatures, whether hot or cold, can cause discomfort, reduce focus and impair our ability to perform well. The optimal temperature for peak performance varies depending on the task at hand.

In a study conducted by Cornell University, it was found that the optimal temperature for office productivity is between 71-77 degrees Fahrenheit. Temperatures outside of this range were found to reduce productivity and increase errors.

To optimise one's environment for peak performance, it's important to ensure that the temperature is appropriate for the task at hand. For example, a cooler temperature may be more appropriate for a physically demanding task, while a warmer temperature may be more appropriate for a creative task.

Ergonomics

Ergonomics refers to the design and arrangement of furniture and equipment to optimise human performance and prevent injury. Poor ergonomics can cause discomfort and pain and reduce productivity, while proper ergonomics can improve comfort, reduce strain and increase performance.

In a study conducted by the National Institute for Occupational Safety and Health, it was found that proper ergonomic design can reduce the incidence of musculoskeletal disorders and improve productivity.

To optimise one's environment for peak performance, it's important to consider ergonomic design when selecting furniture and equipment. For example, an ergonomic chair with adjustable height and lumbar support can reduce back pain and improve posture, while an ergonomic keyboard and mouse can reduce strain on the hands and wrists.

A poorly designed workspace can cause discomfort, pain and even long-term health problems. On the other hand, a well-designed workspace can increase productivity and reduce the risk of injury.

For example, computer users who spend long hours at their desks may experience discomfort or pain in their neck, back, or wrists. This is often caused by poor posture, improper keyboard or mouse placement, or a poorly designed chair. By making adjustments to the height of the desk and chair, using an ergonomic keyboard and mouse and taking regular breaks to stretch, the user can reduce discomfort and improve their productivity.

Similarly, athletes must have access to well-designed equipment that is properly maintained. For example, a runner who trains on a treadmill with a worn-out belt is at risk of injury. The friction between the foot and the belt can cause blisters or even lead to falls. Proper maintenance and replacement of equipment are essential to ensure that athletes can train safely and effectively.

In addition to physical factors, the social and cultural environment can also have an impact on performance. For example, the presence of supportive and encouraging teammates can boost an athlete's confidence and motivation. On the other hand, a negative or unsupportive team culture can undermine an athlete's performance and confidence.

The cultural environment can also influence performance. For example, research has shown that stereotypes and biases can affect how people perceive their own abilities and potential. If an individual belongs to a group that is stereotyped as being less competent or successful in a particular field, he may internalise these stereotypes and perform worse than they would if they did not have these negative beliefs.

CONCLUSION

In conclusion, the environment in which one performs can have a significant impact on his or her performance. By optimising environmental factors such as lighting, noise, temperature and ergonomics, individuals can improve their productivity and reduce the risk of injury. Additionally, by promoting a supportive and positive social and cultural environment, individuals can boost their confidence and motivation, leading to even better performance.

CHAPTER 19

The Impact of Social Connections on Performance

As the famous poet John Donne once wrote, “No man is an island, entire of itself; every man is a piece of the continent.” This timeless phrase accurately captures the essence of how we as human beings rely on each other for support and guidance. In my own life, I have experienced the truth behind these words firsthand. I owe much of my success and peak performance to the social connections that have helped me along the way.

One of the most significant examples of how social connections have helped me is when I joined the Indian Agricultural Research Institute, New Delhi. Without the assistance of my friends who were already studying there, I would have never been able to gain admission into this prestigious institution. They provided me with a place to stay in their hostel rooms and gave me valuable guidance on how to prepare and succeed in the entrance exams. Their support and encouragement were essential in my ability to gain admission to the Institute.

Another instance where social connections have helped me achieve peak performance is when I decided to write the Civil Services exams. The students who had already attempted the exams gave me invaluable tips and shared their study material with me. Discussing the syllabus and hanging out with them made me even more motivated and determined to succeed. Without their mentoring, I would have never been able to crack the Civil Services and reach this far in life.

But social connections have come to my rescue in other ways as well. In dire situations, my connections have been there to help me overcome obstacles and get through challenging times. Whether with career opportunities or personal challenges, I have had a community of people to support me through it all.

The power of social connections cannot be overstated. Having a strong network of people who support and encourage you can make a world of difference. For me, my social connections have provided me with a sense of community and belonging, as well as opportunities to learn and grow.

To me, it's clear that no one can achieve peak performance alone. We all need the support and guidance of others to help us reach our full potential. I am forever grateful to the social connections in my life who have helped me along the way, and I will continue to pay it forward by being a source of support and encouragement for others. Let us remember the importance of cultivating strong social connections, for they are truly the key to achieving peak performance in life.

INTRODUCTION

Social connections and support are critical to our well-being and success. Research has shown that social connections can have a significant impact on our physical and mental health, happiness and performance in various domains of life. In this chapter, we will explore the relationship between social connections and performance and provide strategies for building a supportive network to enhance performance. We will discuss the importance of communication, collaboration and feedback in fostering social connections.

Importance of Social Connections in Performance

Social connections play a vital role in enhancing our performance in different domains of life. Whether it is our personal life, academic, or professional life, having a supportive network can positively impact our performance. Social connections can help us in the following ways:

Motivation: Social connections can act as a source of motivation and inspiration for us. When we see our peers and friends achieving success in their respective fields, it can motivate us to work harder towards our goals.

Accountability: Social connections can help us stay accountable for our actions. When we share our goals and plans with our friends and colleagues, we are more likely to follow through with them as we do not want to let them down.

Emotional Support: Social connections can provide emotional support during difficult times. When we face challenges or setbacks, having someone to talk to and share our feelings can help us cope better.

One inspiring example of social connection providing emotional support to achieve peak performance comes from the movie "A Beautiful Mind" based on the true story of mathematician John Nash.

In the film, Nash is portrayed as a brilliant but troubled mathematician who struggles with schizophrenia. Despite his struggles, Nash is determined to continue his work and make groundbreaking contributions to the field of mathematics. However, he faces numerous challenges, including isolation from his peers and society due to his illness.

It is not until Nash develops strong social connections with his wife Alicia and a close friend and colleague Martin Hansen, that he is able to make significant breakthroughs in his work. With their support and encouragement, Nash is able to overcome his personal struggles and continue his research, eventually receiving the Nobel Prize in Economics for his contributions.

The film's portrayal of Nash's life shows the transformative power of social connection. Without the support and encouragement of his loved ones, Nash may not have been able to achieve his full potential as a mathematician. The story highlights the importance of human connection, even in the face of difficult circumstances. It reminds us that no matter how brilliant or talented we may be, we all need the support and guidance of others to achieve our full potential.

Communication

Effective communication is crucial for building and maintaining social connections. Communication involves not only speaking but also listening actively. Listening actively involves paying attention to the speaker and trying to understand their perspective. Effective communication can help in the following ways:

Building Trust: Effective communication can help build trust between individuals. When individuals communicate openly and honestly, it can create a sense of trust and mutual respect.

Resolving Conflicts: Effective communication can help resolve conflicts and misunderstandings. When individuals communicate their concerns and perspectives, it can help clear any misunderstandings and find a solution that works for both parties.

Enhancing Collaboration: Effective communication can enhance collaboration between individuals. When individuals communicate effectively, they can work together towards a common goal and achieve better outcomes.

Collaboration

Collaboration involves working together towards a common goal. Collaboration can help in the following ways:

Shared Knowledge and Skills: Collaboration allows individuals to share their knowledge and skills. When individuals work together, they can learn from each other and develop new skills.

Innovation: Collaboration can lead to innovation. When individuals from different backgrounds work together, they can bring different perspectives and ideas to the table, leading to new and innovative solutions.

Better Decision-Making: Collaboration can lead to better decision-making. When individuals collaborate, they can consider different perspectives and make more informed decisions.

Feedback

Feedback is essential for improving our performance. Feedback involves providing constructive criticism and suggestions for improvement. Feedback can help in the following ways:

Identifying Areas for Improvement: Feedback can help us identify areas where we need to improve. When we receive feedback, we can reflect on our performance and work on areas where we need to improve.

Motivation: Feedback can act as a source of motivation. When we receive positive feedback, it can motivate us to continue working hard. When we receive constructive feedback, it can motivate us to improve our performance.

Continuous Learning: Feedback can help us in continuous learning. When we receive feedback, we can learn from our mistakes and work on improving our performance.

Social connections can provide constructive feedback that can help us improve our performance. When we seek feedback from our peers and colleagues, we can identify areas where we need to improve and work on them.

STRATEGIES FOR BUILDING A SUPPORTIVE NETWORK

Be proactive: Building a supportive network requires effort and intentionality. Be proactive in reaching out to individuals who share similar interests and values. Attend networking events, join clubs and organisations and participate in social activities.

Maintain relationships: Building relationships takes time and effort. It is essential to maintain these relationships by regularly staying in touch, whether through social media, phone calls, or meetups. Make an effort to remember important events in their lives, such as birthdays or job promotions and send them congratulatory messages.

Seek out mentors: Mentors can provide valuable guidance and advice. Look for individuals who have experience and knowledge in areas you wish to improve. Be respectful of their time and be open to their feedback.

Be a good listener: Listening is a vital component of communication. Be present and attentive when others are speaking and ask questions to gain a better understanding of their perspective. Show empathy and provide support when needed.

Offer help: Building a supportive network is a two-way street. Offer your help and support when others need it. This can create a sense of reciprocity and build stronger relationships.

LEVERAGING SOCIAL CONNECTIONS FOR PEAK PERFORMANCE

Leveraging social connections can enhance performance in many ways. By building a supportive network, we can receive valuable feedback, learn from others' experiences and gain access to resources and opportunities that can help us achieve our goals. Here are some ways to leverage social connections for high performance:

Collaborate on projects: Working with others can bring new ideas and perspectives to a project. By collaborating with individuals who have different skills and experiences, we can create something more significant than what we could have achieved alone.

Seek mentorship: Mentors can provide guidance and support in areas where we lack expertise. By seeking out mentors, we can learn from their experiences and gain insights that can improve our performance.

Receive feedback: Feedback is essential for growth and improvement. By soliciting feedback from our social connections, we can identify areas where we can improve and make necessary changes to enhance our performance.

Gain access to resources and opportunities: Our social connections can provide us with access to resources and opportunities that we might not have otherwise. Whether it's a job opportunity, a potential collaboration, or a new project, our social connections can open doors that can enhance our performance.

One example of a Hollywood movie that shows the importance of social connections for high performance is "The Social Network". The film tells the story of Mark Zuckerberg, the founder of Facebook and his rise to success. Throughout the movie, we see how Zuckerberg leverages his social connections to create Facebook and grow his company. He collaborates with his friend and business partner, Eduardo Saverin and seeks mentorship from Sean Parker, the founder of Napster. These connections help him build a successful company and achieve high performance.

Another example is the famous English novel *"Great Expectations"* by Charles Dickens. The novel tells the story of Pip, a young orphan who dreams of becoming a gentleman. Throughout the novel, we see how Pip's social connections impact his performance. His mentor, Magwitch, provides him with financial support and guidance, which allows him to pursue his dreams. On the other hand, his relationship with Estella, a wealthy and influential woman, opens doors for him but also leads him down a destructive path. The novel shows how our social connections can both support and hinder our performance.

Influence of social networks on the Performance of a Leader or a Team

Social networks can have a significant influence on the performance of a leader or a team. By building strong social connections, leaders can enhance their ability to communicate effectively, collaborate with others and make better decisions. Teams that have strong social networks are better equipped to share information, coordinate their efforts and work together towards common goals. Here are some ways social networks can influence the performance of a leader or a team:

Communication: Leaders who have strong social networks are more effective communicators. They are better able to articulate their vision, build trust with their team members and create a culture of open communication. Team members who have strong social networks are more likely to share information and ideas with each other, leading to better decision-making and problem-solving.

Collaboration: Social networks can enhance collaboration within teams. By building relationships with team members, leaders can encourage cooperation and coordination. Team members who have strong social networks are more likely to work together towards common goals, share responsibilities and support each other.

Knowledge sharing: Social networks can facilitate knowledge sharing within teams. Leaders who have strong social networks can leverage their connections to gain access to new information, ideas and best practices. Team members who have strong social networks are more likely to share their knowledge and expertise with others, leading to improved performance and innovation.

Resource allocation: Social networks can also influence the allocation of resources within teams. Leaders who have strong social networks can leverage their connections to gain access to resources such as funding, expertise and technology.

Team members who have strong social networks are more likely to receive support and resources from others, leading to improved performance and outcomes.

One example of the influence of social networks on team performance is the success of Pixar Animation Studios. Pixar's success can be attributed in part to the strong social networks and collaborative culture within the organisation. The company fosters a culture of openness and collaboration, encouraging employees to share their ideas and knowledge with others. This has led to the development of innovative and successful films such as Toy Story, Finding Nemo and The Incredibles.

CONCLUSION

In conclusion, the impact of social connections on peak performance cannot be overstated. Whether it's in our personal or professional lives, having a supportive network of individuals who encourage and guide us can make all the difference in achieving our goals. By building strong social connections, leaders can enhance their communication, collaboration, knowledge sharing and resource allocation. Teams that have strong social networks are better equipped to work together towards common goals, share information and knowledge and allocate resources effectively. From the inspiring story of John Nash in "A Beautiful Mind" to my own experiences of relying on friends and mentors, it's clear that social connections play a crucial role in helping us reach our full potential. As we move forward, let us continue to cultivate and cherish these connections, for they are truly the key to achieving peak performance in all aspects of our lives.

Social connections and support are crucial to our well-being and success. Building a supportive network requires effort and intentionality, but the benefits are significant. Effective communication, collaboration and feedback are essential components of building and maintaining social connections. By following the strategies outlined above, we can develop a network of individuals who provide emotional support, motivation and feedback to help us achieve our goals and improve our performance.

CHAPTER 20

Cold Exposure for Peak Performance

INTRODUCTION

In the pursuit of optimal physical and mental health, individuals are constantly seeking innovative methods to unlock their full potential. One such practice gaining recognition is cold exposure—a transformative technique that utilises the power of cold temperatures to elicit a wide array of benefits for both the body and mind. I learnt about the benefits of cold exposure when I came across a podcast where Wim Hof the Snow Man was being interviewed. I decided to give it a listen, little realising that it would forever change my perspective on human potential.

As the podcast began, Wim Hof's voice resonated with unwavering confidence and infectious enthusiasm. He spoke of his extraordinary feats achieved through the practice of cold exposure, leaving me in awe of his unparalleled accomplishments. Conquering Mount Everest, the highest peak on Earth, wearing nothing but shorts, seemed unimaginable, yet Wim had done it. Running marathons barefoot in the freezing cold, crossing icy rivers without hesitation and enduring lengthy ice baths as if they were a refreshing dip in a summer lake—Wim Hof had truly mastered the art of embracing the cold.

Listening to Wim's experiences, it became clear that his physical achievements were not the result of superhuman abilities alone. Rather, it was his unwavering spirit, mental resilience and profound understanding of the mind-body connection that propelled him to greatness. He shared insights into the Wim Hof Method, a comprehensive approach combining specific breathing techniques, exposure to cold temperatures and mindset training. Through this method, Wim had not only harnessed the power of the cold but had also discovered a path to unlocking human potential.

The transformative effects of cold exposure on both the body and mind seemed very inspiring to me. The idea that by subjecting ourselves to discomfort, we could unlock hidden depths of strength and resilience resonated deeply within me. Very soon, I was yearning to explore the power of cold exposure firsthand, to tap into my own untapped potential. I have therefore included this chapter in the book which delves into the fascinating world of cold exposure, exploring its profound effects on physical performance, mental well-being and overall health. By understanding the science behind cold exposure and its potential advantages, individuals can integrate this practice into their daily routines, unlocking a wealth of benefits. Prepare to embark on a journey that invigorates the body, sharpens the mind and unveils your true potential.

PHYSICAL BENEFITS OF COLD EXPOSURE

Enhanced Metabolism and Fat Burning

Cold exposure has been scientifically linked to an increased metabolic rate and improved fat burning. When exposed to cold temperatures, the body activates brown fat, a type of fat that generates heat and burns calories. This metabolic boost can aid in weight management and overall metabolic health. For example, taking cold showers or engaging in cold water swimming stimulates brown fat activation, leading to increased calorie expenditure and enhanced metabolic efficiency.

Boosted Immune Function

Cold exposure has long been associated with strengthening the immune system. Exposure to cold temperatures triggers the release of white blood cells and stimulates the production of cytokines, enhancing immune responses. This can result in reduced frequency and severity of common illnesses such as colds and flu. Cold water immersion or cryotherapy sessions are known to stimulate immune function and improve overall resistance to infections.

Accelerated Muscle Recovery and Reduced Inflammation

Cold exposure plays a vital role in post-exercise recovery and reducing inflammation. Cold temperatures constrict blood vessels, reducing swelling and inflammation in muscles. Techniques like ice baths or the use of cold compresses facilitate muscle repair and alleviate exercise-induced inflammation. Athletes often incorporate cold exposure into their recovery routines to minimise muscle soreness and optimise training performance.

MENTAL AND EMOTIONAL BENEFITS OF COLD EXPOSURE

Improved Mood and Mental Resilience

Cold exposure has a remarkable impact on mental well-being, fostering resilience and enhancing mood. Exposure to cold triggers the release of endorphins, natural chemicals that promote a sense of well-being. This practice can reduce symptoms of depression and anxiety, improve stress management and enhance overall mental resilience. Individuals who regularly engage in cold showers or winter swimming often report increased energy levels and a more positive outlook on life.

Enhanced Cognitive Function and Mental Clarity

Cold exposure has been linked to improved cognitive function and mental clarity. The invigorating effects of cold temperatures enhance focus, alertness and concentration. Exposure to cold stimulates the release of neurotransmitters such as norepinephrine, which play a role in cognitive performance. Incorporating breathing techniques, such as the Wim Hof Method, during cold exposure further enhances mental clarity and mindfulness.

Stress Reduction and Resilience Building

Cold exposure serves as a powerful tool for stress reduction and resilience building. The controlled stress response triggered by exposure to cold temperatures helps individuals adapt to stressors in other areas of life. This practice strengthens the body's ability to handle more significant stressors through a process known as hormesis. By regularly exposing themselves to cold temperatures, individuals can build resilience, improve stress-coping mechanisms and enhance mental well-being.

INCORPORATING COLD EXPOSURE INTO YOUR ROUTINE

Gradual Adaptation and Safety Precautions

When incorporating cold exposure into a daily routine, it is crucial to start gradually and take safety precautions. Acclimating the body to cold temperatures gradually, starting with shorter exposures and gradually increasing duration and intensity, is important. Listening to the body and understanding personal limits are essential in ensuring a safe and effective experience. Seeking professional advice, especially for individuals with certain medical conditions, is recommended to ensure that cold exposure is suitable for their specific circumstances. By following these safety precautions and allowing the body to adapt, individuals can reap the benefits of cold exposure without undue risk.

Practical Strategies for Cold Exposure

Incorporating cold exposure into daily life requires practical strategies that suit individual preferences and lifestyles. Several techniques can be utilised, such as cold showers, cold water immersion, outdoor activities in cold environments and cryotherapy sessions. Each method offers unique benefits and experiences. Cold showers can be easily incorporated into morning routines, while cold water immersion and outdoor activities provide opportunities to connect with nature. Cryotherapy sessions offer controlled environments for experiencing cold temperatures. Step-by-step instructions, tips and safety considerations for each method can help individuals incorporate cold exposure seamlessly into their routines.

Mindset and Mental Preparation

Cold exposure is not solely a physical practice; it also involves mental challenges. Developing the right mindset and mental preparation is crucial for embracing and benefiting from cold exposure fully. Visualisation techniques, positive affirmations and mindfulness exercises can help individuals overcome mental barriers, embrace the discomfort and fully experience the transformative effects of cold exposure. Cultivating a resilient mindset and maintaining a positive outlook are key to approaching cold exposure with enthusiasm and unlocking its full potential.

CONCLUSION

Cold exposure offers a multitude of benefits for physical and mental well-being. From enhanced metabolism and immune function to improved mood, cognitive function and stress resilience, the practice of cold exposure can optimise overall health and performance. Understanding the science behind cold exposure and incorporating practical strategies into daily routines empowers individuals to harness the transformative power of cold temperatures. However, it is essential to approach cold exposure with caution, respect personal limits and prioritise safety. With proper guidance and a willingness to embrace the cold, individuals can embark on a journey of self-discovery, pushing their boundaries and unlocking their full potential for improved physical and mental health. Embrace the chill and embrace a new level of vitality and performance.

CHAPTER 21

Biohacking Your Brainwaves for Peak Performance

INTRODUCTION

In the quest for peak performance, harnessing the power of our own brainwaves has emerged as a fascinating frontier. Advances in neuroscience and technology have given rise to a practice known as brainwave entrainment, which offers the potential to optimise brain function and enhance various aspects of performance. For me, binaural beats helped me combat anxiety and job tension in the midst of my demanding Police service days, where anxiety and tension often loomed over me like dark clouds, I stumbled upon this hidden gem called binaural beats that would transform my state of mind, a captivating auditory experience that would become my refuge in moments of chaos. These sonic journeys promised to transport me to realms of tranquillity and inner peace.

I have suffered from anxiety for a long time since my college days. In those moments when anxiety threatened to consume me, I turned to the low-frequency delta binaural beats. As I settled into my meditation practice, the ethereal sounds enveloped me like a gentle mist, casting a spell of serenity over my troubled mind. It was as if each note, perfectly tuned to stimulate my brainwaves, whispered secrets of profound calmness into my soul.

With my trusty companion, yoga nidra, by my side, I embarked on a voyage within, guided by the rhythmic beats that reverberated through my being. The combination of deep relaxation and the soothing vibrations of the binaural beats worked in harmony, dissolving my anxiety and tension like morning mist under the warmth of the rising sun.

But it was during the most challenging law-and-order situations that the true power of binaural beats revealed itself. Amidst the chaos and clamour, I sought solace in a quiet corner. Closing my eyes, I pressed play on my chosen binaural beats composition. As the harmonious frequencies danced delicately in my ears, a remarkable transformation took place.

With each passing minute, the tension melted away, as if carried off on the wings of the enchanting melodies. My mind, once burdened with the weight of responsibility, began to soar with newfound clarity and focus. The binaural beats became my steadfast ally, infusing me with a cool, collected aura that radiated confidence. Armed with this newfound composure, I stood ready to face any challenge that dared to cross my path.

In the realm of binaural beats, I had found an extraordinary sanctuary—a refuge where anxieties were vanquished, and inner strength was unleashed. The carefully crafted symphony of frequencies had become my secret weapon, a key to unlocking the depths of my resilience.

As the final notes of each session echoed through my consciousness, I emerged as a transformed police officer. The weight of the world had been lifted from my shoulders, replaced by an unwavering sense of calm and readiness. With binaural beats as my trusted ally, I was prepared to navigate the turbulent waters of law and order, confident in my ability to bring peace amidst the storm.

So, if ever you find yourself seeking solace in the midst of chaos, I implore you to explore the enchanting world of binaural beats. Let their ethereal melodies wash over you, guiding you to the shores of serenity. Embrace the power of sound, and discover the profound depths of tranquillity that lie within. Brainwave entrainment offers a myriad of practical applications across various domains, including sports, education, stress reduction and business performance. Athletes, students and business professionals have harnessed its potential to unlock peak performance, enhance cognitive function and achieve remarkable success. In this chapter, we will explore the concept of biohacking your brainwaves for peak performance and provide practical guidance on how to use brainwave entrainment techniques effectively.

Brainwaves for Peak Performance

Harnessing brainwaves to achieve peak performance is a fascinating field with incredible potential. Renowned figures like Jim Kwik, Elon Musk, Dave Asprey and Dr Andrew Hill have explored various techniques to optimise cognitive abilities. Jim Kwik's expertise in accelerated learning and brain performance showcases the power of brainwave entrainment and unlocking the brain's potential. Elon Musk's vision for Neuralink, a neural interface merging AI with the human brain, holds promise for enhancing cognitive capabilities. Dave Asprey's biohacking journey and exploration of neurofeedback and brainwave entrainment demonstrate the quest for improved focus and memory. Dr Andrew Hill's neurofeedback training provides real-time feedback to optimise brain function. Even Olympic athletes like Bode Miller have utilised neurofeedback to enhance performance. These stories inspire us to explore the untapped power of our brains and seek professional guidance to unlock our cognitive potential.

Understanding Brainwaves

Before diving into the realm of brainwave entrainment, it is crucial to grasp the basics of brainwave activity. Our brains generate different types of electrical patterns known as brainwaves, which correspond to various mental states and levels of consciousness. These brainwaves, including beta, alpha, theta and delta waves, play a vital role in our cognitive functions, emotions, creativity and overall well-being.

The Science Behind Brainwave Entrainment

Brainwave entrainment is based on the principle of synchronising the brain's electrical activity with external stimuli, such as sound or light, to induce desired brainwave patterns. By exposing the brain to specific frequencies, we can influence its electrical activity and guide it into specific states conducive to improved performance. This process leverages the brain's natural tendency to synchronise with external rhythms, known as the frequency-following response.

When it comes to brainwave entrainment, there are various techniques available, each with its own benefits and suitability. Here's an overview of the most common methods:

Binaural Beats: This technique involves listening to two slightly different frequencies in each ear, which creates a third "binaural" beat in the brain. Binaural beats are known for their ability to induce specific brainwave states, such as relaxation or focus. They can be accessed through specially designed audio recordings or dedicated apps.

Isochronic Tones: Unlike binaural beats, isochronic tones utilise a single tone that pulses on and off at specific frequencies. These distinct pulses create rhythmic patterns that synchronise brainwaves, leading to desired mental states. Isochronic tones are known for their effectiveness and are often preferred by individuals who have difficulty perceiving binaural beats.

Audiovisual Entrainment: This method combines auditory and visual stimuli to synchronise brainwave patterns. It typically involves wearing specialised glasses or watching videos that incorporate flickering lights or pulsating visuals alongside audio entrainment. Audiovisual entrainment provides a multisensory experience, enhancing the effectiveness of brainwave synchronisation.

Choosing the right method depends on your personal preferences, comfort level and response to different stimuli. Experimentation and exploration will help you discover the technique that resonates best with you.

PRACTICAL APPLICATIONS OF BRAINWAVE ENTRAINMENT

Focus and Concentration Enhancement

One of the primary benefits of brainwave entrainment is its ability to improve focus and concentration. By entraining the brain to alpha or theta frequencies, individuals can experience heightened states of alertness and mental clarity. Techniques such as binaural beats, isochronic tones and audiovisual stimulation can be employed to induce these states and optimise cognitive performance during demanding tasks.

Stress Reduction and Relaxation

In our fast-paced modern world, stress has become a ubiquitous challenge. Brainwave entrainment can serve as a powerful tool for stress reduction and relaxation. By entraining the brain to alpha and theta frequencies, individuals can experience a deep sense of calm and tranquillity. This practice can be particularly beneficial before important events or to unwind after a long and demanding day.

Creativity and Flow State Induction

Brainwave entrainment can also unlock the doors to enhanced creativity and the elusive state of flow. By stimulating alpha and theta brainwaves, individuals can tap into their subconscious minds and unleash their creative potential. Artists, writers and innovators can benefit from using brainwave entrainment techniques to access heightened states of inspiration and enter the flow state, where productivity and creativity flourish.

Sleep Optimisation

Quality sleep is essential for peak performance and overall well-being. Brainwave entrainment can aid in improving sleep quality by promoting relaxation and guiding the brain into delta and theta frequencies associated with deep sleep. Techniques such as delta wave stimulation and sleep-inducing soundscapes can help individuals achieve restful and rejuvenating sleep.

Incorporating Brainwave Entrainment into Your Routine

Now that we understand the potential benefits of brainwave entrainment, let's explore practical ways to incorporate it into our daily lives:

Selecting the Right Technique: Experiment with different brainwave entrainment techniques, such as binaural beats, isochronic tones, or audiovisual stimulation, to find the one that resonates with you the most.

Setting Intentions: Before starting a brainwave entrainment session, set clear intentions for the desired outcome, whether it's improved focus, relaxation, creativity, or better sleep.

Creating an Optimal Environment: Find a quiet and comfortable space where you won't be disturbed. Use headphones or a quality speaker system for audio-based entrainment techniques.

Practising Regularly: Consistency is key when it comes to brainwave entrainment. Incorporate it into your daily routine, whether it's during meditation, before a work session, or as part of your bedtime routine.

Monitoring Your Response: Pay attention to how your mind and body respond to different brainwave entrainment techniques. Notice any changes in focus, relaxation, creativity, or sleep quality. Adjust your practice accordingly to find what works best for you.

Real-Life Examples

Let's explore a few examples of how individuals have successfully used brainwave entrainment for peak performance:

Rajeshwari an entrepreneur, uses alpha wave binaural beats before important meetings and presentations to enhance her focus and reduce anxiety. She finds that it improves her confidence and clarity of thought, enabling her to communicate more effectively.

Bhagat, a writer, incorporates theta wave isochronic tones into his creative writing sessions. By entering a relaxed yet highly focused state, he taps into his imagination more effortlessly and produces his best work.

Lakshmi, a professional athlete, utilises delta wave soundscapes before bed to optimise her sleep quality. The deep relaxation induced by brainwave entrainment helps her recover and perform at her peak during training and competitions.

CONCLUSION

Biohacking your brainwaves through the practice of brainwave entrainment offers a promising avenue for optimising your mental states and achieving peak performance. By understanding the science behind brainwave activity and employing specific techniques, you can enhance focus, reduce stress, unleash creativity and improve sleep quality. Incorporate brainwave entrainment into your routine, experiment with different techniques, and observe the transformative effects on your performance and overall well-being. Embrace the power of your own brainwaves and unlock your true potential.

CHAPTER 22

The Impact of Technology on Performance

INTRODUCTION

Technology has revolutionized many aspects of our lives, including how we work, communicate, and entertain ourselves. In recent years, technology has also become increasingly important in the world of sports and performance, with the emergence of wearable devices, biofeedback tools, and digital tracking and optimization tools. While technology has the potential to enhance performance, it is important to use it responsibly and be aware of the potential risks and downsides.

In my life technology has played a great role in accelerating my performance in all areas of my life. Although I use wearables and other digital tools, I have been getting maximum bang for my buck from a game-changing technological tool - the WHOOP 4.0, a wearable device. This unassuming device, without a screen of its own, opened up a world of insights into my daily activity, exercise performance, sleep quality, and heart rate data.

The WHOOP 4.0 operates through an array of sensors that tirelessly measure various vital parameters, including heart rate, temperature, and more. Worn comfortably on my wrist, it became a constant companion, capturing data a staggering 100 times per second. Notably, WHOOP offers diverse wearable options, from wristbands to sports bras, catering to individual preferences.

The magic of WHOOP lies in its ability to transform this data into actionable information. It calculates a Strain Score from my daily activities, whether it's a rigorous workout or simply going about my day. But where it truly shines is in its assessment of recovery.

Every morning, I wake up to a Recovery Score, derived from factors such as resting heart rate, heart rate variability, respiratory rate, and sleep quality. This score becomes the cornerstone of WHOOP's guidance, acting as my personal Strain

Coach. It advises me on how much I should exert myself based on my recovery status, ensuring I optimize my physical efforts.

During exercise and daily activities, WHOOP continues to monitor essential metrics like respiratory rate, blood oxygen levels, current max heart rate, and calories expended. This comprehensive data allows me to fine-tune my workouts, ensuring I stay within the recommended exertion levels.

Come bedtime, WHOOP remains vigilant, assessing sleep performance in detail. It considers factors like sleep duration, efficiency, consistency, latency, sleep debt, and sleep stages (light, REM, deep sleep, awake) alongside disturbances. Armed with this knowledge, I've unlocked the secrets to maximizing my REM sleep and improving my overall sleep quality.

The impact of WHOOP on my life has been profound. By closely monitoring my heart rate variability (HRV), I made the conscious choice to reduce alcohol consumption, recognising its detrimental effect on recovery. My resting heart rate now hovers around 70, a testament to the positive impact of aerobic exercise.

WHOOP doesn't just provide data; it empowers me to make informed decisions about my daily activities. By understanding my strain levels, I can adjust my workouts to prioritize recovery, keeping me in an optimal state for peak performance.

I have no affiliation with WHOOP, and this endorsement is not an endorsement of the product itself. There are several similar products available that may offer comparable tracking capabilities. WHOOP has personally helped me achieve my performance goals, but it's essential to explore various options to find the best fit for your needs.

Another technological tool that has helped me meet my running goals and keep me running consistently is an app. I discovered the Strava app in 2019. At first, I used the app to track my runs and monitor my progress. I was amazed at how easy it was to see my pace, heart rate, and other metrics in real-time. This information helped me set goals and improve my performance over time. I also started to join challenges and connect with other runners on the app.

One challenge, in particular, caught my eye. It was a monthly challenge to run a minimum distance of 300 kilometres. It seemed like an impossible feat, but I decided to give it a try. With the help of the Strava app, I was able to track my progress and stay motivated throughout the month.

At the end of the month, I completed the challenge and felt a sense of accomplishment like never before. This success fueled my passion for running and I started to set bigger goals for myself.

I decided to start running a half or full marathon every week. Again, the Strava app was my go-to tool for tracking my progress and monitoring my performance. The app's features allowed me to compare my current performance with previous years and months, as well as with other runners I followed. This helped me to stay motivated and challenged me to push myself harder every week.

The Strava app has been a game-changer for me. Keeping track of my runs, generating stats, and challenging myself to take on new goals, have made me a consistent performer and instilled the habit of running into me. Without the app, I wouldn't be able to complete a half or full marathon every week or achieve a minimum distance of 300 km every month. Technology has truly made a difference in my life, and I am grateful for the Strava app for helping me become a better and healthier version of myself.

I have no affiliation with WHOOP or STRAVA, and this endorsement is not an endorsement of the product itself. There are several similar products available that may offer comparable tracking capabilities. WHOOP and STRAVA have personally helped me achieve my performance goals, but it's essential to explore various options to find the best fit for your needs.

Further, In both the money Moneyball and the book The Art of Learning, technology played a key role in helping individuals achieve peak performance. By leveraging data analytics and other tools, these individuals were able to gain insights and identify opportunities for improvement that might have been missed using traditional methods. The use of technology allowed them to work smarter, not harder, and achieve better results with less effort.

For instance, Moneyball is the story of how the Oakland A's, a struggling baseball team with a limited budget, turned to data analytics to build a competitive team. The team's general manager, Billy Beane, hired a young economics graduate named Peter Brand to help him identify undervalued players using statistical analysis. Together, they used a computer program to analyze player data and identify players who were likely to perform well based on their performance metrics, rather than relying on traditional scouting methods.

The use of data analytics revolutionized the way baseball teams evaluated players and helped the A's achieve a remarkable level of success despite their limited budget. By focusing on the numbers rather than the conventional wisdom, they were able to identify talented players who were overlooked by other teams and build a team that could compete with much wealthier organizations.

The use of technology was crucial to the success of Moneyball. The computer program used by the A's allowed them to analyze vast amounts of data quickly and efficiently, and identify patterns and trends that would have been difficult or impossible to spot using traditional methods. The program also allowed the A's to simulate various scenarios and predict the likely outcome of different strategies, helping them make better decisions about which players to acquire and how to use them.

And the book Art of Learning is a memoir of Josh Waitzkin, a chess prodigy who later became a world champion in Tai Chi Chuan Push Hands. Waitzkin attributes much of his success to his ability to learn and adapt quickly, which he developed through his training in chess and martial arts.

One of the key strategies Waitzkin used to improve his performance was the use of technology. He used computer programs to analyze his chess games and identify areas where he could improve, and he used video cameras to record his Tai Chi Chuan Push Hands matches so that he could review and analyze his performance.

Waitzkin also used technology to improve his mental and emotional state. He practised meditation and used biofeedback devices to monitor his heart rate and other physiological signals, allowing him to achieve a state of deep relaxation and focus.

TECHNOLOGICAL TOOLS FOR ENHANCING PERFORMANCE

There are various tech tools for enhancing performance, Some of the types of tech tools are discussed below.

Wearable Devices

Wearable devices are electronic devices that can be worn on the body, such as fitness trackers, smartwatches, and heart rate monitors. These devices can track various biometric data points, including heart rate, calories burned, steps taken, and sleep quality. They can also provide real-time feedback and reminders, such as reminding the wearer to stand up and move around if they have been sitting for too long.

Wearable devices can be incredibly useful for athletes and fitness enthusiasts, as they can help them track their progress and identify areas where they can improve. For example, a runner can use a GPS-enabled smartwatch to track their distance, pace, and elevation gain during a run, and use that data to adjust their training regimen. A weightlifter can use a fitness tracker to track their heart rate and calorie burn during a workout and adjust their intensity accordingly.

However, there are potential downsides to wearable devices as well. For example, some people may become too reliant on their devices and lose sight of their instincts and intuition. Additionally, wearable devices can sometimes be inaccurate or unreliable, leading to incorrect data and potentially harmful decisions.

Biofeedback

Biofeedback is a type of therapy that involves using electronic sensors to measure physiological responses such as heart rate, muscle tension, and skin conductance. The goal of biofeedback is to help individuals learn how to control these responses and improve their overall health and well-being.

Biofeedback can be especially useful for athletes and performers, as it can help them learn how to control their stress levels and focus their attention more effectively. For example, a golfer might use biofeedback to learn how to control their heart rate and breathing during a putt, allowing them to stay calm and focused under pressure.

Digital Tools for Tracking and Optimizing Performance

In addition to wearable devices and biofeedback, there are also a variety of digital tools available for tracking and optimizing performance. These tools can include apps for tracking nutrition and hydration, software for analyzing movement and technique, and virtual reality simulators for practising skills and scenarios.

These digital tools can be incredibly helpful for athletes and performers, as they can provide real-time feedback and allow for more precise and effective training. For example, basketball players might use a motion capture system to analyze their shooting form and identify areas where they can improve. A football player might use a virtual reality simulator to practice plays and scenarios in a safe and controlled environment.

Responsible Use of Technology

While technology can be a powerful tool for enhancing performance, it is important to use it responsibly and be aware of the potential risks and downsides. For example, relying too heavily on wearable devices and digital tools can lead to a lack of intuition and instinct, and can potentially lead to overtraining or injury. Additionally, there is always the risk of technology malfunctioning or being inaccurate, which can lead to incorrect data and harmful decisions.

To use technology responsibly, it is important to remember that technology should always be a supplement to, not a replacement for, human intuition and judgment. Athletes and performers should also be aware of the potential risks and downsides of technology and should seek out expert guidance and advice when using new tools or techniques.

USE OF AI FOR PEAK PERFORMANCE

AI (Artificial Intelligence) is increasingly being used in the world of sports and performance to enhance training, strategy, and performance. One example of AI being used for peak performance can be found in the science fiction film "Ex Machina" directed by Alex Garland. In the movie, a brilliant and wealthy tech entrepreneur creates an advanced AI humanoid robot named Ava intending to create the perfect artificial being.

Throughout the film, the entrepreneur uses various techniques to test Ava's intelligence and consciousness, including a series of sophisticated algorithms that allow her to learn and adapt to her environment. The algorithms use machine learning to analyze data and make predictions about how Ava will behave in different situations, allowing her to constantly improve her performance.

While the main focus of the film is on the development of Ava's consciousness, it also demonstrates how AI can be used to optimize performance and achieve peak performance. By analyzing vast amounts of data and making predictions based on that data, AI can help individuals and organizations identify areas where they need to improve, optimize their training and performance, and achieve their goals more efficiently.

And similarly in the book "Superintelligence: Paths, Dangers, Strategies" by Nick Bostrom, AI is discussed as a potential tool for achieving peak performance in various fields. Bostrom argues that AI has the potential to revolutionize many areas of human activity, from medicine and science to business and finance.

For example, AI could be used to analyze massive amounts of data on patient health to identify patterns and trends that could help doctors make more accurate diagnoses and develop more effective treatments. In business and finance, AI could be used to analyze vast amounts of data on markets and consumer behaviour, allowing companies to make more informed decisions about product development and marketing strategies.

Overall, AI has the potential to transform many areas of human activity and help individuals and organizations achieve peak performance in ways that were previously impossible. However, it's important to approach AI with caution and consider the potential risks and ethical implications of its use.

In addition to analyzing performance data, AI can also be used to simulate and predict game scenarios. For example, AI can simulate different scenarios in a football game and provide recommendations for optimal play calling based on the predicted outcomes of each scenario.

Overall, AI has the potential to revolutionize the world of sports and performance by providing athletes and coaches with powerful tools for analysis, optimization, and prediction. However, it is important to use AI responsibly and be aware of the potential risks and downsides, such as over-reliance on data and loss of intuition and instinct. It's important to approach AI with caution and consider the potential risks and ethical implications of its use.

SOME IMPORTANT TECHNOLOGICAL TOOLS/DEVICES FOR ENHANCING PERFORMANCE

There are many technological gadgets and devices available in the market that can be used to enhance peak performance in various fields. Some of these devices include:

Wearable Fitness Trackers: We have already discussed this above.

Smartwatches: Smartwatches are similar to fitness trackers but also have additional features such as GPS tracking, mobile payments, and the ability to receive notifications from smartphones.

Biometric Sensors: These sensors can be used to measure various biometric data such as muscle activity, skin conductance, and brain waves. They can be used to provide feedback on stress levels, relaxation techniques, and optimal training intensity.

Virtual Reality (VR) and Augmented Reality (AR) Headsets: VR and AR headsets can be used to create immersive training experiences and simulate real-life scenarios. For example, VR headsets can be used to simulate high-pressure game situations in sports.

Electronic Muscle Stimulators: These devices use electrical impulses to stimulate muscles and improve muscle strength and recovery. They can be used to target specific muscle groups and improve performance in sports and other physical activities.

Cognitive Training Apps: These apps use games and exercises to improve cognitive function and mental agility. They can be used to improve focus, memory, and decision-making skills in sports and other performance-related fields.

Smart Recovery Tools: These devices use vibration therapy, compression therapy, and other techniques to aid in recovery and reduce soreness and inflammation after physical activity. They can be used to speed up recovery time and improve overall performance.

Overall, these devices can be powerful tools for enhancing performance in various fields, but it is important to use them responsibly and be aware of potential downsides such as over-reliance on data and loss of intuition and instinct.

NEW GAME-CHANGING TECH TOOLS IN DEVELOPMENT FOR THE FUTURE

The field of peak performance is constantly evolving, and new game-changing tech tools are being developed all the time. Here are a few examples of cutting-edge tech tools that are currently in development and have the potential to revolutionize the world of peak performance:

Brain-Computer Interfaces (BCIs): BCIs are devices that allow direct communication between the brain and external devices. They can be used to control prosthetic limbs, communicate with computers, and even control virtual environments. In the world of peak performance, BCIs could be used to enhance cognitive function and improve reaction time and decision-making skills.

Wearable Tech for Mental Health: Wearable devices are currently being developed that can monitor biometric data related to mental health, such as heart rate variability, sleep quality, and stress levels. This data can be used to provide personalized recommendations for improving mental health and cognitive function.

Smart Clothing: Smart clothing is being developed that can monitor biometric data such as heart rate, breathing rate, and body temperature. This data can be used to provide real-time feedback on training intensity and recovery time, as well as monitor for signs of injury or illness.

AI-Assisted Training: AI is being used to develop personalized training programs that take into account an individual's unique physiological and psychological profile. By analyzing biometric data and other performance metrics, AI can provide recommendations for optimal training intensity, duration, and recovery time.

Virtual Reality Training: Virtual reality is being used to create immersive training experiences that simulate real-world scenarios. For example, virtual reality can be used to simulate high-pressure game situations in sports, allowing athletes to train under conditions that closely mimic the demands of competition.

These are just a few examples of the exciting new tech tools that are currently in development and have the potential to revolutionize the world of peak performance. As technology continues to advance, we can expect to see even more innovative tools and techniques that can help us reach our full potential in sports, work, and life.

CONCLUSION

Technology has the potential to revolutionize the world of sports and performance conclusion, technology has had a significant impact on performance, both positive and negative. From wearable fitness trackers to brain-computer interfaces, countless technological gadgets and devices can be used to enhance performance in various fields. These tools can help us monitor progress, improve cognitive function, and create immersive training experiences that simulate real-world scenarios. However, it is important to use these tools responsibly and be aware of potential downsides such as over-reliance on data and loss of intuition and instinct.

As technology continues to evolve, we can expect to see even more innovative tools and techniques that can help us reach our full potential in sports, work, and life. However, we must also be mindful of the potential risks and ensure that we use technology in a way that supports our overall health and well-being. By using technology responsibly and in conjunction with traditional training methods, we can achieve peak performance and reach our safely and sustainably.

CHAPTER 23

The Role of Positive Psychology in Peak Performance

INTRODUCTION

Positive psychology is a relatively new field of study that focuses on the factors that contribute to human well-being and flourishing. Rather than solely looking at what is wrong with people and how to fix it, positive psychology aims to identify the strengths and positive aspects of individuals and how to enhance them.

One area where positive psychology has gained a lot of attention is in the field of peak performance. Peak performance is the state where individuals perform at their highest level, achieving optimal outcomes in their chosen field. Positive psychology can play a critical role in helping individuals achieve peak performance by cultivating positive emotions, building resilience and developing a sense of purpose and meaning in their work.

As a police officer, I have always believed in the power of positive psychology. Throughout my various postings, I have deployed this strategy to scale my performance and undertake several community policing initiatives. But it was during my tenure as ADGP-Armed Police in 2021 that I had the most outstanding experience with positive psychology.

The COVID-19 pandemic had taken a significant toll on individuals and families across the country. As a police officer and a human being, I was appalled at the suffering that people were facing. I knew that it was my duty to protect and serve my community, but I wanted to do more than just that. I wanted to alleviate their suffering, to offer them a glimmer of hope in these dark times.

That's when I decided to employ positive psychology to uplift those around me. I launched the www.letsfightcorona.com initiative, a platform that aimed to alleviate people's suffering during the ongoing pandemic by rendering a bouquet of humanitarian services. With the help of more than 10,000 personnel under me, police vehicles and kitchens, we were able to provide essential supplies and resources to those in need.

The initiative went above and beyond our call of duty. We became the conduits to facilitate the transfer of resources from the haves to the have-nots. There were a lot of volunteers who had resources such as money and supplies, but they were unable to distribute them. We stepped up to the challenge, and our efforts paid off. In just 40 days, we were able to distribute relief worth more than Rs 50 lakhs.

But I didn't stop there. With a heart full of compassion, I decided to raise funds for a dialysis machine for the Tanker Foundation. I embarked on a 50 km run, pushing myself to the limit to make a difference in someone else's life. And my hard work paid off, as I raised a staggering 10 lakh rupees, contributing to the installation of the much-needed machine.

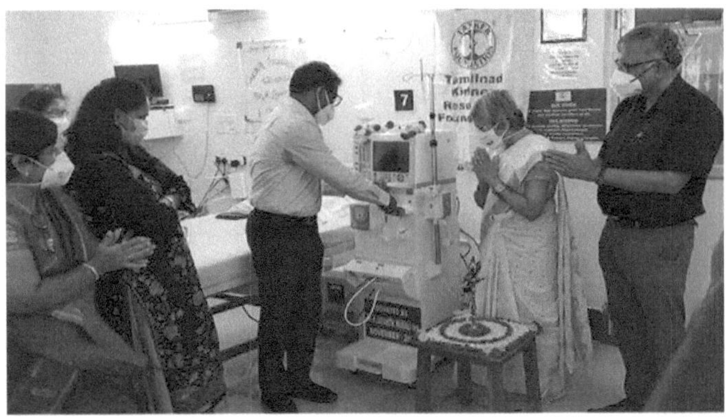

The experience was both physically and emotionally challenging. But seeing the impact of our efforts made it all worth it. The joy and gratitude on the faces of the people we helped filled my heart with a sense of purpose and fulfilment that I will never forget.

Through this experience, I learnt that positive psychology could be a powerful tool, not just for personal growth, but for making the world a better place. And although the pandemic has receded, my legacy lives on as a reminder that even in the darkest of times, hope and kindness can prevail.

One of the most famous books on positive psychology and peak performance is *"Flow: The Psychology of Optimal Experience"* by Mihaly Csikszentmihalyi. Published in 1990, the book became a landmark in the field of positive psychology and has inspired countless people to pursue their passions and achieve peak performance.

The book introduces the concept of "flow," which is the state of mind that people enter when they are fully immersed in an activity and experience a sense of energised focus, complete involvement and enjoyment in the process. According to Csikszentmihalyi, flow is the key to achieving optimal experience and peak performance in any area of life.

Csikszentmihalyi also explores the factors that contribute to flow, such as setting clear goals, having immediate feedback and facing challenging tasks that match one's skill level. He also discusses how flow can lead to increased creativity, productivity and happiness.

"Flow" has become a classic in the field of positive psychology and its insights and practical advice continue to be relevant and inspiring today. It is a must-read for anyone interested in achieving peak performance and living a fulfilling life.

Cultivating Positive Emotions

Positive emotions such as joy, gratitude and optimism can play a crucial role in achieving peak performance. These emotions can broaden an individual's thought-action repertoire, enhance creativity and promote cognitive flexibility. Therefore, it is essential to cultivate these emotions intentionally.

An inspiring story of how positive psychology contributed to peak performance is that of Nick Vujicic, a motivational speaker and author who was born without arms or legs.

Despite facing seemingly insurmountable challenges from birth, Vujicic never gave up on his dreams. He learnt to adapt to his limitations and developed a positive attitude that allowed him to overcome adversity and achieve incredible things.

Vujicic's positive mindset was particularly evident in his approach to sports. Despite his physical limitations, he became an accomplished swimmer, winning numerous medals in competitions around the world. He also became a talented surfer and even learnt to play golf and tennis.

But perhaps Vujicic's greatest achievement was in his career as a motivational speaker. He travels the world, sharing his story and inspiring others to overcome their challenges and live their best lives. Through his positive outlook, Vujicic has touched the hearts of millions of people and shown them that anything is possible with the right mindset and attitude.

In his book, **"Life Without Limits,"** Vujicic explains how he uses positive psychology to maintain a sense of purpose and fulfilment in his life. He emphasises the importance of focusing on one's strengths, developing a sense of gratitude and cultivating a positive mindset. By following these principles, Vujicic has been able to achieve peak performance in his personal and professional life, inspiring others to do the same.

Gratitude is one positive emotion that has been shown to have numerous benefits. Gratitude is the practice of focusing on the good things in life and acknowledging them with a sense of appreciation. Studies have shown that individuals who practise gratitude regularly have increased levels of happiness, lower levels of stress and greater life satisfaction.

For example, in one study, participants were asked to write a letter expressing gratitude to someone who had made a significant impact on their lives. After just three weeks of the intervention, the participants reported increased levels of happiness and decreased symptoms of depression.

Another positive emotion that can help individuals achieve peak performance is optimism. Optimism is the belief that good things will happen in the future and that one's actions can make a positive difference. Optimistic individuals tend to be more resilient and better able to cope with setbacks.

For example, in a study of Olympic athletes, researchers found that those who had a more optimistic outlook before the competition performed better and were less likely to experience negative emotions during the competition. Optimism can be cultivated through cognitive restructuring techniques, such as reframing negative situations in a more positive light.

Building Resilience

Resilience is the ability to bounce back from setbacks, adapt to change and cope with stress. Resilient individuals are better able to maintain their focus and perform well under pressure, making them more likely to achieve peak performance.

One way to build resilience is through the practice of mindfulness. Mindfulness is the practice of paying attention to the present moment, without judgement. Mindfulness has been shown to reduce stress, improve emotional regulation and enhance cognitive functioning.

For example, in a study of elite athletes, those who practised mindfulness had better attentional control, were more able to regulate their emotions and performed better under pressure. Mindfulness can be practised through formal meditation or informal practices, such as mindful breathing or mindful movement.

Another way to build resilience is through the development of a growth mindset. A growth mindset is a belief that abilities and intelligence can be developed through hard work and dedication. Individuals with a growth mindset tend to view challenges as opportunities for growth, rather than as threats to their self-esteem.

For example, in a study of college students, those who had a growth mindset were more likely to persist in the face of challenges and had higher levels of academic achievement. Developing a growth mindset can be done through deliberate practice, seeking feedback and reframing failures as opportunities for growth.

Developing a Sense of Purpose and Meaning

Developing a sense of purpose and meaning in one's work can also contribute to achieving peak performance. When individuals feel that their work is meaningful and aligned with their values, they are more motivated, engaged and committed to their work.

One way to develop a sense of purpose and meaning is to identify one's values and connect them to one's work. Values are the guiding principles that give meaning and direction to our lives. When individuals can identify their values and connect them to their work, they are more likely to find their work meaningful and fulfilling.

For example, in a study of healthcare workers, those who connected their work to their values reported higher levels of job satisfaction and lower levels of burnout. To connect one's work to their values, individuals can reflect on what they find most important in life and how their work aligns with those values.

Another way to develop a sense of purpose and meaning is to set goals that are aligned with one's values. Goals that are aligned with one's values are more likely to be motivating and provide a sense of purpose.

For example, in a study of college students, those who set goals that were aligned with their values reported higher levels of motivation and achievement. To set goals that are aligned with one's values, individuals can reflect on what is most important to them and set goals that are consistent with those values.

CONCLUSION

Positive psychology can play a crucial role in achieving peak performance by cultivating positive emotions, building resilience and developing a sense of purpose and meaning in one's work. Cultivating positive emotions such as gratitude and optimism can broaden an individual's thought-action repertoire, enhance creativity and promote cognitive flexibility. Building resilience through mindfulness and a growth mindset can help individuals bounce back from setbacks, adapt to change and cope with stress. Developing a sense of purpose and meaning in one's work can provide motivation, engagement and commitment. By applying the principles of positive psychology, individuals can achieve their highest level of performance and live a more fulfilling life.

CHAPTER 24

How to set and achieve goals for peak performance

INTRODUCTION

Setting and achieving goals is an important aspect of peak performance, whether it be in sports, business, or personal development. The science of goal-setting has been extensively studied, and research has shown that setting specific, measurable, achievable, relevant, and time-bound (SMART) goals increases the likelihood of success.

For instance, I had always dreamed of becoming a civil servant, and passing the preliminary examination was just the first step towards achieving my goal. However, I only had four months to prepare for the main examination, which seemed daunting given the vast syllabus that needed to be covered.

To tackle this challenge, I decided to set daily, weekly, and monthly goals for myself. I knew that I needed to be disciplined and consistent with my efforts if I wanted to succeed. I also divided my day into three four-hourly sessions, one for General Studies, one for Agriculture, and one for Botany, which were my two optional subjects.

Despite the overwhelming amount of material, I had to cover, I remained 8 focused on my goals and persevered through the challenges. I made sure to use every available resource, including textbooks, study materials, and the university library to make the most of my preparation time.

As the exam approached, I reserved the last month for revision and mock tests. I knew that this was a critical period, and I couldn't afford to waste any time. I studied previous years' question papers and simulated test environments to prepare myself for the actual exam.

In the end, my hard work paid off. I cleared the civil services examination with flying colours, and I realized that anything is possible with determination, discipline, and a clear plan of action. Similarly, in the world of endurance and human achievements, where the limits of the body and mind merge into an ever-expanding horizon, I have another take to recite my relentless determination and thirst for noble goals. This is the story of my pursuit of two Asian Records in the realm of marathon running, a journey inspired by the fervent desire to make a difference, one breath at a time.

It all began in 2018, amid the bustling streets of Chennai, during the Dream Runners Marathon, an event that beckoned not just the fleet-footed, but also the dreamers who dared to defy convention. MOHAN Foundation, a beacon of hope in the organ donation landscape, was orchestrating an enrollment drive, seeking those willing to pledge the precious gift of life through organ donation.

The cause was noble, the mission clear - every Indian in need of a life-saving organ deserved a chance at life. And so, I embarked on a mission to bridge the gap between awareness and action.

Running a full marathon (42 km) in the WIPRO Marathon, I wove the narrative of organ donation into each stride, advocating for a cause that could redefine lives. It was a journey of self-discovery, resilience, and a determination to bring about change. My voice echoed through every step, and my heart pounded with a rhythm that spoke of hope.

But one marathon wasn't enough. In 2019, I set my sights on a new challenge - the Dream Runners Half Marathon. This time, it wasn't just about creating awareness; it was about setting a record that would resonate with the world. A challenge that no one had attempted before - running an entire half marathon with my mouth taped shut.

The science was clear; taping the mouth meant breathing only through the nose, an endeavor known to make long-distance running incredibly arduous. Runners typically rely on mouth breathing for the influx of oxygen needed during their athletic pursuits. Nasal breathing restricts oxygen delivery, tightens the jaw, and induces breathlessness. It was a feat that had never been attempted on the global stage.

My journey to achieve this incredible goal was a testament to the power of setting SMART goals. Specific - an Asian Record in a half marathon with a taped mouth. Measurable - the distance covered and the time taken. Achievable - with rigorous training and preparation. Relevant - for the noble cause of organ donation. Time-bound - a fixed date for the record attempt.

Hours were spent in the pool, practicing breath holds, honing my lung capacity, and training my body to adapt to this unconventional breathing technique. I meticulously planned my training regimen, ensuring that each day brought me closer to my goal.

As the day of reckoning arrived, the streets of Chennai bore witness to an unprecedented feat. With every stride, I defied not just physical limitations but the skepticism of naysayers. I ran, breathless yet determined, a beacon of inspiration for those who dared to dream and strive for the extraordinary. In the following year, I repeated the same feat but in the full marathon category and found my way into the Asian Book of Records again.

Two Asian Records, each a testament to the boundless potential of human determination, were etched into history. My journey was a symphony of setting goals, crafting a plan of action, and executing it with surgical precision. The records were not just personal achievements; they were dedications to the noble cause of organ donation, made possible by the unwavering belief that change begins with setting goals and daring to achieve them.

My abovementioned success stories have inspired many others to set their own goals and pursue their dreams with passion and commitment. So let's explore the science of goal-setting and the practical strategies for setting and achieving goals to optimize performance.

THE SCIENCE OF GOAL-SETTING

The Importance of Goal-Setting for Peak Performance

Goal-setting is a powerful tool for achieving peak performance. Research has shown that setting goals can enhance motivation, increase effort, and improve performance. Goals provide individuals with a clear direction and a sense of purpose, allowing them to focus their attention and effort on the task at hand.

The SMART Model of Goal-Setting

The SMART model of goal-setting is a popular framework for setting goals. SMART goals are specific, measurable, achievable, relevant, and time-bound. Specific goals are clear and well-defined, measurable goals can be quantified and tracked, achievable goals are realistic and attainable, relevant goals align with personal values and priorities, and time-bound goals have a specific deadline for completion.

Goal-Setting Theory

Goal-setting theory suggests that setting specific and challenging goals can enhance performance by providing individuals with a clear target to strive for. The theory proposes that goals should be challenging but attainable, and that feedback and support are critical for goal attainment.

The Role of Self-Efficacy in Goal-Setting

Self-efficacy, or an individual's belief in their ability to succeed, is an important factor in goal-setting. Research has shown that individuals with higher levels of self-efficacy are more likely to set and achieve challenging goals.

STRATEGIES FOR GOAL-SETTING AND GOAL ACHIEVEMENT

Developing a Goal-Setting Action Plan

Developing an action plan is an essential component of goal-setting. An action plan outlines the steps needed to achieve a goal, including specific actions, timelines, and resources needed.

Visualizing Success

Visualizing success is a powerful tool for goal-setting. Visualization involves imagining oneself successfully achieving a goal, including the emotions and sensations associated with success.

Using Positive Self-Talk

Positive self-talk can be used to enhance motivation and confidence in goal-setting. Positive self-talk involves using positive affirmations and statements to encourage oneself and build confidence.

Seeking Social Support

Social support can be a valuable resource in goal-setting. Seeking support from friends, family, or colleagues can provide encouragement, feedback, and accountability.

Monitoring Progress

Monitoring progress is a critical component of goal-setting. Regularly tracking progress can help individuals stay on track, adjust their action plans as needed, and celebrate small successes along the way.

EXAMPLES OF GOAL-SETTING FOR PEAK PERFORMANCE

Goal-Setting in Sports

Goal-setting is commonly used in sports to enhance performance. Athletes may set specific goals related to performance metrics such as time, distance, speed or physical fitness.

Shah Rukh Khan, also known as the "King of Bollywood," set a peak performance goal to improve his physical fitness and transform his body for his role in the movie

"Happy New Year." His goal was to lose weight and build muscle to portray a character who was a former athlete.

To achieve this goal, Khan used the SMART goal-setting process. He made his goal Specific by identifying the amount of weight he wanted to lose and the muscle he wanted to gain. He made it Measurable by setting a deadline for his goal and tracking his progress using body measurements and fitness tests. He made it Achievable by working with a team of personal trainers, nutritionists, and fitness experts to develop a customized workout and diet plan. He made it Relevant by tying his goal to his professional aspirations as an actor. Finally, he made it Time-bound by setting a deadline for his transformation to coincide with the filming schedule of the movie.

Khan documented his journey on social media, sharing updates on his progress and motivating his fans to prioritize their health and fitness. He eventually achieved his goal, losing several pounds of weight and gaining muscle mass in the process. His physical transformation was widely praised by audiences and critics alike, and he continues to inspire others to set and achieve their peak performance goals.

Goal-Setting in Business

Goal-setting is a common practice in business to enhance performance and productivity. Businesses may set specific goals related to sales targets, customer satisfaction, or product development. Goal-setting can also be used to enhance employee motivation and engagement.

Goal-Setting in Personal Development

Goal-setting can be used in personal development as an effective tool to help individuals identify their objectives, create a plan of action, and track their progress towards achieving their desired outcomes. Setting goals can help individuals clarify their aspirations and provide motivation to work towards achieving them.

Here are some steps that individuals can take when setting goals for personal development:

Identify your long-term goals: Start by identifying your long-term aspirations, the things that you want to achieve over the next few years or even decades. These can be related to your career, personal life, relationships, health, or any other aspect of your life.

Break down your long-term goals into short-term objectives: Once you have identified your long-term goals, break them down into smaller, more manageable objectives that you can work on in the short term. This will make it easier to track your progress and stay motivated.

Make your goals specific and measurable: Ensure that your goals are specific and measurable so that you can track your progress towards achieving them. For example, if your goal is to lose weight, specify the amount of weight you want to lose and by what date.

Create an action plan: Develop a plan of action that outlines the steps you need to take to achieve your goals. This may include developing new habits, learning new skills, or seeking out support from others.

Track your progress: Regularly track your progress towards achieving your goals. This can help you stay motivated and identify any areas where you need to make adjustments to your plan of action.

Remember, goal-setting is not a one-time activity, but an ongoing process. As you achieve your goals, you can set new ones to continue your personal development journey.

Here are some additional tips to keep in mind when setting goals for personal development

Set realistic goals: Ensure that your goals are realistic and achievable based on your current skills, resources, and circumstances. Setting unrealistic goals can lead to disappointment and discouragement.

Focus on the process, not just the outcome: While it's important to have a clear outcome in mind, focusing solely on the result can be overwhelming. Focus on the process of achieving your goals and celebrate small victories along the way.

Be flexible: Life is unpredictable, and circumstances can change. Be open to adjusting your goals and plans as needed to stay on track.

Seek support: Personal development can be challenging, and having a support system can help you stay motivated and accountable. Consider seeking support from friends, family, a mentor, or a coach.

PEAK PERFORMANCE GOALS

Peak performance goals are designed to push individuals to reach their full potential in a particular area of their lives. These goals are not just about achieving success, but also about continuous growth and improvement. They can be related to any aspect of life, including physical fitness, mental performance, career success, personal development, and relationships.

To set peak performance goals, it's important to first identify your strengths and weaknesses in the area you want to improve. Next, consider what steps you need to take to achieve your desired outcome, and break down those steps into smaller, actionable goals. It's also important to set a timeline for achieving your goals and to track your progress along the way.

Here are a few examples of peak performance goals

Running a Marathon: A peak performance goal for a runner might be to complete a marathon within a specific time frame. To achieve this goal, they might break down their training into smaller goals, such as increasing their weekly mileage, improving their speed, and building their endurance.

Increasing Sales Performance: A sales professional might set a peak performance goal of increasing their monthly sales by a certain percentage. To achieve this goal, they might focus on developing their sales skills, building their network, and identifying growth opportunities.

Improving Mental Performance: An individual looking to improve their mental performance might set a peak performance goal of learning a new language or mastering a musical instrument. They could break down this goal into smaller, measurable steps, such as practising for a certain amount of time each day or completing a specific number of lessons.

Achieving a Health and Fitness Milestone: A peak performance goal for someone looking to improve their health and fitness might be to complete a certain number of push-ups or pull-ups or to run a certain distance without stopping. They might break down this goal into smaller goals, such as increasing the number of reps they can do each week or gradually increasing their running distance.

CONCLUSION

In conclusion, setting peak performance goals can help individuals push themselves to achieve their full potential in all aspects of life. By identifying specific, measurable targets and breaking them down into smaller, actionable steps, individuals can track their progress and continuously improve their performance over time.

In the finale, goal-setting is a valuable tool for peak performance. By identifying your aspirations, creating a plan of action, and tracking your progress, you can achieve your goals and continue to grow and develop as a person. Remember to set realistic goals, focus on the process, be flexible, and seek support when needed.

CHAPTER 25

Time Management and Productivity for Peak Performance

INTRODUCTION

Time is a finite resource, and managing it effectively is crucial for achieving peak performance. Effective time management can help you maximise productivity, reduce stress and achieve your goals more efficiently like the way it did for me. In this chapter, we will explore the principles of effective time management and provide practical strategies for optimising productivity.

For the first 50 years of my life, I felt like time was always slipping through my fingers. I was constantly stressed and overwhelmed, struggling to keep up with my responsibilities and feeling like I was never making progress on my goals. I was a chronic procrastinator, always putting things off until the last minute and struggling to stay focused.

But when I turned 49, a friend gave me a gift that would change my life forever. It was a book called *"Getting Things Done"* by David Allen, and it provided a comprehensive system for managing tasks, projects and responsibilities. I was sceptical at first, but as I began to implement the GTD system, I started to see amazing results.

One of the key principles of the GTD system is the idea of capturing and organising all of your tasks and commitments, rather than just prioritising and executing them. I started using an external system to capture all of my tasks and ideas and then processed them to determine their next actions and organise them into actionable lists. This helped me stay on top of my to-do list and avoid getting bogged down by distractions.

I also started implementing other time management strategies, like breaking tasks down into smaller, actionable steps and using time-blocking to schedule my day effectively. And I started waking up early and implementing the SAVERS system from Hal Elrod's book *"The Miracle Morning,"* which involved practices like meditation, affirmations, visualisation, exercise, reading and journaling.

As I continued to implement these systems in my life, I started to see incredible results. I became more productive, more focused and more disciplined. I found that I had more time for the things that mattered to me, like spending time with my family and pursuing my passions. And I started achieving things that I never thought were possible, like becoming a columnist, marathon runner, author, painter and farmer.

The most inspiring thing about my journey is that it's never too late to start managing your time effectively. Even at 50, I was able to transform my life and achieve peak performance in all areas of my life. And the benefits of effective time management go far beyond just getting more done—it's about living a more fulfilling and purposeful life. So if you're struggling with time management or feeling overwhelmed by your responsibilities, take heart—there is a way to take control of your time and achieve your dreams. To help you control your time and manage it effectively, we will explore the principles of effective time management and provide practical strategies for optimising productivity.

STRATEGIES FOR OPTIMISING PRODUCTIVITY

One of the most important principles of effective time management is prioritisation. It is important to identify which tasks are most important and require your immediate attention. This can be done by using the Eisenhower matrix, which involves dividing tasks into four categories: urgent and important, important but not urgent, urgent but not important and neither urgent nor important. This matrix helps you prioritise tasks based on their importance and urgency.

Minimising distractions

Distractions are one of the biggest obstacles to effective time management. To optimise productivity, it is important to minimise distractions and maintain focus on the task at hand. This can be done by eliminating unnecessary notifications, scheduling specific times to check email and social media and creating a quiet and organised workspace.

As someone who has always struggled with distractions and finding focus in my work, I was blown away by the insights in Cal Newport's book *"Deep Work."* The book provided a comprehensive framework for overcoming distractions and achieving a state of deep focus and productivity that I had never experienced before.

One of the key concepts in the book is the idea of "deep work"—a state of intense focus and concentration on a task that requires cognitive effort. Newport argues that in today's hyper-connected world, distractions are everywhere, and our ability to focus on deep work is constantly being eroded. However, by intentionally carving out time for deep work and eliminating distractions, we can achieve a level of productivity and creativity that is truly remarkable.

One of the most powerful techniques I learnt from the book was the idea of block time for deep work. This involves scheduling chunks of time—anywhere from 1-4 hours—for focused, uninterrupted work on a specific task. During this time, all distractions are eliminated—no email, no social media, no phone calls—so that I can fully immerse myself in the task at hand.

At first, I was sceptical about this approach. I didn't think I could go for hours without checking my email or social media. But as I started to implement block time for deep work, I found that it was incredibly effective. Not only was I able to get more done in less time, but the quality of my work improved as well. I was able to think more deeply and creatively about the problems I was working on, and I felt more focused and energised throughout the day.

Of course, implementing block time for deep work isn't always easy. It requires discipline and a willingness to say no to distractions. But the benefits are undeniable. By intentionally setting aside time for deep work, I could achieve a level of productivity and focus that I never thought was possible. And as I continue to practise this technique, I know that my work will only continue to improve.

Pomodoro Technique

The Pomodoro Technique is a popular time management strategy that involves breaking work into 25-minute intervals, known as Pomodoros, separated by short breaks. This technique can help you maintain focus, increase productivity and manage time effectively.

Time-blocking

Time-blocking is a strategy that involves scheduling specific blocks of time for different tasks throughout the day. This can help you stay organised, maintain focus and ensure that important tasks are completed on time. Time-blocking can be done using a digital calendar or a physical planner.

Create a routine

Establish a consistent routine for your day-to-day activities. This can help you develop good habits and eliminate decision fatigue, making it easier to stay focused and productive.

Avoid multitasking

Multitasking can reduce your productivity and increase stress levels. Instead, focus on one task at a time and complete it before moving on to the next one.

Take breaks

Regular breaks can help you recharge and maintain your focus throughout the day. Use the Pomodoro Technique or other similar methods to take short breaks between blocks of work.

Using technology to manage time

There are many technological tools available that can help you manage time effectively, such as time-tracking apps, productivity apps and project management tools. These tools can help you monitor progress, track time spent on different tasks and collaborate with team members.

TIME MANAGEMENT FOR PEAK PERFORMANCE

A famous book on time management for peak performance is *"Eat That Frog!"* by Brian Tracy. In this book, Tracy provides practical advice for overcoming procrastination and getting more done in less time.

The title of the book is based on a famous quote by Mark Twain: "Eat a live frog first thing in the morning and nothing worse will happen to you the rest of the day." Tracy uses this quote as a metaphor for tackling your most important and challenging task first thing in the morning so that you can get it out of the way and free up mental energy for the rest of your day.

The book is divided into 21 short chapters, each of which contains a specific time management strategy or technique. Some of the key ideas include:

The 80/20 rule: Focus on the 20% of tasks that will give you 80% of the results.

Set clear goals: Write down your goals and create a plan for achieving them.

Prioritise your tasks: Use the ABCDE method to prioritise your tasks based on their importance and urgency.

Focus on high-value activities: Identify the activities that will have the biggest impact on your goals and prioritise them.

Use the power of deadlines: Set deadlines for yourself and use them to stay focused and motivated.

Overcome procrastination: Use the "Swiss cheese" method to break down big tasks into smaller, more manageable pieces.

Overall, "Eat That Frog!" is a practical and easy-to-read book that provides a wealth of strategies and techniques for improving your time management skills and achieving peak performance.

We can also learn about time management for peak performance from the lives of several celebrities who are known for their exceptional time management skills, but one notable example is Dwayne "The Rock" Johnson.

Despite his busy schedule as a Hollywood actor, producer and former professional wrestler, Johnson is known for being extremely disciplined and productive with his time. He reportedly wakes up at 4 a.m. every day to start his day with a workout and often shares his daily schedule on social media to inspire his fans and followers.

In addition to his strict fitness regimen, Johnson is also a prolific actor and producer, often juggling multiple projects simultaneously. He has spoken publicly about his commitment to staying organised and focused, using tools such as a daily planner to manage his schedule and stay on top of his commitments.

Overall, Johnson's success as a celebrity and entrepreneur can be attributed in part to his exceptional time management skills and disciplined approach to productivity. His dedication to maintaining a healthy lifestyle and managing his time effectively serves as a role model for others looking to achieve peak performance in their own lives.

The other real-life examples are Elon Musk and Barack Obama. Elon Musk is a master of time management and productivity. He is known for working long hours and achieving remarkable results in multiple industries. Musk uses time-blocking to schedule his day and prioritise tasks, and he maintains focus by minimising distractions and working in a quiet environment. And Barack Obama, the former President of the United States, is well-known for effective time management. Obama is known for his rigorous schedule, which includes early morning workouts, daily briefings and scheduled blocks of time for tasks such as reading and writing.

TIME MANAGEMENT TOOLS FOR PEAK PERFORMANCE

Time management tools can be incredibly useful for achieving peak performance. Here are some popular tools that can help you manage your time more effectively:

Todoist: A task management app that lets you organise your tasks and projects, set deadlines and track your progress. You can use it to prioritise your tasks, create sub-tasks and set reminders.

Trello: A visual project management tool that allows you to organise your projects into boards, lists and cards. You can use it to create checklists, assign tasks to team members and track progress.

RescueTime: A time-tracking tool that helps you understand how you spend your time on your computer and mobile devices. It provides detailed reports on your daily habits and helps you identify areas where you can improve your productivity.

Forest: A mobile app that encourages you to stay focused by planting virtual trees. When you start a work session, you plant a tree that grows over time. If you leave the app before the session ends, your tree dies.

Pomodoro Technique: We have already discussed in this chapter under strategies for time management.

CONCLUSION

Effective time management and productivity are crucial for achieving peak performance in any field. By prioritising tasks, minimising distractions and using tools such as the Pomodoro Technique and time-blocking, you can optimise productivity and achieve your goals more efficiently. By following the examples of successful individuals such as Elon Musk, Barack Obama and Bill Gates, you can learn to manage your time effectively and reach your full potential.

CHAPTER 26

Creativity for Peak Performance

INTRODUCTION

Peak performance is the ability to perform at one's best, consistently achieving superior results in a chosen field. Creativity, on the other hand, is the ability to come up with novel and innovative ideas. While peak performance is often associated with excellence in a particular skill or domain, creativity is essential for achieving sustained success. This is because, to maintain a competitive edge, individuals must be able to think outside the box, adapt to changing circumstances and find new and innovative solutions to problems. I wanted to write and give value to my readers, but my creative channels remained locked and I could find no innovative key to open them up and start writing.

As a result, I became a terrible procrastinator when it came to writing. I had a burning desire to write and get my articles published, but every time I sat down to write, I found myself confronting a debilitating resistance that made me put off my writing or tear up whatever I had written. This went on for several years, and I felt like I was stuck in a rut. That's when I discovered Steven Pressfield's book, *"The War of Art"*, and everything changed.

I first heard about the book when I stumbled upon an interview with Steven Pressfield on the Spartan Up podcast back in 2017. His words resonated with me, and I was immediately intrigued. I decided to purchase the book and read it in a single day.

As I delved deeper into the book, I found answers as to why my creativity was getting impeded, and I learnt how to overcome it. The book provided valuable insights and strategies for overcoming resistance and tapping into my creative potential. Armed with this knowledge, I was able to finally break through the resistance and start writing again.

"The War of Art" was a powerful resource for me, and it helped me overcome my creative blocks and procrastination. It taught me that resistance is a natural part of the creative process and that I need to push through it to achieve my goals. The book provided me with a roadmap for unlocking my creative potential and helped me turn into a published author of four books.

Today, I am proud to say that I have published several articles, and I am well on my way to achieving my writing goals. "The War of Art" was the catalyst that helped me transform my life and tap into my full potential. I am forever grateful for the lessons I learnt from this incredible book.

Books and movies can be powerful tools for exploring the role of creativity in peak performance. "Creative Confidence" and "The War of Art" provide practical insights and strategies for leveraging creativity to achieve success. By exploring these resources, individuals can cultivate their creativity and achieve their full potential in their chosen fields.

I was particularly fascinated by the movie "Dead Poets Society" which tells the story of an English teacher who inspires his students to think creatively and pursue their passions. It demonstrates the power of creative thinking in transforming lives and inspiring change. The movie also explores the challenges of maintaining a creative vision in the face of societal norms and expectations.

The book *"Creative Confidence"* by Tom Kelley and David Kelley is my top pick. This book explores the role of creativity in problem-solving and innovation. The authors, who are the founders of the design firm IDEO, share their insights and experiences in helping individuals and organisations unlock their creative potential. The book provides practical strategies for overcoming creative blocks and fostering a culture of innovation, making it a valuable resource for anyone looking to leverage their creativity for peak performance. Having overcome my creative block, I believe for peak performance it is imperative to explore the science of creativity and provide strategies for cultivating creativity to enhance performance.

Divergent Thinking

Divergent thinking is the ability to generate multiple solutions to a problem, often by thinking outside the box. This type of thinking is crucial for creativity because it allows individuals to consider multiple perspectives and come up with unique solutions. In contrast, convergent thinking is the process of finding a single solution to a problem. While convergent thinking is necessary for some tasks, such as solving a math problem or following a recipe, divergent thinking is essential for creative problem-solving.

To cultivate divergent thinking, individuals can engage in activities that encourage exploration and experimentation. For example, brainstorming sessions can be a powerful tool for generating a wide range of ideas. During a brainstorming session, individuals are encouraged to share their ideas without fear of judgement. This allows for a free-flowing exchange of ideas, which can lead to innovative solutions. Another way to encourage divergent thinking is to engage in creative exercises, such as drawing or writing prompts, which challenge individuals to think outside the box.

Brainstorming

Brainstorming is a powerful tool for generating creative ideas. During a brainstorming session, individuals are encouraged to share their ideas without fear of judgement. This allows for a free-flowing exchange of ideas, which can lead to innovative solutions. Brainstorming can be used for a wide range of tasks, from developing new products to solving complex problems.

To facilitate a successful brainstorming session, it is important to create a safe and supportive environment. This means that all ideas should be welcomed and respected, even if they seem unrealistic or impractical. It is also important to set clear goals and guidelines for the session so that everyone is on the same page. Finally, it is important to follow up on the ideas generated during the session, by evaluating their feasibility and developing a plan of action.

Incubation

Incubation is the process of letting an idea or problem simmer in the mind, without actively thinking about it. This allows the subconscious mind to work on the problem in the background, leading to new insights and solutions. Incubation is an important part of the creative process because it allows individuals to take a break from actively thinking about a problem, which can lead to new perspectives and insights.

To cultivate incubation, individuals can engage in activities that promote relaxation and downtime, such as meditation or taking a walk in nature. It is also important to permit oneself to take a break from actively thinking about a problem and to trust that the subconscious mind will continue to work on it in the background.

Examples

The role of creativity in peak performance can be seen in a wide range of fields, from business to the arts. For example, Steve Jobs, the co-founder of Apple, was known for his creativity and innovative thinking. He was able to transform the technology industry by introducing new products, such as the iPhone and iPad, that revolutionised the way people interact with technology.

Similarly, J.K. Rowling, the author of the Harry Potter series, used her creativity to create a rich and complex world that has captured the imaginations of millions of readers worldwide. Her ability to think outside the box and create a unique and engaging story has made her one of the most successful authors of all time.

In the world of sports, creativity is also essential for peak performance. For example, Brazilian soccer player Pelé was known for his creative and innovative style of play, which allowed him to dominate the field and score goals in new and unexpected ways. Similarly, basketball player Michael Jordan was able to use his creativity and innovative thinking to develop new strategies and techniques that helped him become one of the most successful players in NBA history.

LEVERAGING CREATIVITY IN THE MODERN TECHNOLOGICAL ERA

In the modern technological era, there are various ways that we can leverage creativity for peak performance. Here are some strategies:

Use Technology for Inspiration: Technology has made it easier than ever to find inspiration and generate new ideas. Social media platforms, search engines and online communities can provide access to a wealth of information and perspectives. By using these resources, individuals can stay up-to-date on the latest trends and developments and draw inspiration from diverse sources.

Collaborate Virtually: Technology has also made it possible to collaborate with individuals from around the world, regardless of location. This can provide access to diverse perspectives and skill sets, leading to more innovative and effective solutions. Virtual collaboration tools such as video conferencing, shared workspaces and project management software can help facilitate this process.

Use Creative Software: There are various creative software tools available that can help individuals bring their ideas to life. For example, graphic design software, video editing software and animation software can all be used to create visually engaging content. These tools can be especially useful for individuals in fields such as marketing, advertising and content creation.

Embrace Emerging Technologies: Emerging technologies such as artificial intelligence, virtual reality and Blockchain are changing the way we work and create. By embracing these technologies and exploring their potential applications, individuals can stay at the forefront of innovation and find new ways to leverage creativity for peak performance.

Make Time for Creative Activities: With the constant demands of work and technology, it can be easy to neglect creative pursuits. However, making time for activities such as writing, painting, or music can help individuals maintain their creative spark and develop new skills that can be applied in their work. By prioritising creative activities, individuals can foster a more innovative and creative mindset, leading to enhanced performance.

CAN CREATIVITY BE BIOHACKED FOR PEAK PERFORMANCE?

While creativity is often associated with innate talent or inspiration, there are certainly ways to enhance creative abilities through biohacking. Here are some methods that may help biohack creativity for peak performance:

Optimise sleep: Getting adequate sleep is crucial for creative thinking. Sleep helps consolidate memories and clears the mind, allowing for fresh ideas to surface. To optimise sleep, consider using tools like blue-light-blocking glasses, optimising the sleeping environment and implementing a consistent sleep schedule.

Exercise: Regular exercise has been shown to enhance cognitive function, including creativity. Exercise increases blood flow and oxygen to the brain, which can improve focus and generate new ideas. Additionally, exercise has been shown to reduce stress and anxiety, which can be major barriers to creativity.

Nootropics: Nootropics are supplements or drugs that are believed to enhance cognitive performance. Some nootropics, such as caffeine and Modafinil, have been shown to improve creativity by increasing alertness and reducing fatigue. However, it's important to do research and consult a healthcare professional before experimenting with nootropics.

Mindfulness: Mindfulness meditation has been shown to improve divergent thinking, which is a key component of creative thinking. Mindfulness can help reduce distractions and increase focus, allowing for more innovative ideas to emerge.

Brainstorming techniques: Several brainstorming techniques can help facilitate creativity, such as mind mapping, reverse brainstorming and random word association. These techniques can help break down mental barriers and encourage novel thinking.

Creativity exercises: There are a variety of creativity exercises that can be used to train the brain to think more creatively. For example, the "six thinking hats" exercise involves wearing different "hats" to approach a problem from different perspectives. Another exercise is "random word stimulation", where a random word is chosen and used as a starting point for generating new ideas.

Overall, creativity can be biohacked for peak performance. However, it's important to remember that creativity is a complex and multifaceted process, and what works for one person may not work for another.

CONCLUSION

In conclusion, creativity is an essential component of peak performance. It allows individuals to approach problems in new and innovative ways, leading to superior results and sustained success. By cultivating divergent thinking, engaging in brainstorming sessions and promoting incubation, individuals can enhance their creativity and achieve peak performance in their chosen field. The examples of Steve Jobs, J.K. Rowling, Pelé and Michael Jordan demonstrate how creativity can lead to exceptional success, both in business and in sports. By harnessing the power of creativity, individuals can achieve their full potential and make a lasting impact in their field.

CHAPTER 27

Developing a Personalised Peak Performance Plan

INTRODUCTION

Developing a personalised peak performance plan is a process that requires careful consideration of an individual's strengths, weaknesses and goals. This plan can help individuals optimise their performance, improve productivity and achieve their objectives more effectively. In this chapter, we will explore the process of developing a personalised peak performance plan and provide strategies for creating a plan that is tailored to individual needs and preferences.

Before we dive deep into the subject, let's take a peek into the peak performance measurement plans that some famous people from various fields followed. Benjamin Franklin developed a plan to measure his performance in the pursuit of self-improvement. He identified 13 virtues that he wanted to cultivate and measure daily, including temperance, industry and frugality. He tracked his progress on a chart and focused on one virtue per week to achieve mastery. Tim Ferriss, author of "The 4-Hour Work Week", developed a plan to measure and achieve his goals. His Dreamlining plan involves identifying and defining specific goals, prioritising them and creating a timeline for achieving them. He also recommends developing action steps for each goal and measuring progress weekly.

Michael Jordan, a retired NBA superstar, had a rigorous practice plan that helped him achieve peak performance on the court. His plan involved practising for several hours each day and focusing on specific skills and drills, such as shooting and defensive techniques. He also incorporated visualisation and mental preparation into his practice routine. And Arianna Huffington, founder of the Huffington Post, developed a sleep plan to optimise her performance and productivity. Her plan involves prioritising sleep by setting a consistent sleep schedule, creating a sleep-conducive environment and practising relaxation techniques before bed. She also recommends avoiding electronics before sleep and prioritising restful activities, such as reading, to wind down before bed.

Warren Buffett, billionaire investor and CEO of Berkshire Hathaway, developed a learning plan to achieve peak performance in his field. His plan involves reading extensively about investment and finance, attending conferences and seminars and seeking out mentorship and guidance from experienced investors. He also prioritises continuous learning and personal development to stay ahead in his field. These plans illustrate the importance of developing personalised strategies and measurement systems to achieve peak performance in various fields. By focusing on specific goals and measuring progress regularly, individuals can optimise their performance and achieve their objectives more effectively. Like, all of them, I too have developed a personalised peak performance plan which you can take a look at here.

Every morning, I kickstart my day with a power-packed routine. I hit the gym or go for a run, followed by a rejuvenating meditation session. This helps me to awaken my body and mind, setting the stage for an energetic and focused day ahead.

I am mindful of what I put into my body, fuelling it with healthy and nutritious foods. I steer clear of junk food and prioritise whole, nutrient-rich meals that provide me with the energy and vitality I need to perform at my peak.

I am relentless in my pursuit of improvement, dedicating six days a week to training and honing my skills. I push myself beyond my comfort zone, constantly striving to surpass my previous best. I also challenge myself with a long run every week, pushing my limits and breaking through barriers.

I understand the importance of mental clarity for peak performance. I practise journaling and reading, which helps me to declutter my mind and enhance my focus. Journaling allows me to reflect on my thoughts and emotions while reading exposes me to new ideas and perspectives, expanding my horizons.

I prioritise my sleep and take regular breaks from social media to ensure that my mind and body are adequately rested and recharged. I seek guidance and mentorship from successful individuals in my field, learning from their experiences and applying their wisdom to my journey. My personalised peak performance plan is a holistic approach that encompasses physical exercise, meditation, healthy eating, training, mental clarity, rest and guidance. Following this plan has unlocked my potential and transformed my life.

STEPS IN DEVELOPING A PERSONALISED PEAK PERFORMANCE PLAN

Given below are three steps for developing a personalised peak performance plan:

Understanding Personal Strengths and Weaknesses

The first step in developing a personalised peak performance plan is to identify one's strengths and weaknesses. This is essential as it provides a foundation for creating a plan that is tailored to an individual's unique needs and preferences. Identifying one's strengths and weaknesses requires introspection and self-reflection. One way to do this is by conducting a SWOT analysis.

SWOT stands for Strengths, Weaknesses, Opportunities and Threats. This analysis involves identifying the strengths and weaknesses of an individual and the opportunities and threats that may impact their performance. By conducting a SWOT analysis, individuals can identify their unique strengths and weaknesses and develop strategies to capitalise on their strengths and overcome their weaknesses.

For example, some individuals may identify that they have excellent communication skills but struggle with time management. In this case, they can develop a plan that focuses on improving their time management skills while leveraging their communication skills to achieve their goals.

Setting Goals

The next step in developing a personalised peak performance plan is to set goals. Goals provide a clear direction and purpose for an individual's efforts. When setting goals, it is essential to ensure that they are SMART—specific, measurable, achievable, relevant and time-bound.

Specific: The goal should be clear and specific. For example, instead of setting a goal to "improve productivity", an individual may set a goal to "increase productivity by 20% in the next six months".

Measurable: The goal should be measurable. This means that an individual should be able to track progress and measure success. For example, an individual can measure productivity by tracking the number of tasks completed in a day.

Achievable: The goal should be realistic and achievable. Setting unrealistic goals can lead to frustration and demotivation. For example, it may not be feasible to increase productivity by 100% in a week.

Relevant: The goal should be relevant to an individual's overall objectives. For example, if an individual's objective is to get a promotion, then setting a goal to improve his coding skills may be relevant.

Time-bound: The goal should have a specific deadline. This helps to create a sense of urgency and accountability. For example, an individual may set a goal to increase productivity by 20% in the next six months.

Developing Strategies

Once an individual has identified his strengths and weaknesses and set goals, the next step is to develop strategies to achieve those goals. Strategies should be specific and tailored to an individual's unique needs and preferences. Some strategies that can be used to optimise performance include:

Prioritising Tasks: Prioritising tasks is essential to maximise productivity. Individuals can use tools such as to-do lists, calendars and task managers to prioritise tasks and stay organised.

Managing Time: Time management is critical to achieving goals. Individuals can use time management tools such as Pomodoro timers, time-tracking apps and scheduling tools to manage their time effectively.

Improving Skills: Improving skills is an excellent way to optimise performance. Individuals can take courses, attend workshops, or read books to develop new skills and improve existing ones.

Seeking Feedback: Feedback is essential to identify areas of improvement. Individuals can seek feedback from colleagues, mentors, or coaches to gain insight into their performance and identify areas for improvement.

Managing Stress: Managing stress is critical to maintaining optimal performance.

Dwayne "The Rock" Johnson is an actor, producer and former professional wrestler who is known for his impressive physical feats and charismatic personality. In addition to his success in the entertainment industry, he has also achieved success as an entrepreneur and philanthropist. His peak performance plan is a crucial part of his success and has helped him maintain his peak performance throughout his career. Johnson is known for his impressive physique and rigorous workout routine. He trains six days a week, focusing on a combination of weightlifting, cardio and circuit training. He also pays close attention to his diet, consuming a high-protein, low-carb diet with plenty of fruits and vegetables. He works with a personal trainer to help him reach his fitness goals and tracks his progress using a fitness app.

Johnson also prioritises his mental health and well-being. He practises daily meditation and visualisation, which he credits with helping him stay focused and motivated. He also uses affirmations to maintain a positive mindset and overcome challenges. He prioritises sleep, aiming for seven to eight hours of sleep each night and takes regular breaks from social media and technology to reduce stress and improve his mental health. He is known for his busy schedule, juggling multiple projects and commitments. To stay on top of his game, he carefully manages his time, prioritising his most important tasks and scheduling his day in advance. He also uses technology to stay organised, using a productivity app to manage his schedule, to-do list and goals.

Johnson has also built a successful personal brand, leveraging his unique personality, physique and work ethic to create a loyal fan base. He uses social media to connect with his fans, sharing behind-the-scenes glimpses of his life and work. He also carefully selects the projects he works on, focusing on those that align with his values and goals. Despite his success, Johnson never stops learning and growing. He seeks out mentorship and guidance from successful entrepreneurs and industry leaders and reads extensively about business, leadership and personal development. He also uses his platform to inspire and educate others, sharing his knowledge and experiences through his social media channels and charitable work. Dwayne Johnson's peak performance plan is a comprehensive approach to maintaining his physical, mental and emotional well-being while achieving his goals. By prioritising fitness, mental health, time management, personal branding and continuous learning, he has built a successful career and inspired millions of fans around the world.

PEAK PERFORMANCE QUESTIONNAIRE

Developing a personalised peak performance plan requires understanding your strengths, weaknesses, goals and preferences. One way to gain clarity in these areas is through a peak performance plan questionnaire. Here's an outline of a peak performance plan questionnaire that you can use to identify areas for improvement and create a personalised plan:

Strengths and Weaknesses

a. What are your top strengths? How do they contribute to your performance?
b. What are your top weaknesses? How do they hinder your performance?
c. What strategies have you used to improve your weaknesses in the past? Were they effective?

Goals

a. What are your short-term and long-term goals? (e.g., personal, professional, financial, health, etc.)
b. How do your goals align with your values and priorities?
c. What specific steps can you take to achieve your goals? What resources do you need?

Habits and Routines

a. What are your daily habits and routines? How do they impact your performance?
b. What habits and routines would you like to improve or establish to support your goals?
c. How can you make these changes sustainable?

Mental and Emotional Health

a. How do you manage stress and pressure? What coping strategies do you use?
b. What mental and emotional states help you perform at your best? How can you cultivate them?
c. Are there any mental or emotional blocks that hinder your performance? How can you address them?

Physical Health

a. How do you prioritise physical health in your life? What areas need improvement?
b. What physical activities do you enjoy? How can you incorporate them into your routine?
c. What changes can you make to your diet, sleep, or exercise habits to optimise your performance?

Support System

a. Who are the people that support and encourage you? How do they contribute to your performance?
b. Who are the people that hinder your performance? How can you limit their impact?
c. Are there any mentors or coaches that can help you achieve your goals? How can you seek their guidance?

By answering these questions, you can gain a deeper understanding of yourself and identify areas for improvement. From there, you can create a personalised peak performance plan that incorporates strategies and measurement systems to optimise your performance and achieve your goals.

It is important to remember that developing a personalised peak performance plan is not a one-time event, but rather an ongoing process that requires dedication, commitment and continuous evaluation and adjustment. It may take time and effort to fine-tune your plan and make it truly effective for you. However, the benefits of investing in your personal growth and performance can be immense, leading to improved outcomes, increased confidence and enhanced overall well-being.

In addition, it is essential to recognise that everyone's journey towards peak performance is unique. What works for one person may not work for another, and it is crucial to customise your plan according to your strengths, weaknesses and preferences. It is also important to seek support from mentors, coaches, or trusted individuals who can provide guidance, feedback and accountability as you work towards your peak performance goals.

CONCLUSION

In conclusion, developing a personalised peak performance plan is a powerful tool that can help you achieve your full potential, excel in your endeavours and live a more fulfilled and successful life. By following the principles outlined in this chapter and consistently applying them in your daily life, you can unlock your peak performance capabilities and reach new heights of success. Remember, you have the power to shape your destiny, and with a well-designed and customised peak performance plan, you can take control of your performance and achieve extraordinary results. So, start today, commit to your growth and unleash your true potential!

CHAPTER 28

Measuring and Tracking Performance Progress

INTRODUCTION

Measuring and tracking performance progress involves evaluating and quantifying the results and outcomes of efforts made towards achieving a particular goal or objective. It is a critical process that allows individuals, teams and organisations to assess their performance, identify strengths and weaknesses and make data-driven decisions to improve performance.

There are several key principles of performance measurement and tracking:

Clear and measurable goals: Performance measurement starts with setting clear and specific goals that are measurable. A well-defined goal should be specific, measurable, achievable, relevant and time-bound (often referred to as SMART criteria). This allows for easy tracking and assessment of progress towards achieving the goal.

Selecting appropriate performance indicators: Performance indicators are the quantifiable measures that are used to track progress towards a goal. It is important to carefully select performance indicators that are relevant to the goal and provide meaningful insights. Performance indicators should be aligned with the overall objectives and should be easily measurable and understandable.

Collecting accurate and reliable data: Accurate and reliable data is crucial for effective performance measurement. Data should be collected using standardised methods and processes to ensure consistency and reliability. Data should be based on factual and objective information, rather than subjective opinions or assumptions. It is important to regularly review and validate the data to ensure its accuracy and reliability.

Analysing and interpreting data: Once the data is collected, it needs to be analysed and interpreted to derive meaningful insights. Data analysis involves examining the data to identify patterns, trends and anomalies. Interpretation involves making sense of the data and drawing conclusions based on the analysis. Data visualisation techniques, such as charts and graphs, can help present clearly and understandably.

Regular and timely feedback: Timely feedback is essential for effective performance tracking. Regular feedback allows for real-time monitoring of progress and provides an opportunity to make adjustments or improvements as needed. Feedback should be constructive, specific and focused on areas for improvement. It should also acknowledge achievements and successes to maintain motivation.

Continuous improvement: Performance measurement and tracking should be viewed as an ongoing process of continuous improvement. It is important to regularly review and analyse performance data, identify areas for improvement and implement appropriate actions to optimise performance. This may involve revising goals, adjusting strategies, or providing additional resources or support.

STRATEGIES FOR TRACKING PROGRESS AND OPTIMISING PERFORMANCE INCLUDE:

Setting up a performance tracking system: Establish a system for collecting, storing and analysing performance data. This may involve using performance tracking software, spreadsheets, or other tools that allow for easy data collection and analysis.

Creating performance dashboards: Performance dashboards are visual representations of performance data that provide a snapshot of key performance indicators (KPIs) in a concise and accessible manner. Dashboards can help track progress towards goals and facilitate data-driven decision-making.

Regular performance reviews: Conduct regular performance reviews to assess progress towards goals, provide feedback and identify areas for improvement. These reviews can be conducted individually or as a team and should involve a thorough analysis of performance data.

Benchmarking and comparison: Benchmarking involves comparing performance data against industry standards, best practices, or previous performance to identify areas for improvement. This allows for a contextual understanding of performance and helps set realistic targets for improvement.

Utilising technology: Technology can be a valuable tool for tracking performance progress. There are various software applications and tools available that can automate data collection, analysis and reporting, making performance tracking more efficient and effective.

Regularly updating goals and strategies: Goals and strategies should be regularly reviewed and updated based on performance data and feedback. If performance is not meeting expectations, goals and strategies may need to be revised to ensure they are achievable and aligned with the overall objectives.

To understand better let's consider an example of measuring and tracking performance for a marathon runner. The marathon runner has set a goal to complete a marathon race within a certain time frame and wants to track their progress towards achieving this goal.

Clear and measurable goal: The marathon runner's goal is to complete a marathon race within a specific time frame, such as finishing the race in under four hours.

Performance indicators: The performance indicators for the marathon runner could include the time taken to complete each training run, the distance covered in each training session, heart rate during training and other relevant metrics such as pace, speed and endurance.

Data collection: The marathon runner collects data during each training session, recording the time taken, distance covered, heart rate and other relevant metrics using a GPS watch or a running app on their smartphone.

Data analysis and interpretation: The marathon runner reviews the collected data regularly, analysing the time taken, distance covered, heart rate and other metrics to assess their performance progress. They may use data visualisation tools, such as charts or graphs, to visually analyse the data and identify patterns or trends.

Regular feedback: The marathon runner seeks feedback from a coach or fellow runners, who can provide insights on their performance and suggest areas for improvement. They may also reflect on their performance and set personal targets based on the feedback received.

Benchmarking and comparison: The marathon runner may compare their performance data against previous races or personal bests to assess their progress over time. They may also compare their performance against established benchmarks, such as average race times for their age group or gender, to set realistic targets for improvement.

Utilising technology: The marathon runner may use technology, such as GPS watches, heart rate monitors, or running apps, to track their performance data accurately and consistently. They may also use online platforms or spreadsheets to store and analyse their performance data.

Regularly updating goals and strategies: Based on the performance data and feedback received, the marathon runner may revise their goals and training strategies.

For example, they may adjust their training plan, focus on improving specific aspects of their performance, or set new targets based on their progress.

In summary, marathon runner measures and tracks their performance progress by setting clear goals, collecting and analysing relevant data, seeking feedback, benchmarking against established standards, utilising technology and regularly updating their goals and strategies. This enables them to make informed decisions, identify areas for improvement and optimise their performance to achieve their marathon race goal.

Metrics, such as Key Performance Indicators (KPIs), are essential tools for measuring progress and making data-driven decisions in various contexts, including business, sports and personal performance. Here are some reasons why using metrics is important:

Objective measurement: Metrics provide an objective way to measure progress and performance. They allow for quantifiable assessment of performance, which helps to eliminate bias, subjectivity and ambiguity in evaluating progress. Metrics provide concrete, measurable data that can be used to accurately assess performance and track progress over time.

Clarity and focus: Metrics, especially KPIs, provide clarity and focus by identifying specific, relevant and measurable goals. They help individuals and organisations to clearly define what needs to be achieved and provide a benchmark for evaluating progress. This clarity and focus enable individuals and organisations to align their efforts towards achieving the desired outcomes.

Data-driven decision-making: Metrics enable data-driven decision-making, which is based on evidence and facts rather than subjective opinions or gut feelings. By tracking relevant metrics, individuals and organisations can collect and analyse data to make informed decisions about their performance strategies, resource allocation and goal-setting. Data-driven decision-making allows for more effective and efficient decision-making, leading to better outcomes.

Performance improvement: Metrics facilitate performance improvement by identifying areas that need improvement and tracking progress over time. By regularly measuring and analysing performance metrics, individuals and organisations can identify strengths and weaknesses, uncover patterns or trends and take necessary actions to optimise performance. Metrics also serve as motivators, as they provide a sense of accomplishment when progress is made and highlight areas that require further effort.

Accountability and transparency: Metrics promote accountability and transparency in performance management. By setting clear performance metrics and tracking progress against them, individuals and organisations can hold themselves accountable for their performance. Metrics also enable transparency, as they provide a clear picture of performance to stakeholders, including managers, team members and customers, fostering trust and accountability.

Continuous improvement: Metrics support a culture of continuous improvement. By regularly measuring and tracking performance, individuals and organisations can identify areas for improvement and take corrective actions to optimise performance. Metrics provide a feedback loop that enables ongoing learning and adaptation, leading to continuous improvement and innovation.

Communication and alignment: Metrics facilitate communication and alignment among team members and stakeholders. They provide a common language for discussing performance, setting expectations and evaluating progress. Metrics also help to align efforts and resources towards common goals, ensuring that everyone is working towards the same objectives.

MEASURING AND TRACKING PERFORMANCE PROGRESS

The following are some more examples of measuring and tracking performance progress:

Personal Fitness: A person interested in improving their fitness level can set a goal to run a 5k race. A relevant metric could be the time it takes to run a 5k race. The person can track their progress by regularly monitoring their running time and by making adjustments to their training routine.

Sales Team Performance: A sales team can set a goal to increase sales by 10% in the next quarter. A relevant KPI could be the volume of sales per month. The team can track their progress by monitoring the number of sales and make adjustments to their sales strategy.

Project Management: A project manager can set a goal to complete a project on time and within budget. Relevant metrics could include project milestones, project costs and project risks. The project manager can track progress by regularly monitoring these metrics and making adjustments to the project plan as necessary.

A model table for measuring and tracking progress:

Goal/ Objective	KPI/Metric	Target	Current Status	Progress
Increase website traffic	Website visits	10% increase in monthly website visits	5% increase in monthly website visits	50% achieved
Reduce customer complaints	Complaints per month	25% decrease in monthly customer complaints	10% decrease in monthly customer complaints	40% achieved
Improve employee productivity	Sales per employee	5% increase in sales per employee	3% increase in sales per employee	60% achieved
Enhance customer satisfaction	Net Promoter Score (NPS)	10% increase in NPS score	8% increase in NPS score	80% achieved

This table includes columns for the goal or objective, the KPI or metric used to track progress towards the goal, the target for the KPI, the current status of the KPI and the progress made towards achieving the target. This model table can be customised based on the specific goals and objectives being measured and tracked.

A model table for measuring and tracking progress for a marathon runner

Goal/ Objective	KPI/Metric	Target	Current Status	Progress
Improve marathon finish time	Marathon finish time	10% decrease in marathon finish time compared to the previous race	5% decrease in marathon finish time compared to the previous race	50% achieved
Increase weekly mileage	Weekly mileage	5% increase in weekly mileage	3% increase in weekly mileage	60% achieved
Improve running speed	Average pace per mile	5 seconds decrease in average pace per mile	3 seconds decrease in average pace per mile	60% achieved
Enhance endurance	Longest run distance	10% increase in longest run distance	8% increase in longest run distance	80% achieved

This table includes columns for the goal or objective, the KPI or metric used to track progress towards the goal, the target for the KPI, the current status of the KPI and the progress made towards achieving the target. The goals and KPIs in this model table are specific to a marathon runner's training and performance. This model table can be customised based on the specific goals and objectives of the individual marathon runner.

A blank table for first-timers to enter and measure progress (athletes, businessmen and students)

Goal/ Objective	KPI/Metric	Target	Current Status	Progress

This table can be used by athletes, businessmen, students or anyone else who is a first-timer and wants to track their progress towards their goals. The user can fill in the headers according to their specific goals and KPIs. The 'Target' column can be used to set a realistic target that the user wants to achieve. The 'Current Status' column can be used to track the current status of the KPI. The 'Progress' column can be used to monitor the progress made towards achieving the target.

To learn more about measuring and tracking performance progress, here are a few books which can serve as a reference and make you better.

"Measure What Matters: How Google, Bono, and the Gates Foundation Rock the World with OKRs" by John Doerr - This book introduces the concept of Objectives and Key Results (OKRs) and how they can be used to measure progress and achieve ambitious goals.

"The Lean Startup: How Today's Entrepreneurs Use Continuous Innovation to Create Radically Successful Businesses" by Eric Ries: This book discusses the importance of measuring and tracking progress in the context of starting and growing a business. It emphasises the use of lean principles to develop and test ideas quickly and efficiently.

"Atomic Habits: An Easy & Proven Way to Build Good Habits & Break Bad Ones" by James Clear: This book provides practical advice on how to build good habits and break bad ones. It emphasises the importance of measuring and tracking progress in order to achieve lasting behaviour change.

"High-Performance Habits: How Extraordinary People Become That Way" by Brendon Burchard: This book explores the habits and behaviours of high performers across various fields and provides practical strategies for achieving high performance. It emphasises the use of metrics and measurement to track progress and achieve goals.

"The 4 Disciplines of Execution: Achieving Your Wildly Important Goals" by Chris McChesney, Sean Covey and Jim Huling: This book presents a framework for achieving ambitious goals by focusing on the most important actions and measuring progress through lead and lag measures. It provides practical advice on how to implement this framework in a variety of contexts, including business and personal goals.

CONCLUSION

Measuring and tracking performance progress is a crucial aspect of optimising performance. It involves setting clear and measurable goals, selecting appropriate performance indicators, collecting accurate and reliable data, analysing and interpreting data, providing regular feedback and embracing a mindset of continuous improvement. By implementing effective strategies for tracking progress and optimising performance, individuals, teams and organisations can identify areas for improvement, make data-driven decisions and achieve better outcomes. Regular monitoring and evaluation of performance progress can lead to increased motivation, enhanced productivity and ultimately, improved performance results. By leveraging the power of metrics, individuals and organisations can optimise performance, achieve desired outcomes and drive success. It is important to approach performance measurement and tracking as an ongoing process, utilising technology and best practices to ensure that performance is constantly monitored, evaluated and improved upon.

CHAPTER 29

Ethics of Performance Enhancement and the Importance of Responsible Use

INTRODUCTION

Performance enhancement has become an increasingly popular topic in sports, fitness and other competitive arenas. People are always looking for ways to gain an edge, whether it be through training harder, using special equipment, or even taking substances to improve their performance. However, the use of performance-enhancing techniques and substances raises ethical and moral questions. In the present chapter, we will explore the ethical considerations surrounding performance enhancement and the importance of responsible use.

What is Performance Enhancement?

Performance enhancement refers to the use of various techniques or substances to improve an individual's physical or mental performance. These techniques and substances can range from legal and accepted methods like physical training, specialised equipment and dietary supplements to more controversial methods like the use of anabolic steroids, blood doping and cognitive enhancers.

Benefits and Risks of Performance Enhancement

The use of performance enhancement can offer several potential benefits, such as increased muscle mass, improved endurance, enhanced cognitive function and improved overall physical and mental performance. These benefits can be particularly important for athletes and individuals competing in high-stress environments, such as military personnel or emergency responders.

However, performance enhancement also carries significant risks. For example, the use of anabolic steroids can lead to liver damage, heart disease and other serious health problems. Similarly, blood doping can increase the risk of heart attacks, stroke and other cardiovascular issues. Additionally, the use of cognitive enhancers can lead to addiction, insomnia and other mental health problems.

Ethical Considerations

The use of performance-enhancing techniques and substances raises several ethical questions, including fairness, health and safety and the integrity of the competition.

Fairness

One of the most significant ethical concerns surrounding performance enhancement is fairness. If some athletes or competitors are using substances or techniques to enhance their performance, it creates an unfair advantage over those who do not use these methods. This can lead to a sense of unfairness and disillusionment among competitors who feel that they cannot compete on an equal playing field.

Health and Safety

Another significant ethical concern is the health and safety of individuals who use performance-enhancing substances or techniques. Some of these methods can be harmful or even fatal, particularly when used incorrectly or without proper medical supervision. It is important to consider the potential long-term health consequences of these practices and ensure that individuals who use them are fully informed of the risks involved.

Integrity of Competition

The use of performance-enhancing techniques and substances can also raise concerns about the integrity of the competition. If individuals are using substances or techniques that are not allowed, it can undermine the credibility and fairness of the competition. It can also lead to a perception that the competition is less legitimate or less meaningful.

Responsible Use

While the use of performance-enhancing techniques and substances can carry significant risks, it is possible to use these methods responsibly. Responsible use involves making informed decisions about the potential risks and benefits of these practices, as well as understanding the rules and regulations governing their use.

Making Informed Decisions

One of the most critical aspects of responsible use is making informed decisions about the potential risks and benefits of performance enhancement. Individuals should fully understand the risks and benefits of any substance or technique they are considering using and make an informed decision based on this information.

Following Regulations and Policies

Another important aspect of responsible use is following the regulations and policies governing the use of performance-enhancing substances and techniques. These regulations and policies are in place to protect the health and safety of individuals and ensure the fairness and integrity of the competition.

PERFORMANCE-ENHANCING DRUGS AND THEIR CONSEQUENCES

Performance-enhancing drugs (PEDs) are substances or methods that are used to improve athletic performance, cognitive abilities, or productivity. Here is a list of some common PEDs and their potential consequences:

Anabolic Steroids: Anabolic steroids are synthetic substances that mimic the effects of testosterone. They can increase muscle mass, strength and endurance. However, long-term use of anabolic steroids can have serious health consequences, including liver damage, kidney failure and heart disease.

Human Growth Hormone (HGH): HGH is a hormone produced naturally by the body that is responsible for growth and development. Synthetic HGH can increase muscle mass, reduce body fat and improve endurance. However, long-term use of HGH can cause diabetes, joint pain and heart disease.

Stimulants: Stimulants such as amphetamines and caffeine can increase alertness, focus and energy. However, long-term use of stimulants can cause addiction, insomnia, anxiety and heart problems.

Blood Doping: Blood doping involves increasing the number of red blood cells in the body, which can improve endurance. However, blood doping can cause blood clots, stroke and heart attacks.

Beta-Blockers: Beta-blockers are drugs that can lower heart rate and blood pressure. They are used in some sports to reduce performance anxiety and improve accuracy. However, beta-blockers can cause fatigue, depression and other side effects.

Erythropoietin (EPO): EPO is a hormone that stimulates the production of red blood cells. It is used to improve endurance and recovery. However, EPO can cause blood clots, stroke and heart attacks.

Diuretics: Diuretics are drugs that increase urine production and can help athletes lose weight quickly. However, diuretics can cause dehydration, electrolyte imbalances and kidney damage.

Overall, the use of PEDs can have serious health consequences, including liver damage, kidney failure, heart disease and other health issues. Additionally, the use of

PEDs is considered cheating and is banned in most sports. It is essential to promote responsible use and educate individuals about the potential risks and benefits of these practices. Additionally, regulations and policies should be in place to control the use of PEDs and prevent their misuse.

Performance-enhancing drugs (PEDs) are often associated with sports, but their use is not limited to athletic competition. PEDs are also used by students and business professionals to improve their cognitive abilities, focus and productivity. However, the use of PEDs in these contexts raises significant ethical concerns.

Sports: The use of PEDs in sports is perhaps the most well-known form of performance enhancement. Athletes may use PEDs to improve their strength, endurance, or speed, giving them a competitive advantage. However, the use of PEDs is considered cheating and can have serious legal consequences for the athlete apart from harmful health issues.

Students: Students may use PEDs to enhance their cognitive abilities, such as memory, attention and focus. This is known as cognitive enhancement. The use of PEDs in this context raises ethical concerns because it may create an unfair advantage for those who use them. Additionally, the long-term health consequences of cognitive enhancement drugs are not yet fully understood.

Business: Some business professionals use PEDs to improve their productivity and focus. This may involve the use of stimulants or other drugs to stay awake and alert for long periods.

Overall, the use of PEDs in sports, students and business contexts raises significant ethical concerns. It is essential to promote responsible use and educate individuals about the potential risks and benefits of these practices. Additionally, regulations and policies should be in place to control the use of PEDs and prevent their misuse. Education and prevention efforts can help individuals make informed decisions about the use of PEDs and promote responsible behaviour.

The use of performance-enhancing drugs (PEDs) has been a significant issue in the world of sports for many years. Several athletes who were once considered peak performers have been caught abusing PEDs and lost their titles and reputations as a result. Lance Armstrong is perhaps the most well-known case of an athlete caught using PEDs. Armstrong won the Tour de France seven times between 1999 and 2005, but in 2012, he was stripped of all his titles and banned from the sport for life after he admitted to using PEDs. Similarly, Marion Jones, an Olympic gold medallist in track and field was caught using PEDs in 2007. Jones was stripped of her medals, and she served time in prison for lying to investigators about her PED use.

Ben Johnson was a Canadian sprinter who won the gold medal in the 100 metres at the 1988 Olympics in Seoul, South Korea. However, he was later stripped of his medal after he tested positive for steroids. Further, Rafael Palmeiro was a Major League Baseball player who hit more than 500 home runs during his career. However, in 2005, he tested positive for steroids and was suspended from the game. And Alex Rodriguez was a professional baseball player who was caught using PEDs in 2014 was suspended for the entire 2014 season and was later released by his team.

There have also been several cases of Indian athletes being caught using performance-enhancing drugs (PEDs) over the years. Narsingh Yadav, an Indian wrestler, was banned for four years in 2016 after testing positive for steroids. Yadav was set to compete in the 2016 Rio Olympics but was banned from the event as a result of his PED use. Inderjeet Singh, a shot putter, was banned for four years in 2018 after testing positive for steroids. Singh had won the gold medal at the 2015 Asian Championships and was considered a promising young athlete in Indian sports. Sanjita Chanu, a weightlifter, was banned for two years in 2018 after testing positive for steroids. Chanu had won gold medals at the 2014 Commonwealth Games and the 2018 Commonwealth Games, but her victories were tarnished by her PED use.

These cases demonstrate the serious consequences of using PEDs. Athletes who use PEDs not only risk their health but also risk losing their titles, reputations and careers. The use of PEDs is considered cheating and is not tolerated in most sports. It is essential for athletes to make informed decisions about their performance and avoid using PEDs to gain an unfair advantage. Additionally, regulations and policies should be in place to control the use of PEDs and prevent their misuse.

Performance enhancement in bodybuilding is a controversial issue, and the legality of such practices varies depending on the specific substances or methods being used. There are a few reasons why performance enhancement is generally more accepted and allowed in the sport of bodybuilding than in other sports:

Bodybuilding is a sport that is primarily focused on the aesthetics of the body, rather than on athletic performance. This means that there is less concern about the potential health risks associated with certain performance-enhancing substances, as the focus is on achieving a certain look rather than on enhancing athletic ability.

Further, bodybuilding is largely an unregulated sport, meaning that there are no strict rules or regulations governing what substances or methods athletes can use to enhance their performance. While some bodybuilding organisations may have their own rules and guidelines, there is no universal standard for what is considered legal or illegal in the sport. And there is a culture of acceptance surrounding performance enhancement in bodybuilding, with many athletes openly discussing their use of anabolic steroids or other substances. This culture of acceptance has made it more difficult to enforce bans or restrictions on performance-enhancing substances in the sport.

It is important to note, however, that the use of performance-enhancing substances in bodybuilding is still a controversial and potentially dangerous practice. While some athletes may argue that such substances are necessary to achieve their goals in the sport, there are numerous health risks associated with their use, including liver damage, cardiovascular disease and other serious health conditions. Athletes should always be aware of the potential risks associated with performance-enhancing substances and make informed decisions about their use.

POLICING PERFORMANCE ENHANCEMENT

Performance enhancement is a challenging issue for police for several reasons. While there are laws and regulations in place to restrict the use of certain substances and techniques, enforcing these regulations can be difficult. Here are some reasons why performance enhancement is not easily policed:

Difficulty in Detection: Some performance-enhancing substances and techniques are difficult to detect through standard drug tests or other methods of screening. This can make it challenging to identify individuals who are using these methods.

Evolving Nature of Performance Enhancement: Performance enhancement is a constantly evolving field, with new substances and techniques being developed all the time. This can make it challenging for regulatory bodies to keep up with the latest developments and ensure that their regulations are up-to-date.

Availability of Performance-Enhancing Substances: Performance-enhancing substances can be purchased easily through the Internet or other sources, making it difficult to control their distribution and use.

Lack of International Consensus: There is no international consensus on the regulation of performance enhancement. Different countries have different regulations and laws regarding performance enhancement, making it challenging to enforce a unified approach.

Cultural and Social Attitudes: Some cultures and societies may have more permissive attitudes towards performance enhancement, which can make it difficult to enforce regulations in these contexts.

Overall, while there are regulations and policies in place to restrict the use of performance-enhancing substances and techniques, enforcement can be challenging due to the difficulty in detecting these substances, the evolving nature of performance enhancement, the availability of these substances, the lack of international consensus and cultural and social attitudes towards performance enhancement. As such, it is essential to promote responsible use and educate individuals about the potential risks and benefits of these practices.

WHY IS BIOHACKING ETHICAL PERFORMANCE ENHANCEMENT?

Biohacking is a term used to describe the practice of making changes to one's body or lifestyle to enhance performance. Biohacking is often seen as a more ethical form of performance enhancement when compared to the use of performance-enhancing drugs (PEDs) for several reasons:

Healthier: Biohacking typically involves making changes to one's diet, exercise routine, or sleep habits to improve performance. These changes are often considered healthier than the use of PEDs, which can have negative effects on the body and may even be life-threatening in some cases.

Transparency: Biohacking is often a transparent process, meaning that individuals who engage in biohacking are open about the changes they are making to their bodies and lifestyles. This transparency allows others to make informed decisions about whether they want to engage in similar practices and ensures a level playing field for all individuals.

Natural: Biohacking typically involves natural methods of performance enhancement rather than artificial or synthetic substances. This means that biohacking is often seen as a more natural form of performance enhancement that is in line with the body's natural processes.

Sustainable: Biohacking is often focused on making long-term changes to one's lifestyle or habits rather than seeking short-term gains. This focus on sustainability means that biohacking is often a more responsible and ethical form of performance enhancement.

Overall, biohacking is often seen as a more ethical form of performance enhancement when compared to the use of PEDs. However, it is important to note that there are still ethical considerations and risks associated with biohacking, and individuals should always make informed decisions about any changes they make to their bodies or lifestyles.

Are the rules and regulations adequate? Should new rules and laws be enacted?

The rules and regulations surrounding performance enhancement in sports are constantly evolving, and there is an ongoing debate about whether these rules and regulations are adequate. While some may argue that current rules and regulations are sufficient to ensure fair play and protect the health and safety of athletes, others believe that more needs to be done to address the issue of performance enhancement in sports.

One of the main challenges with current rules and regulations is that they can be difficult to enforce. Athletes may be able to find ways to circumvent testing or to use substances that are not currently on the banned substances list. Additionally, the lack of standardisation across different sports and organisations can make it difficult to ensure a level playing field for all athletes.

In response to these challenges, there have been calls for new rules and laws to be enacted to address performance enhancement in sports. Some of the potential solutions that have been proposed include:

Stricter testing protocols: This could involve more frequent and comprehensive testing of athletes, as well as increased penalties for those who are found to be using performance-enhancing substances.

Increased education and awareness: Athletes may be more likely to make responsible decisions about performance enhancement if they are better informed about the risks and benefits of different substances and methods.

Standardisation across sports and organisations: Establishing a universal set of rules and regulations for performance enhancement in sports could help to ensure a level playing field for all athletes and reduce the likelihood of cheating.

Collaboration between athletes, coaches and governing bodies: By working together, athletes, coaches and governing bodies can create a more transparent and collaborative environment that promotes the responsible use of performance-enhancing substances.

CONCLUSION

Performance enhancement is a complex and controversial issue that spans a wide range of domains, from sports and academics to business and everyday life. While performance enhancement can offer numerous benefits, including improved physical and cognitive performance, there are also significant risks associated with the use of performance-enhancing substances and techniques.

One of the main ethical considerations surrounding performance enhancement is the issue of fairness. When some individuals have access to performance-enhancing substances or techniques that others do not, it can create an uneven playing field and undermine the integrity of competitions or other performance-based activities.

Additionally, the use of performance-enhancing substances can pose serious health risks, including liver damage, cardiovascular disease and other potentially life-threatening conditions.

Despite these risks, performance enhancement remains a common practice in many domains. Athletes may turn to performance-enhancing substances to gain a competitive edge, while students and professionals may use cognitive enhancers to improve their academic or work performance. Similarly, biohackers may experiment with different techniques to optimise their health and well-being.

While performance enhancement is not necessarily illegal in all domains, it is important to approach it with caution and make informed decisions about its use. This includes understanding the potential risks and benefits associated with different substances and techniques, as well as following any rules and regulations that are in place to govern their use. Additionally, it is important to consider the ethical implications of performance enhancement and to work towards promoting responsible use that is fair and safe for all individuals involved.

Overall, the issue of performance enhancement raises several important ethical and moral questions that require ongoing discussion and collaboration between individuals, organisations and society as a whole. By working together to find effective solutions and promote responsible use of performance-enhancing substances and techniques, we can help to ensure a fair and safe playing field for all individuals, while also respecting individual autonomy and the pursuit of excellence.

Conclusion

As I sit down to write this final chapter, I am filled with a sense of satisfaction and gratitude. It has been an incredible journey exploring the art of peak performance and discovering the myriad of ways we can optimise our bodies and minds to achieve success. Throughout the previous 29 chapters, we have delved into various aspects of peak performance, from understanding the biology of the brain and the impact of genetics and epigenetics to the role of nutrition, sleep, exercise and mindfulness in optimising our performance.

We have explored the impact of stress on performance and how to manage it, the importance of mindset and cultivating a growth mindset and the role of emotion, visualisation and mental rehearsal in peak performance. We have also examined the impact of environment, social connections and technology on performance and how to set and achieve goals for success.

As I reflect on this journey, I am struck by the incredible potential we all have to achieve greatness in our lives. By understanding the art of peak performance and implementing the strategies outlined in this book, we can unlock our full potential and achieve the success we desire.

But our journey is far from over. The art of peak performance is a rapidly evolving field, and new research is continually emerging that sheds light on how we can further optimise our performance. In this final chapter, I will discuss some of the new frontiers in peak performance and how technology could revolutionise some of the areas we have explored.

One area that is receiving increasing attention is the role of the microbiome in peak performance. The microbiome refers to the trillions of bacteria, viruses and fungi that reside in our gut and play a critical role in regulating our immune system, metabolism and brain function. Emerging research suggests that optimising our gut microbiome could enhance our cognitive and physical performance, reduce stress and improve our overall health and well-being.

Another exciting area of research is the use of wearable technology to monitor and optimise our performance. From fitness trackers to brain-sensing headbands, wearable technology provides real-time feedback on our performance and allows us to track our progress over time. This technology could help us identify areas where we need to improve and provide us with the motivation to continue striving for success.

Furthermore, advances in artificial intelligence and machine learning could revolutionise the way we approach peak performance. By analysing vast amounts of data on human performance, AI algorithms could identify patterns and insights that humans alone might miss. This could help us develop more effective strategies for achieving success and optimising our performance in ways we could not have imagined before.

As we look to the future, it is clear that the art of peak performance will continue to evolve and provide us with new tools and strategies for achieving success. But ultimately, the key to success lies within ourselves. By cultivating a growth mindset, practising mindfulness and prioritising our physical and mental health, we can unlock our full potential and achieve greatness in our lives.

I hope this book has provided you with the knowledge, inspiration and motivation to become a peak performer. Remember that success is not a destination but a journey, and the journey is always more rewarding than the destination. I encourage you to continue learning, growing and striving for success, and I wish you all the best on your journey.

Thank you for allowing me to be a part of your journey to peak performance!

About the Author

Dr. K. Jayanth Murali, IPS (Retd.), is a dynamic and charismatic leader who has left an indelible mark in the realm of law enforcement and beyond. Hailing from the vibrant city of Golconda Fort, India, Dr. Murali's career has been nothing short of extraordinary, brimming with excitement, accomplishments, and unwavering dedication to public service.

A trailblazer from the very beginning, Dr. Murali's insatiable thirst for knowledge led him to pursue a PhD in microbiology from the prestigious Indian Agricultural Research Institute, New Delhi where he emerged as a brilliant scientific scholar. However, destiny had other plans for him, and he was handpicked for the prestigious Indian Police Service in 1991, setting the stage for an illustrious career that spanned over three decades of unparalleled achievements.

With his larger-than-life personality and exceptional leadership skills, Dr. Murali served in a diverse array of policing assignments that left a lasting impact. From tackling complex law and order situations to spearheading high-stakes crime investigations and providing VIP security, Dr. Murali's unwavering commitment to duty earned him widespread recognition and admiration. As Chief of Crime Branch CID, Director of Vigilance and Anti-Corruption, and Additional Director General of Police, Law and Order, and Director General of Police for the Government of Tamil Nadu, he carved a niche for himself as an exemplary law enforcement professional.

But Dr. Murali's contributions go far beyond his official duties. He is a prolific writer, whose thought-provoking articles have graced the pages of leading newspapers and e-magazines, capturing the imagination of readers with his diverse interests and deep insights. As a gifted writer, Jayanth's words resonate with depth and insight. His critically acclaimed book, "42 Monday's: On Emerging Technologies in Policing," is a testament to his profound understanding of the evolving landscape of law enforcement. In addition, he has authored three other captivating books, namely "Soliloquies on Future Policing," "Enkindling the Endorphins of Endurance," and "Marathon" (Tamil). His writings on policing, security, technology, sports, science fiction, health, and fitness are nothing short of captivating, igniting a spark of inspiration in the hearts of his readers.

In addition to his literary pursuits, Dr. Murali is a man of many talents. An avid farmer, he nurtures his passion for the land and has a green thumb that is the envy of many. He is also a renowned coach for running, nutrition, and health, helping countless individuals achieve their fitness goals and lead healthier lives. As a painter and cook, he unleashes his creative genius, delighting others with his artistic flair and culinary expertise.

Dr. Murali's indomitable spirit and unwavering determination are further exemplified by his exceptional achievements in the field of marathon running. He has completed over 50 half and full marathons, and holds prestigious records in the India Book of Records and Asia Book of Records, showcasing his unparalleled prowess as an athlete. His dedication to the cause of organ donation, through marathons and other initiatives, is a testament to his compassionate heart and desire to make a positive impact on society.

Beyond his professional accomplishments and athletic pursuits, Dr. Murali's humanitarian endeavors are truly awe-inspiring. As ADGP, Armed Police, he launched the www.letsfightcorona.com initiative during the ongoing pandemic, leading a remarkable effort to distribute relief worth more than Rs. 50 lakhs in just 40 days, providing much-needed aid to those in need. His selfless acts of kindness and unwavering commitment to serving humanity have earned him the respect and admiration of people from all walks of life.

In his personal life, Jayanth is a loving husband to his college mate Dr. Jayanthi, IFS, and a proud father to two accomplished daughters, Tanya, an architect in Mumbai, and Sonya, a postgraduate student at Jawaharlal National University, New Delhi. Jayanth's extraordinary journey is a shining example of resilience, determination, and compassion, making him a true inspiration to all. To learn more about this remarkable individual and his incredible achievements, visit www.jayanthmurali.com and prepare to be inspired.

In conclusion, Dr. K. Jayanth Murali, IPS, is a trailblazer and an inspiration to many. His unwavering commitment to public service, exceptional leadership skills, diverse talents, and humanitarian endeavors make him a true force to be reckoned with. His journey is a testament to the power of determination, resilience, and unwavering passion to make a positive impact on society

Website - https://www.jayanthmurali.com/

www.ingramcontent.com/pod-product-compliance
Lightning Source LLC
LaVergne TN
LVHW041016150826
845672LV00001B/111

* 9 7 9 8 8 9 1 3 3 7 7 8 7 *